SLAVERY, COLONIALISM, AND CONNOISSEURSHIP

Slavery, Colonialism, and Connoisseurship

Gender and Eighteenth-Century Literary Transnationalism

NANDINI BHATTACHARYA
University of Toledo, USA

ASHGATE

Published by
Ashgate Publishing Limited
Gower House
Croft Road
Aldershot
Hants GU11 3HR
England

Ashgate Publishing Company
Suite 420
101 Cherry Street
Burlington, VT 05401-4405
USA

Ashgate website: http://www.ashgate.com

British Library Cataloguing in Publication Data
Bhattacharya, Nandini
Slavery, colonialism and connoisseurship : gender and eighteenth-century literary transnationalism
    1.English literature – 18th century – History and criticism 2.Transnationalism
    3.Imperialism in literature 4.Globalization in literature 5.Slavery in literature
    I.Title
    820.9'355'09033

Library of Congress Cataloging-in-Publication Data
Bhattacharya, Nandini.
  Slavery, colonialism, and connoisseurship : gender and eighteenth-century literary transnationalism / by Nandini Bhattacharya.
      p. cm.
  Includes bibliographical references and index.
  ISBN 0-7546-0353-9 (alk. paper)
    1. English literature—18th century—History and criticism. 2. Colonies in literature.
3. Nationalism in literature. 4. Slavery in literature. 5. Women and literature—England—History—18th century. 6. Literature and society—England—History—18th century.
7. Transnationalism—England. 8. England—Civilization—18th century. I. Title.

  PR448.C64B47 2006
  820.9'358—dc22

ISBN-13: 978-0-7546-0353-5
ISBN-10: 0-7546-0353-9

2005032499

Printed and bound in Great Britain by Antony Rowe Ltd, Chippenham, Wiltshire.

Contents

List of Figures

Acknowledgments

I am deeply grateful to my transnational family, my inspiration for this book. Thank you, Ma, Baba, Tuli, Paromita, Manu, Jona, Roktim, Lopa, June, Apurba, Babu, Pipey, Dadus, Mashis, and the little ones. You have always believed in me when I have wondered and wandered. To you this book is dedicated.

In addition, I have many people to thank for advice, editing, critical scrutiny, feedback and reference help at various stages of progress of this manuscript. In particular, I would like to thank Dr. Paula Backscheider, my dissertation advisor, for her continued support of my scholarship. My heartfelt thanks go to colleagues and librarians at Valparaiso University, who always read, discussed and critiqued my work with enthusiasm. In particular I would like to thank Betsy Burow Flak, Renu Juneja, Maire Mullins, Jon Pahl, David Morgan, and David Rowland for their friendship and support. Several research grants from Valparaiso University – including a research professorship leave – enabled the inception and evolution of this book. I would also like to thank colleagues and mentors at the University of Toledo for their cooperation and help in getting this book "done." For generous travel and research support I thank David Stern, and for their support and confidence and interest I thank Marietta Morrissey, Joan Mullins, Sue Ott Rowlands, Roger Ray, and the Humanities Institute seminarians – a great group on whom to try out unfinished ideas. The University of Toledo gave me a Kohler grant, which enabled me to travel to complete research for this book, and I thank the committee. My thanks also go to Asma Abdel Halim, Renee Heberle, Pat Murphy, and Ashley Pryor, great colleagues in the University of Toledo's Women's and Gender Studies department.

Friends and colleagues at other institutions have, naturally, been invaluable too. I thank Kevin Berland, Mita Choudhury, Bidyut Chakraborty, Morris Eaves, Richard Maxwell, Linda Merians, Kumkum Sangari, Beth Fowkes Tobin, Katie Trumpener, and Kenneth Warren for conversations, hospitality, and encouragement at critical moments in writing. I can only attempt to suggest, moreover, the debt of thanks I bear to Arjun Appadurai, leader of the Ford Foundation Project on Globalization at the University of Chicago, where I had the good fortune to have a fellowship; his ideas inspire and permeate this book. Thanks also go to Jacqueline Bhabha, Dipesh Chakraborty, Prasenjit Duara, Steve Collins, Malathi de Alwis, Farhat Haq, and other scholars and colleagues at the Globalization Project. Especial thanks to Homi Bhabha for encouraging and inspiring me to an extent possibly unknown to himself, and well beyond even the range of his cited works in this book.

For assistance with locating materials, hunting down images, and answering various queries in general, I thank the staff and services of the American Antiquarian Society, the Asiatic Society Calcutta, the Beinecke Rare Books and Manuscript Library, the British Museum, the British Library, the Huntington Library, the Houghton Library, and especially the Harvard Theatre Collection staff, the Lady Level Gallery, and the

Oriental and India Office Collections. To the Huntington Library I am also grateful for the Andrew Mellon postdoctoral research fellowship that jump-started this book; many thanks to the director Dr. Robert Ritchie for his interest and hospitality.

To Ashgate's anonymous reader of the manuscript, my heartfelt thanks for broadening my scholarly reach and perspective on a project which, in four years of continuous co-existence, had become sometimes too intimate a companion for me to imagine alternative analyses of its intellectual challenges.

No one could have a better editor than Erika Gaffney at Ashgate Publishing. To her, heartfelt thanks for discovery, encouragement, and guidance of my work.

Personal friends can never be thanked enough for the times that writing had me both preoccupied and demanding of them. These friends, who must know but never remind me that I owe them so much, are Marisa Garcia Verdugo, Alex and Jane Geisinger, Jim Kingsland, Elizabeth Lynn, Irene Dhar Malik, Bill Marion, Zahra Nwabara, Lisa Pahl, Marian Rubchak, Urmi Sen, Srilata Mukherjee, Sharon Rowley, and, last but not least, my soul-sister Nelly Zamora Bello.

Audiences at many conferences have been dynamic and electrifying. I thank the listeners who made wonderful suggestions at the East-Central American Society for Eighteenth-century Studies conferences, the McMaster Taylor Conference, the Northeast American Society for Eighteenth-century Studies conferences, and the British Society for Eighteenth-century Studies conferences over the years. If I had known your individual names I would necessarily have included them, as your intellectual contributions have enriched this book.

I thank Adam Myers for his counsel and support, and especially thank my son Khoka for giving me the joy in life which made it possible to write this book.

Chapter 1

Introduction

muse that difference sing[1]

This book explores a nascent eighteenth-century diasporic and transnational identity discourse by exploring cultural debates on value, taste, and commerce. These debates expressed metropolitan desire to refigure the excesses and breaches of transnational commerce and colonization as cultural surplus value. As strange things and stranger people became commodities in European systems of value, a concomitant economy and nexus of material collecting and connoisseurship provided a helpful analogous schema for the revaluation and refiguration of the exotic and the unfamiliar – the transnational curiosity – within eighteenth-century western culture. While examining the debates on value, taste and commerce and their attendant discontents, this book's focus is upon eighteenth-century metropolitan and marginal voices speaking within and across national territories in this age of empire, colonialism, and slave-trading. The focus does not lead to articulating such "global uniformities" as C.A. Bayly argues existed in the early modern world and modern worlds,[2] but to emphasizing a particular range of intercultural differentials of value, taste, and commerce as articulated by the marginalized and the oppressed.

The experience of the marginalized, oppressed, and colonized, of the repeatedly and involuntarily "translated" or "transnationalized," is the original churning mud of a transnational theory.[3] In recontextualizing race, gender, and national sentiment within nascent transnationalisms, the works discussed in this book offer suggestive precursors to postcolonial discourse by foregrounding the fluid and resituated nature of objects, people, and movements of debated or questioned cultural significance, moral provenance, and commercial valence. Within the contemporary critical discourse on transnationality, Paul Gilroy has captured the essence of such fluidity by stating, "different nationalist paradigms for thinking about cultural history fail when confronted by the intercultural and transnational formation that I call the black Atlantic."[4] I have attempted to show that such a destabilizing of national boundaries and categories operated in the literary domain and in everyday practices at different points along the Euro-American imperial rim in the eighteenth century.

This pre-national or pre-transnational phase has been alternatively conceptualized as "archaic globalization."[5] Within such archaic globalization, according to C.A. Bayly, "Neither race nor nationality, as understood at the end of the nineteenth century, was yet a dominant concept … embodied status remained the key discriminator in the interaction of peoples in the archaic and early modern diasporas. It operated at a deeper level than nationality, which remained a flexible and rather indistinct category at this period."[6] Bayly thus appears to offer a historical analogy for an argument made by Saskia Sassen about contemporary globalization's deterritorialized nature: "globalization – as illustrated by the space economy of advanced information industries – denationalizes national territory."[7] Thus framed, the age of nationalism in the nineteenth century may seem to be just an aberrant blip in the otherwise seamless continuum of world history as globalization at different speeds. Moreover, in the tracing of globalizations past and present, it may seem as though books such as Bayly's, and this one, are doing no more than staking that claim about the continuity and archaic origins of globalization in world history. It is, therefore, important to extract and develop fully another strand that might get lost in the endless clamor about globalizations old and new. This strand is the yet emergent and complex idea of transnationalism.

By transnationalism, I intend a consciousness and a movement, as studied by Saskia Sassen, Bruce Robbins, Pheng Cheah, and others.[8] Transnationalism engages with the global flux as both a macro-reality and an everyday subjective conundrum; it is discursive as well as material and hyper-real.[9] This book endeavors not to make an undifferentiated survey of early modern global entities and imaginations; it aims to pick out those voices that most closely approach the specific modality of transnationalism as an engaged, articulate, reflexive discourse on globality. I have therefore coined the term "transnation" as a key thematic for this book. Transnation reflects the transcendence of national boundaries, the rearrangement of "national" identities, the revaluation of aesthetic objects, and the renegotiation of cultural concepts in a hyper-commercial age, by metropolitan as well as marginalized subjects of that transnational imperium who largely *consciously* engage with a *concept* of transnationality. As the term transnation suggests, I conflate the meanings of "translation" and "nationality" to produce as a "proper" noun, as a nominative force, the dynamics of two significant acts in history, that of reproducing an original text in a different linguistic context, and that of binding or finding oneself bound to a certain concept of an original context or text called the nation. The migratory impetus of translation and the territorial impetus of nationality converge to produce a ground in perpetual motion, a mechanism of crosscultural identity that speaks its name always as a difference, an elsewhere, an other. Whereas the concept of the migrant or intercultural subject, the tropicopolitan, has already become an influential trope and term in eighteenth-century postcolonial and diaspora studies, my attempt in this book is to introduce and deploy the idea of transnation as a trope for the political and social transformation of those subjects, agents, nations, and nationalities in the vast global flows of things and people that characterized the early modern era, particularly the eighteenth century.[10]

This is not to make a claim that Richard Brinsley Sheridan, Phillis Wheatley, James Cobb, and George Colman Jr. – the authors whose works will be discussed in subsequent chapters – discourse on globality more critically or articulately than others. It is, however, my claim that these authors articulate nascent transnationality in significant and symptomatic ways that deserve attention as a new direction in rereading eighteenth-century colonialism and globalization. However, it might be asked, why focus on literature? In her excellent book on eighteenth-century anxieties about import-dependent lifestyles and the rise of a "discriminating" taste closely associated with abolitionism, Charlotte Sussman points out the literary as a powerful ground for the manifestation of these refigurations and contestations: "During most of the eighteenth century, moreover, the distinction between political and literary material in the public sphere was quite fluid … questions about the legitimacy of certain kinds of consumerism entered public discussion not divorced from the literary, but on a continuum with it."[11] Sussman is at pains to retain the discussion within the framework of distinct national boundaries and consumerist identities. My attempt, on the other hand, is to take the discussion beyond national boundaries, into transactional border zones, and eighteenth-century literature in particular happens to provide an excellent ground for investigating the recontextualization of familiar and novel objects within fluid and extraterritorial material cultures.[12]

This recontextualization concerns "the uneven entanglement of local and global power relations on colonial peripheries, particularly as these have been manifested in capacities to define and appropriate the meanings of material things."[13] In works of literature that occupy and represent the zones of indeterminacy and cultural crosspollination, one sees clearly that the way in which "objects are not what they were made to be but what they have become"[14] is also true of persons, subjectivities, identities; they too follow the fate of objects in culture, experiencing "mutability … in recontextualization."[15] Sussman notes the revaluation attendant on such recontextualization when she writes about "a decline in the glorification of indiscriminate accumulation, and … an increasing fear that Britain's consumption of colonial goods was compromising its self-sufficiency… Often, even at times when accumulation and expansion were being glorified, those reactions were characterized by a nebulous anxiety, and by a suspicion that such objects retained traces of the violence with which they were appropriated from foreign locations, or produced by captive labor."[16]

These consumer anxieties were produced, of course, by eighteenth-century fears of what Saskia Sassen describes today as: "denationalization, which to a large extent materializes in global cities, [and] has become legitimate for capital and has indeed been imbued with positive value by many government elites and their economic advisors. It is the opposite when it comes to people, as is perhaps most sharply illustrated in the rise of anti-immigrant feeling and the renationalizing of politics."[17] Anxieties about consumerism paralleled, therefore, anxieties about collecting and possessing both things and people that psychologically and physically invaded British identity in the process of being collected. Such anxieties presage and mobilize, as Sussman shows, the renationalizing of politics, particularly with regard to a notion of citizenry and national belonging, as well as the revaluing of migrating bodies and things.

Despite renationalizing, the anxiety was a conscious or unconscious response to the reality of transnational contexts and consciousnesses, what Sussman calls "transculturation."[18] The fate of a literary persona, sometime Wedgwood teapot and sometime Amerindian beauty, as in George Colman Jr.'s play *Inkle and Yarico* (discussed here in Chapter 2), or that of a Phillis Wheatley, sometime slave and sometime gifted young poet (discussed here in Chapter 5), or that of a Turk and no Turk in a Florence that is England (Chapter 3), or that of a portrait in Georgian England that clings to its inalienability in the very moment of imminent commodification (Chapter 4), all attest to the literary dispersal of transnational recontextualizations triggered by active material cultural border zones: "a succession of uses and recontextualizations."[19]

It is helpful to recognize that the type of conscious engagement with recontextualizing migrations, border crossings, and polyphonic transnational identities that is under review in this book is the precursor to the located yet fluid "reattachment, multiple attachment, or attachment at a distance" that Bruce Robbins discusses in *Cosmopolitics*.[20] If metropolitan renationalizing was territorial, some migrant transnationals were involuntary peripatetics or self-situating as well. Indeed, transnational voices like Wheatley and Sheridan, beyond their own different experiences of migration and transculturation, speak also from the context of a conscious rootedness in place.[21] Often such places are cities like London, Boston, and Kingston, then as now, in Sassen's terms, producing differential human destinies and uneven globalizations.[22] Saskia Sassen has surreally delineated this scenario as "about the possibility of a new type of transnational politics, a politics of those who lack power but … have 'presence.'"[23] It is often in such places, I would say, that the crosspollination of a migrant presence and either voluntary or involuntary situatedness engenders what I will call "strategic transnationalism."

It will be evident that my term "strategic transnationalism," which I intend to use interchangeably with "transnation," draws upon Gayatri C. Spivak's now famous concept of "strategic essentialism."[24] In her articulation of this concept, Spivak writes of the "project to retrieve the subaltern consciousness as the attempt to undo a massive historiographic metalepsis and 'situate' the effect of the subject as subaltern … as a *strategic* use of positivist essentialism in a scrupulously visible political interest."[25] It is in this light of repeating the original accents of murderous languages while tracing discontinuities and ruptures that Donna Landry sees Phillis Wheatley – gifted, young, black, and slave – deploying the very trope of memory as a form of "affirmative deconstruction,"[26] to invoke Spivak again. Hortense Spillers introduces a similar strategic thinking in her theory of the history of black female flesh,[27] and one that is also redolent in Spivak's citation of Foucauldian "practical ontology."[28] I introduce the echo deliberately; Spivak redrew the frontiers of identity-discourse long before globalization theory became current to enable inclusion of seemingly fractal and contradictory political stances and articulations with her purchase on the "strategic" potential of an essentialist pose. I aim to capture the "strategic" character of a transnationalism that must navigate multiple matrices and vectors of race, gender, and national ontologies, and migratory, colonial, hybrid, transcultural, and colonial teleologies, and yet retain some purchase on the possibilities of individual identity and action for collective justice. Phillis Wheatley's deployment of the concept of flight (Chapter 5), or Sheridan's deployment of the auction as an alienating yet renationalizing space (Chapter 4), exemplify such strategic practices.

It is in that sense that the transnational actors and speakers in this book have distinguished themselves from merely "globalized" entities. They strategically represent and are represented in transnational discourse so it becomes a discourse, a politics, and an aesthetic. Once again, in the sense of an enacted "strategy," a "practical ontology," this sort of transnationalism knows itself as an elusive or fugitive subjectivity and yet forges patterns of power and traces paths of action out of its migrations and disappearances, its knowledge "strategically adhering to the essentialist notion of consciousness, that would fall prey to an anti-humanist critique, within a historiographic practice that draws many of its strengths from that very critique."[29]

The theorization of such transnationalism, which I discuss more fully as transnation in Chapter 4, embodies colonial and postcolonial modalities and aesthetic praxes of repetition with a difference as indubitable signatures of transnational and postcolonial identity-making, of transforming identity from involuntarily transported to autonomously "transnationalized." More on these aesthetic praxes shortly; at present it is important to stress that at the very core of such phenomena of reproductions of identities with a difference, of a politicizing repetition, is the transportation, violation, and multiplication of Africans as a slave diaspora in the New World – a history of the flesh as Hortense Spillers has called it[30] – which has become an irreducible and unreduced remainder of the slave trade and slave systems. Its cultural and political effects continue to transform and transnationalize Atlantic and European worlds, as Stuart Hall and Paul Gilroy have demonstrated.[31] In Gilroy's words, for example, "the diaspora concept ... should be cherished for its ability to pose the relationship between ethnic sameness and differentiation: a *changing* same."[32] Another such reproduction of identities has occurred in the context of colonial aggressions, of metropolitan outreach into the tropics and peripheries, where mimic men and women have produced anticolonial revolutions, postcolonialities, and transnationalities. Thus the theory that glosses such experiences as plantation culture is embedded in a modality of repetitive labor that has been described by Bayly as "the ultimate, forced, industrious revolution."[33] The record of such "repetitions, traces, convergences ... migrations" can be erased only at extreme cost to history, or only with "'separations' as a primary agenda."[34]

In counterpoint to the situated discourses of metropolitan nationalisms and other subjectivities, though, the historical muting and mutation of slaves, migrants and the colonized are the grounds from which a contemporary theory of transnationalism dismantles received geographies. The historian Richard Sheridan goes so far as to say that "it can be argued that instead of separating the people of West Africa and the Caribbean, the transatlantic slave trade served as a bridge to join together the oppressed peoples in common resistance to chattel slavery."[35] Bayly's world-historical lens too affirms that "the marginal has always worked to construct the grand narratives as much as the converse has been true. Especially before the mid-nineteenth century, it was common for people on 'the fringes' to become historically central."[36] In tracing the pre-history of contemporary western migration patterns and immigration crises, Sassen writes perceptively that "during the course of the later eighteenth century temporary migrations for work expanded throughout Europe, creating a mobile – and therefore mobilizable – mass of bodies ... migrants circulated more effectively than merchandise."[37] My concept of transnation points to a theoretical threshold for speaking of translated and transported and migrant subjects and their so-called "origins" or "homelands" by rereading the locations and migrations of eighteenth-century British texts, nationalisms, and cultural artifacts as subject-formations that "do not always make for harmony."[38] They do, however, create, a compelling polyphony, and sometimes a fascinating cacophony: a literary transnationalism. The drama of eighteenth-century imperializing Britain and the voices echoing across the Atlantic are found to be preoccupied with translating experiences that cannot "be conceived ... primarily in terms of domination, subordination or 'subalternization,' but in terms of slipperiness, elsewhereness ... constantly eluding the terms of the discussion."[39]

Gayatri C. Spivak's now-echoing concept/metaphor of the "subaltern" as a site of representation, of articulation of repressed memory and consciousness – the theatre of *darstellung* or the podium of *vertretung*? – also evokes the ongoing controversy over the concept of the speaking erased subject.[40] What I concern myself with in this book is not so much the concept of "agency," for this may and perhaps should forever remain a contested term lest its potency petrify in co-opted terrain, but with the effect of transnationality generated by a combination of putative agents and germinal spaces and movements, engendering, at the very least, consciousness. Outside of elite metropolitan speaking spaces, the transnational is a subaltern. It is the consciousness of transnationality that should in some degree rewrite the modern histories of nations in so far as "it is the subaltern who provides the model for a general theory of unconsciousness. And yet, since the 'subaltern' cannot appear without the thought of the 'elite,' the generalization is by definition incomplete ... This 'instituted trace at the origin' is a representation of the deconstructive critique of simple origins."[41]

Speaking of simple origins, scholars of eighteenth- and nineteenth-century British literature have drawn attention to the trope of culture as transculturation, and of transculturation as culture. Life forces commodified through labor value, and fetishized objects metamorphosed in commercial exchange have long signified transformed national identity.[42] I read in the dappling of Britain and its commerce the transformation of national image from dystopia to heterotopia and into an incomplete utopia, a complex process enabled by gendered and racial narratives of transformation of value itself. Gary Kelly has described the creation of an early nineteenth-century British national identity through an emergent hegemonic fiction of national culture thus:

> In the Revolutionary aftermath national identity was a continuing cause of political and cultural anxiety. A single 'national' identity had to be created without provoking local rebellion. This was done by celebrating and even inventing local and regional identities but subsuming them in a larger 'national' identity and interest, defined not so much from within the 'nation' but from external, global and historical, Revolutionary and post-Revolutionary struggles against France, America, Russia, and other rivals. The 'nation' was constituted as its 'destiny' to rule and civilize alien peoples throughout the world, to 'protect' them from themselves and from predatory neighbours.[43]

Kelly captures here an important ideological complex of nineteenth-century British national culture, namely that national identity was constructed out of a resurrection and then partial suppression of "other" national cultures, indigenous narratives, histories, and performances, and by representing as universal yet local truths the experiences of global encounters with diversity.

This book attempts to trace this complex further back in the eighteenth century, when memory may have seemed failing, or unreliable, or simply frightening. The failure of memory or the memory of failure,[44] or the production and representation of identity as a form of amnesiac wandering, a cultural and national forgetfulness, also marks some of the works discussed in this book, notably James Cobb's *Strangers at Home* and George Colman Jr.'s *Inkle and Yarico*. In late eighteenth-century plays preceding the French revolution, but starting with the American Revolution, dramatists including Colman, Cobb, and Sheridan were already developing a drama that concerned itself with re-inventions of national culture through the stories and performances of surrogated foreign cultures, or transculturation.

An example of the complex dynamics of transnation as transculturation can be sought in the construction of English topography itself. In her complex and rich account of the evolution and naturalization of the proto-industrial and industrial era "English" countryside, Donna Landry demonstrates anti-cruelty and environmentalist sentiments as the twin vectors within which the new landscape took shape. While anti-cruelty sentiment is deconstructed by her as decontextualized and sentimental,[45] she also indicates its points of analogy with anti-slavery sentiment, which defended another kind of captive or hunted creature.[46] While Landry's insight alerts us already to the dangerous conflation of beasts and slaves, her argument favoring the robustness of sporting culture is relevant to this book for a further reason.

She talks about the attitudes to nature and animals that characterized the invention of the English countryside in the eighteenth century and finds conclusively that the anti-cruelty movement was often oblivious to the fact that animals were hunted with an attitude of respect for them and for their demise, with concurrent attention to the not necessarily negative ecological (in the Georgic sense) implications of hunting and sporting.[47]

The part of her argument that is interesting for my purposes is its asymmetrical textual application to the British attitudes towards slaves and natives within the context of slavery and colonialism. While the anti-cruelty movement may have been superficial and decontextualized because hunting entailed a certain degree of identification with animals and with nature, surely the anti-slavery movement addressed a qualitatively different and critical dis-identification.[48] Slaves and hapless natives were not hunted and destroyed with any empathic dynamic in place or with any regard for natural conservation or ecological wellbeing; the motive seems to have been purely one of immediate profit. If animals were hunted with respect, thus repositioning the anti-cruelty movement as merely sentimental and superficial at worst and environmentalist not ecological at best, slaves were not hunted with respect, and thus the anti-slavery movement actually aligns up exactly athwart the anti-cruelty movement in that sense.

Moreover, gaming became a mark of English privilege and rank, not merely of nouveaux financial clout. Landry writes that "Game stood for land ... By limiting access to sporting privileges, the game laws succeeded in privileging inherited rank and land over mere financial clout, which was becoming increasingly a matter of capital investments other than landed property as the eighteenth century wore on ... A final battle of the English revolution had been fought and won by the men of landed property against commercially successful tradesmen and artisans, stock-brokers and financiers, political office-holders and great urban merchants."[49] In this sense, animals of the hunt were apparently perceived as more of a part of the nexus of immoveable symbolic capital – of landed status, of the true national self – than slaves who belonged to the nexus of mobile and transferable thus exchangeable labor and capital. Safe to say, then, the abolition movement was rescuing humans who were being treated worse than beasts as English life and social hierarchies were shifting in the late eighteenth century. Ultimately, it is hard to justify a sporting culture perhaps so rooted in the valorized domestic end of a spectrum of cruelties, no matter how much it underpinned Englishness; said Englishness, outside of England, took far less "sporting" forms, regrettably.[50] Transnation, in the case described by Landry, becomes a dominant metropolitan enterprise linked to transatlantic social movements. Landry's somewhat incidental linkage of anti-cruelty and anti-slavery offers one instance of the fractured linkage between English nationalism and unfavorable English attitudes to "others." In the cases I have described in this book, the appropriation, transportation, reclassification, and transformations of foreign agents and objects realize the conditions for the differential reproduction of commodified subalternities that were as much linked as separated from the dominant races and groups.[51]

These commodified subalternities were, again, emerging globally. Historians of slavery and the slave trade write in consonance with such a concept of transnation. Walvin writes of the "complex consumer tastes [that] had developed on the [eighteenth-century] African coast, demanding (and getting) from European traders a range of material goods (many trans-shipped from Asia) in return for slaves ... It was a remarkable irony that the fruits of slave labour in the Americas – sugar, rum, and tobacco – should find their way back to West Africa and on to the westbound slave ships; slave-made produce shipped back and forth across the Atlantic in order to accumulate and then pacify yet more cargoes of Africans."[52] Walvin also writes: "What is surprising, however, is the degree to which Caribbean slaves, like West African middlemen, became addicted to the material artefacts of the outside world. Both regions were, in effect, part of a broader Atlantic world of material consumption. The history of modern material consumption has focused primarily on modern Europe and North America, but it is a story which was also evident in the slave islands; slaves, like their free British contemporaries, became consumers."[53] Blackburn has described these phenomena as follows: "The dynamic of the Atlantic economy was sustained by new webs of social trust, and gave birth to new social identities. It required business planning and methods for discounting risk; it was associated with distinctive modern traditions of reflexive self-consciousness."[54] Paul Lovejoy and David Richardson have also documented, for instance, that some West African slave traders trusted English merchants and business partners with the transportation and education of their own children in England.[55]

On the other hand, writers upon the slave trade gave voice to subaltern consciousness of the great chain of commerce, which brought luxury to some and repetitive, forced toil to others. Thus, M. Kerr, the author of *Reflections on the Present State of the Slaves in the British Plantations, and the Slave Trade from Africa* so ventriloquized the slave: "Our lives are spent in daily toil to raise commodities which serve to supply your commerce – encrease [sic] your seamen and your shipping – enrich your merchants – augment your treasury – recruit and man your navy; to repel your enemy and defend your coasts ...."[56] *Transnation* evolved as a defining shorthand for the dynamic of transnationality in this book after it became evident that there were texts – some dramatic, some poetic – from Britain's imperial and theatrical age that were confronting head on the phenomenon of becoming national while relating to an Other, and reacting in some measure to a swelling murmur of voices from other shores that were attempting an account of what had happened to them as slaves, colonized, and yet also "moderns."

As we view our world and times, we know that massive migrations inevitably link to vast changes of political sensibility and representational technes and aesthetics. This book discusses a part of that vast transformation of sensibility and techne during late eighteenth-century migrations – forced and unforced – and their generative and generated politics and aesthetics of marginality, by focusing on materialist aesthetics as represented within literary transnationalisms. If – as I amplify in the chapter on Phillis Wheatley – the aesthetic mode of transnational identity is the colonial and postcolonial reproduction or repetition of a copy with a politicized difference, then imperial cultures must always already be read in terms of their production through the ambiguities of a politics of difference, through subject-formations that "do not always make for harmony."

In Walter Benjamin's sense of reproductions of an aura-laden original in his 1935 essay "The Work of Art in the Age of Mechanical Reproduction," such repeated reproductions of "subjects" – uneven links upon a great chain of commerce – created not merely clones but unique articulations about the possibilities of early modern transnational consciousness, possibilities that transcended totalitarian and murderous demands on humanity, then as later. Benjamin writes, "Mankind ... can experience its own destruction as an aesthetic pleasure of the first order. This is the situation of politics which Fascism is rendering aesthetic. Communism responds by politicizing art." [57] He inspires the critique of a critique that sees the reproduction of Tradition as a devaluation of it. Instead, one must become educated to see reproduction and repetition, as experienced by colonial and postcolonial subjects – their hybridity, their mimicry, their copies with a difference – like the displaced and reversing effect of the subaltern in history, as the ultimate consciousness effect.[58]

Benjamin's work of art in the age of mechanical reproduction – "mechanical reproduction" certainly characterizing the eighteenth century's prolific and relentless reproduction of material, visual, textual, social, and human resources – is transformed by two dominant coexistent modalities: politics and repetition. Benjamin writes:

> for the first time in world history, mechanical reproduction emancipates the work of art from its parasitical dependence on ritual. To an ever greater degree the work of art reproduced becomes the work of art designed for reproducibility. From a photographic negative, for example, one can make any number of prints; to ask for the "authentic" print makes no sense. But the instant the criterion of authenticity ceases to be applicable to artistic production, the total function of art is reversed. Instead of being based on ritual, it begins to be based on another practice – politics.[59]

Benjamin's cultural modulation of the political is a critical locus for my articulations of transnation. Though Benjamin was thinking about photography and the cinema when he wrote "reproduction,"[60] his point about mechanical reproduction characterizing modernity is only too relevant for the eighteenth century, an age of commerce and transnational reproductions and representations of trade goods as well as connoisseurial objects, and of repetitive and transnational literary and visual print cultures. Metropolitan colonizing, slaveholding, and slave-trading societies were also compelled to duplicate subjects and slaves to meet bureaucratic, market and labor needs, as well as to reproduce the themes and mechanisms of domination and interculturalism.[61] Reading the political through the cultural, then, transnationality in this regard must be seen as the spatially and temporally widespread reproduction of national gendered, raced, and classed subjects with a difference; that is, it is always already intimately implicated in the heart of early modern western national projects.

To further explore the role of repetition/reproduction in transnational aesthetics, I would invoke Fredric Jameson's now famous point about postcolonial national production: that its distinguishing characteristic is its political orientation and agenda.[62] Indira Karamcheti has noted that a postcolonial – hence "minor" – literature is one of becoming political rather than merely aesthetic.[63] Karamcheti articulates the primary distinction of postcolonial literature as "political" rather than "aesthetic," adding that the best of such postcolonial literature, such as Salman Rushdie's *Satanic Verses*, does not enforce a dissociation of political and aesthetic sensibilities. Still, within postcolonial literary criticism the political clearly becomes a category impossible to confuse with an erstwhile categorization of art as "art," and unlike, say, Walter Benjamin's "ritual" artifact or "work of art," today's postcolonial artifact seems to be posited upon its political urgency and utterance. This dominance of the political over the "ritually" artistic, the "aura-laden" in Benjamin's sense of the term,[64] becomes manifest in eighteenth-century literary transnationalism. The linkage of politics and repetition is particularly productive in defining the early modern transnational, both political and repetitive in the crosscultural reproduction of subjectivities and identities with a difference: slaves, colonials, migrants, and artists. Thus, Marcus Wood draws attention to the proliferation of slavery-related drama on the British stage alone between 1787 and 1808.[65]

The sort of aura that is contested when an object loses its "cult value" to gain "exhibition value," as Benjamin speaks of these things,[66] is transferable to slavery, colonialism, and connoisseurship in the eighteenth-century context. As will be examined in detail in the chapter on George Colman's *Inkle and Yarico*, connoisseurship and collection had become polarities on a continuum of acquisition, evaluation, and fetishization of "novel" and strange objects. The collecting mania that had evolved within the "cabinet of curiosities" tradition in the seventeenth century had split – as Charlotte Sussman, Nicholas Thomas, and others have indicated[67] – into cultures of discriminating connoisseurship and indiscriminate collection.[68] In part this polarity was defined along lines of the bifurcation of "artistic" versus "natural" objects, respectively. Nature in the raw and culture in the artistic realm defined the differences, in a sense, between the objects of the collector's and the connoisseur's curiosity, respectively. Another useful distinction between collections and connoisseurial caches was that of the "exhibition" versus "cult" values of these holdings. Things merely curious and the faculty of curiosity itself, perceived as a lower-class and effeminate passion, was noted as a problem among sailors on James Cook's Pacific voyages, as Thomas notes: "'It was astonishing to see with what eagerness everyone [the sailors] catched at every thing they saw, it even went so far as to become the ridicule of the Natives by offering pieces of sticks stones and what not to exchange, one waggish Boy took a piece of human excrement on a stick and hild it out to every one of our people he met with.'"[69] Thomas has inverted the anthropological conceit of the "native" as the curious and indiscriminate consumer of trifles exhibited by Europeans, and instead tellingly emphasized that it was Europeans who entered a trance of "curiosity," one generally associated with "exhibitions," "displays," and "shows," so to speak, when they entered non-western cultures.[70]

Broadly speaking, Thomas transnationalizes the activity of collecting, displacing the emphasis usually placed upon the metropolitan appropriation of indigenous things. Returning to Europe, though, Thomas also finds that early travelers' encounters with "savagery" were not inlaid or framed by metropolitan cultural discourses of aesthetic standards. Thomas' observations alert us to the possibility that "collecting" curiosities may even have gained an indirect and notorious association with a primitive form of aesthetic value judgment or the lack of a refined one.[71] What was encountered was absorbed as such, without attempts to organize material hoards into hierarchies of cultural capital.[72] Hence, such "collecting" encounters missed the opportunity to establish "cult" scenarios and value systems. The same was true of the early spirit of "curious" collection. There was an element of scientific and taxonomical interest in non-specific collections, but the translation of materiality into aesthetic capital and value systems was absent.[73]

The criterion of refinement and the idea of adding value was, in contrast, a central paradigmatic feature of the connoisseurial spirit. Throughout the later eighteenth century, collecting activities became increasingly discredited and marginalized by connoisseurial values. The pursuit of meaning and the pleasure of ownership of foreign objects and collectibles became increasingly entangled with the need to define and refine values. But the polarized twinning of discourses of collection and connoisseurship operated in a very consequential and real context, as Chapter 2 primarily demonstrates. Sometimes, the axis separating inanimate nature and culture was not the only dividing line between collected and connoisseurial value systems. In the "value-added" mode wherein "refined" connoisseurship came to perch above "mere" collecting, slaves and colonial bodies came under scrutiny as having or lacking the potential for such classification, as connoisseurial objects or as mere collectibles. Humans demonstrated as much slipperiness as objects in their containment within these hierarchies determined by overlapping commercial and aesthetic languages of materiality. The questions of function and utility associated with either collected or connoisseurial objects also gave rise to gendering and race-ing of such objects and activities. Thus, within connoisseurship, objects and activities that had a more significant public life often became gendered male, whereas those that remained more private, however collectively and significantly, were feminized. In fact, gender and race intersect all transnational longings and imaginings in this history. A gendered distinction obtains in such other international eighteenth-century pursuits as botanical science, for instance, wherein male participation became classified as serious and scientific whereas female enterprise became private and amateurish.[74]

Thus, slaves and colonials were perceived as either trifles or treasures, depending on the reigning political discourse. Such oscillations made such human commodities either fetishized or devalued, making their ownership or domination either "cult" or "exhibition" phenomena, respectively. At other times, however, the west allowed a proximity to this other, permitting some mimicry and sharing of their effects and affects, thereby moving to a civilizational attitude whereby difference was disavowed in favor of a more universalist, monoculturalist, and familializing vision, often mediated by feminine figures. Using the theories of Homi Bhabha and Robert J.C. Young, I argue that the colonizing and masculinist west, under pressure to constantly redefine its relations with the non-dominant races and genders (what Bhabha calls "repetition" of the recognition and disavowal of otherness as universal sameness or difference) labeled the other culturally and racially different, hybrid or stereotypical, categories that foreground their non-universal, biologized difference, threatening the west's identity.[75] If in the realm of biology, of the gendered and racial hybrid and the stereotype, the denial of difference required the mobilization of stereotypical sexualities to avert catastrophic miscegenation, in the realm of civilization, culture, and mimicry, women mobilized the familialization and absorption of the other as a feminized figure. The travails of women and foreign races were alternately yet simultaneously explained by their own perfidy (that is, their essential, biological difference and sexual deviancy) or as the perfidy of the west (hence mandating a civilizational flurry). Due to the latter phenomenon, the racial other sometimes became a familial subordinate or servant, masking the subordination of both women and racial others in this paternalist fiction. In this regard, gender became the modality for living race.

This feminization and familialization of difference, a strategic civilizing containment of threats of radical hybridity, partiality, racial otherness, and the stereotype, are exemplified in the figure of Yarico in Colman's play (Chapter 2). Yarico's story sees the absorption of the female other as a daughter of the family, desexualized and familiarized. This familiarization and familialization is symptomatic, of course, of the aforementioned oscillation between nature and culture – race versus civilization, or the amoral perfidy of the non-western other versus the rational morality of the west – throughout the eighteenth century. However, its apparent resolution, at the century's end, is a civilizational moment: women of other cultures are absorbed into the national body reorganized as a universal civilizational family, the equivalent of today's "multicultural" societies. The commercial flows and exchanges of the century go underground in this symbolic zone of the family; this is analogous to the sentimental "family values" ideology that triumphed at the end of the twentieth century.

Thus, projects of tasteful sentiment and civilizationism attempted reconciling imperialist consciousness to the reality of African slavery on the one hand; mercantile rhetoric obfuscated the terrible realities of slavery in British plantocracies on the other hand. In this context, the growing distinction over the century between collecting and connoisseurship paralleled the growing divergence between the projects of racialization or biology and familialization/domestication or civilizationalism, or between nature and culture.

Charles Smith writes that what distinguishes collectibles from one-of-a-kind connoisseurial objects is that "in order for an item to be considered a collectible there must be a sufficient number of them to allow for some system of categorization. While the uniqueness of a work of art usually enhances its value, such uniqueness can work against collectibles ...."[76] Smith also writes: "judgments regarding inherent value tend to be more important in art and one-of-a-kind auctions; classification and equivalency judgments, in collectible auctions ...."[77] Analogously, the commercial capitalist venture commodified people and things – as a collector would do – and made no particular attempt to "individualize" and "value" them individually. The connoisseur on the other hand attempted to pin more refined sensibilities, values and associations on things and people, and to accommodate them thus more within a universal human familial schema of "worth."

Hence, in the 1736 "Speech of Mr. John Talbot Campo-bell," purportedly a free African's work, but actually written by a pro-slavery clergyman in Nevis island named Robert Robertson, the fictional African describes the slave trade and African and plantation societies as fairly identical, lateral and equitable flows of slaves, sugar, and white labor. Thus:

> Men, Women, and Children, are consider'd with us [Africans] as the Growth or Manufacture of the Country, and are treated accordingly by their Owners, i.e. by their Princes, Masters, or Parents; and if at any time this is thought inconvenient, or not sufficient for the Purposes of Trade, the Prince and People of one Nation are easily persuaded to pick a Quarrel, and to go to Blows, with the Prince and People of another Nation, and then the Victors dispose of the Vanquish'd, just as the *white* People here dispose of their

Sugar, Rum, and Molasses, to those that will give most for them. Some of you were *Slaves* in Africa, where Servitude, as you know, is propagated from Father to Son for ever, and where the Masters or Owners sell their Slaves to one another, or to Foreigners, on the same Condition on which themselves possess them. Among us, bare suspicion in the Husband will justify him in selling his Wife for a Slave. A small matter of Theft will, in many of our Countries, condemn both the guilty Person and his whole Family to Servitude, or, if Purchasers cannot be found, to present Death: and there are many other Laws with us, the Violation whereof will have the same Effect, as you see some *Whites* are banish'd to this Place from *England*, for breaking the Laws of the Country.[78]

In this discourse, issuing from an "African" mouthpiece, addressed to his "Countrymen," the pro-slavery white writer's agenda is transparently to mitigate the specific problem of slavery by placing the slave trade on an equal footing with the sugar trade or white bonded servitude. Within this transactional nexus, the human being is stripped of family, community, and inalienable human rights; she becomes a purely exchangeable commodity. Placed within the continuum of other global commodity and labor flows, slavery is made to appear no better or worse than say exporting sugar or British migration to colonies. Similarly, the depiction of the plantation slave as yet another commodity in the vast global flow of things obviously demonstrates the mindset of the commercially motivated collector of slaves who is able to use criteria of "classification and equivalency," and not to concern himself with "inherent worth" issues.[79]

The morally tasteful and symbolic sentimentalist venture did in fact invest in the uniqueness of such entities. However, the latter, though in this and in other ways engaged in a "connoisseurship" and not a mere "collection" of exotica, did not individualize such individuals as slaves sufficiently to free them entirely. Instead, their status was more or less of the one-of-a-kind valuable, which had been valued out of the market but not out of the museum. It would take the Phillis Wheatleys, and to some extent the abolitionists, to do both; to free slaves altogether from nexuses of evaluation by others, and at least theoretically to grant them self-determination.

When commodified humans like Wheatley or those sensitive to their commodification spoke, a politics of deritualization of aura became transformed, at least in certain cases, into a new political aesthetic of repetition. Such a politics of repetition transformed the criteria of aura and "cult" into tools for appropriation and rewriting of such originary "aura." By debunking the connoisseurial schema, voices like Phillis Wheatley's and even James Cobb's could displace an entire scheme of cultural valuations based on the elevation of privileged symbolic concepts like tradition, aura, uniqueness, originality, and racial dominance, and replace them with what might be called a proletarian art. As in any progressive cultural debate, there were voices such Colman's and to some extent Sheridan's that would not or did not comprehend the full potential of the contest between collection and connoisseurial culture; nevertheless, they too participated, and in some cases like Sheridan's, seemed to lend much ammunition to ideologies operating unconsciously. That the contest within material culture was progressive is confirmed by noting its common ground of revaluation of politics as a sort of moral aesthetic, within the abolition movement as also within literary transnationalisms.

A word on "material culture" is appropriate here. Our world continues to struggle with the fate of culture within materialism; my hope is that we will recognize what a powerful debate and struggle the culture of materiality and the materiality of culture – symbolic and commercial capital yoked in interdependence – engendered in eighteenth-century Britain. This debate and struggle are captured in the ascendancy of connoisseurship over collecting, which momentarily appeared to augur the triumph of the cultural – and high culture – within materiality. The contest between collecting and connoisseurship is testament to the jostling paradox of the concept of "material culture," a concept struggling to contain a mutable, protean paradox.

The transnational and the postcolonial manifest the cultural and political practices of repetitions of subjectivities and sensibilities that are semblant – "repetitions/ reproductions" – but different, British but colonized or slave, Homi Bhabha's mimic hybrids.[80] These are repetitions that respond to "a crisis of intercultural representation," "catachresis for agency arising at a felt moment of disculturation."[81] That some of the metropolitan voices speaking such a transnational consciousness were resistant and racist does not negate the fact that such a consciousness was nevertheless in process. The output of scholars such as Linda Colley, Srinivas Aravamudan, and Felicity Nussbaum and others provide ample testimony to the operations of such "identity-in-difference"[82] in the eighteenth century.

Quoting the definition of Trope in Ephraim Chambers' 1741 *Cyclopaedia* ("to *wash the black-moor white, or a fruitless undertaking*"), Aravamudan has written:

> trope is transitive ... it swerves from self-adequation to surplus and, while doing so, moves from the "proper and natural" to another meaning with "some advantage" ... Who would want to wash the blackamoor white, and who would be in the position of realizing that such an act was a fruitless undertaking? ... the aspiration of the racially minded progressive or assimilationist ... having assumed that in all contexts white is desirable over black, attempts to render the black skin white. This attitude, reminiscent of Michael McKeon''s definition of "naïve empiricism," interprets racial debasement as corrigible through amelioration. However, alongside this very attitude is ... "extreme skepticism," recognizing the attempted washing as revelatory of a *fruitless undertaking*. The trope, therefore, encapsulates an attitudinal shift. It guards a collective memory, gained through cumulative empirical experiment, that the epidermis cannot be changed through washing, only in order to process this into something a of a moral lesson ... Who exactly do these so-called blackamoors refer to, and how were they treated? ... What is the significance of ... reliance on a pre-existing cultural knowledge of failed efforts to whiten the black?[83]

Aravamudan's conceit or trope, it would seem, can be renamed the crisis of repetition as the political reproduction (versus erasure) of difference, and this is the matter of transnation, a term that encapsulates transformative representations and resistant agencies[84] in its meanings. This book examines four voices of Enlightenment cosmopolitanism for their voicing of the transformation, the trans-identification, and the transnationality of subjects and subalterns in processes and acts of cultural representation and self-representation. Representations of transnationality effect identities that refuse or fail to be situated within boundarized national parameters, whatever they are, and instead offer masquerades or reproductions of identity with a difference[85] that blur lines between the black, the brown, and the red; the metropolis and the colony; European, American, and Caribbean; commerce and culture; commodity and treasure; the hoard and the connoisseurial; the antique and the household; and the dead and the living.

In April 1998, Jeremy Rifkin, then president of the Foundation on Economic Trends in Washington, DC, drew our attention to a new phenomenon of global exchange and corporate takeover that will, he argued, define human and institutional life in the coming centuries: that phenomenon is the commodification of the human genome. He also argued that the twenty-first century would be the Biotech century. In it neo-Darwinian theory will be challenged by "a new cosmological narrative about evolution ... with a view of nature compatible with the operating assumptions of the new technologies and the new global economy."[86] According to Rifkin, then, nature and culture, instead of remaining discrete binaries, will merge. Nature itself will be the realm of culture, and culture will provide the narrative of nature in an absolute and literal sense far transcending any notion of ideology. Not only does Rifkin compare this epochal revolution to earlier great ages of worldwide expeditions and cultural revolution, but he also assures us that North-South hierarchies will remain intact in this new redefinition of human civilization: "While the technological expertise needed to manipulate the new green gold resides in scientific laboratories and corporate boardrooms in the North, most of the genetic resources that are essential to fuel the new revolution lie in the tropical ecosystems of the South."[87]

A startling narrative of skewed progress, does this not after all sound highly familiar? The simultaneous appropriation, erasure and revaluation of the "other" is a story much repeated in history, and only most lately in a global activity of mining the South to add to the economic revolution of the North, to which Rifkin himself refers:

> The last great debate of this kind occurred in the nineteenth century, over the issue of human slavery, with abolitionists arguing that every human being has intrinsic value and "God-given rights" and cannot be made the personal commercial property of another human being. During this time the abolitionist discourse merged with the sentimental anti-cruelty discourse, which however troublingly conflated slaves and animals in advocating for them. The abolitionists' argument ultimately prevailed, and legally sanctioned slavery was abolished in every country in the world where it was still being practiced. Like the anti-slavery abolitionists of the nineteenth-century, a new generation of genetic activists is beginning to challenge the very concept of patenting life, arguing that life is imbued with intrinsic value and therefore can never be legitimately reduced to commercial intellectual property controlled by global life-science conglomerates and traded as mere utilities in the marketplace.[88]

To a student of eighteenth- and nineteenth-century literatures and cultures, Rifkin's narrative will have additional interest because of its intersection with the history he notes of a past global circulation and transvaluation of value as embodied in the human being herself. Exchange and transformation of things and people are the dominant processes of nation-formation, according to the literature surveyed in this book. Foreign plunder becomes British wealth; marauding foreigners stand aside to give place to energetic Britons. Robin Blackburn writes:

> Fifty thousand Africans toiled in the sweltering sun of the Caribbean to produce twenty thousand tons of sugar a year for the English table. Over a hundred ships-of-the-line, requiring for their construction the felling of 2,500 trees and each capable of hurling half a ton of hot metal a quarter of a mile in broadsides every few minutes, patrolled the seas to make them safe for the English merchant-men ... the drawing-room now commanded global resources to satisfy its whims and cravings ... The serving of tea or coffee, with sugar, became a sociable and respectable domestic ritual ... Sugar consumption per head in Britain rose from 2 lb in the 1660s to 4 lb in the 1690s, and to 8 lb in the period 1710 to 1719 ... The salience of exotic produce in the new order of things is neatly symbolized by the fact that the newly established institutions of the City of London – the Bank of England, the Stock Exchange, Lloyd's Underwriters, several of the merchant banks – had been founded on the premises of coffee houses.[89]

One must react to the empirical but sensational impact of the above and recognize the intimacy and transfusions of the social and commercial lives of things and people. Indeed, if commerce maybe said to have a psychology, here it is: a world of dark despair and primal terror opened up for Africans to disappear into European maws during these centuries. To quote Blackburn again: "By the last years of the [eighteenth] century Britain was importing £6 million annually from the British West Indies ... To stock new plantations, between 50,000 and 100,000 slaves were brought across the Atlantic each year ... Between 1756 and 1770 the Company and its officials directly remitted £2.7 million from India to Britain: these direct remittances rose to £5.4 million between 1770 and 1784, or at a rate of some £386,000 annually."[90]

Postcolonial critics recognize, of course, the West's continued reality and impact on decolonized realms through material and ideological practices. These practices range from material neo-colonialism, to the academic appropriation of postcolonial practice and strategy, to poststructuralist and other reorganizations of the west. Some, like Stephen Slemon, have argued for an all-out rejection of this harnessing of specific and local postcolonial constructs as a modality for the concerns and purposes of the west, while others such as Helen Tiffin, while recognizing the validity of Slemon's position, have argued nevertheless that such a position's "danger ... lies in the reintroduction of a covert form of essentialism."[91] Embracing the discourse of identity that Spivak has also claimed as ready for engagement, Tiffin has instead recommended a practice of "canonical counterdiscourse," recognizing that subversion entails engagement with the west, for "pre-colonial cultural purity can never be fully recovered."[92]

Yet, as in the use of "fully" in that sentence, Tiffin's statement of her assertion bristles with qualifications. I quote at length: "*if* the impulse behind much post-colonial literature is seen to be *broadly* counter-discursive, *and* [*if*] *it is recognised* that the resulting strategies *may* take many forms in different cultures, I *think* we have a *more* satisfactory model than national, racial, or cultural groupings based on marginalisation can offer, and one which *perhaps* avoids *some* of the pitfalls of earlier collective models or paradigms."[93] This sounds like we can hope, but we cannot be too sure, that the counter-discursive approach too will not somehow fall prey to the West's neo-assimilation.

This is why the liminality and interstitiality of transnation – of strategic transnationality as a translation of the nation between the lines – seems to offer a theoretical construct dismantling the impasse of the questions of "authenticity" and "agency" in identity-construction. It eliminates the dominance of canons altogether (be they discourse or counter-discourse) and seeks for identity instead in the political pleasures and power of repetitions of canon and of identity with an irreducible difference.

Such controversies, however, help me approach my work in this book with a deepened sense of its stakes for the transnational debate on postcoloniality. I propose this book to be an instance of colonial discourse analysis from a post-postcolonial and transnational perspective. However, it remains also in many ways a study of the culture of Great Britain in the eighteenth century. Many eighteenth-century scholars of British culture and literature who come from postcolonial contexts experience the ethical unease of wondering what knowledge production they are furthering, and the loyalties and implications thereof.[94] Whatever may be the best approach – counter-discursive, or the postcolonial local or the transnational – the engagement of the rest with the west cannot end, since ideologies and practices still interlock and reproduce each other, repeating history, so to speak.

Notes

[1]   From James Grainger's *The Sugar Cane* (1764), in Marcus Wood, *The Poetry of Slavery: An Anglo-American Anthology 1764–1865* (Oxford, 2003), p. 11.

[2]   C.A. Bayly, *The Birth of the Modern World 1780–1914: Global Connections and Comparisons* (Malden, 2004), p. 1. Though Bayly's study encompasses a larger ambit and a more general argument than this book does, I have generally found his discussions – especially those on "archaic globalization" – extremely thought provoking. Points where the broader argument of his work are different from mine might be illustrated by citing language such as the following: "The violence and cruelty of the slave trade and of the exploitation of slaves cannot obscure the fact that this was a flexible, financially sophisticated, consumer-oriented, technologically innovative form of human beastliness" (Bayly, *The Birth of the Modern World*, pp. 40–41).

[3]   Of particular significance as such oppressed, marginalized, colonized, or transnationalized entities are Carole Boyce Davies' paradigmatic "Black Women" in Davies, *Black Women, Writing and Identity: Migrations of the Subject* (London, 1994), p. 29, and Srinivas

Aravamudan's "tropicopolitans" in *Tropicopolitans: Colonialism and Agency* (Durham; London, 1999).

[4]   Gilroy, *The Black Atlantic: Modernity and Double Consciousness* (Cambridge, MA, 1993), p. ix.

[5]   C.A. Bayly, *The Birth of the Modern World*, pp. 27–47. Of the now immense literature on globalization, some of the foundational texts that repay reading for a representation of the political alignments of globalization critique are Arjun Appadurai, *Modernity at Large: Cultural Dimensions of Globalization* (Minneapolis, 1996); Fredric Jameson and Masao Miyoshi (eds), *The Cultures of Globalization* (Durham, 1998); Saskia Sassen, *Globalization and its Discontents* (New York, 1998); Frederick Buell, *National Culture and the New Global System* (Baltimore, 1994); and A.G. Hopkins, *Globalization in World History* (New York, 2002). The major debate captured within these articulations concerns the liberatory versus neocolonial character of globalization.

[6]   Bayly, *The Birth of the Modern World*, pp. 46–4.

[7]   Sassen, *Globalization*, p. xxviii.

[8]   Sassen, *Globalization*. See also Jameson and Miyoshi (eds), *The Cultures of Globalization*, and Bruce Robbins and Pheng Cheah (eds), *Cosmopolitics: Thinking and Feeling Beyond the Nation* (Minnesota, 1998).

[9]   For a description – albeit ironic – of such postnationalism and globalization see Pheng Cheah, "Introduction Part II: The Cosmopolitan Today," in Robbins and Cheah (eds), *Cosmopolitics*, p. 20.

[10] See Robin Blackburn's Chapter 3 – "Slavery and Spanish America" – in Robin Blackburn, *The Making of New World Slavery: From the Baroque to the Modern, 1492–1800* (London, 1997), pp. 129–60.

[11] Charlotte Sussman, *Consuming Anxieties: Consumer Protest, Gender, and British Slavery, 1713–1833* (Stanford, 2000), p. 2. Sussman underscores the particular importance of the literary for the anti-slavery movement (pp. 2–4, 15–20).

[12] On "recontextualization" see Nicholas Thomas, *Entangled Objects: Exchange, Material Culture, and Colonialism in the Pacific* (Cambridge, MA, 1991), pp. 2–5. For Sussman on "the value of goods and people in tense, intercultural settings," see *Consuming Anxieties*, p. 50.

[13] Nicholas Thomas, *Entangled Objects*, p. xi.

[14] Ibid., p. 4.

[15] Ibid., p. 28.

[16] Sussman, *Consuming Anxieties*, pp. 13–14; see also pp. 58–9, and 81–109.

[17] Sassen, *Globalization*, p. xxviii; see also p. xxx.

[18] Sussman, *Consuming Anxieties*, p. 109.

[19] Thomas, *Entangled Objects*, p. 29.

[20] Bruce Robbins, "Introduction Part 1," in Bruce Robbins and Pheng Cheah (eds), *Cosmopolitics*, p. 3.

[21] A rootedness such as Robbins has discussed in "Introduction Part 1," *Cosmopolitics*, p. 3.

[22] Sassen, *Globalization*, pp. xx–xxvii; Sassen, *Guests and Aliens* (New York, 1999), pp. 14–16; Robbins and Cheah, (eds), *Cosmopolitics*, pp. 8, 34. See also Lisa Lowe, *Immigrant Acts* (Durham, 1996).

[23] Sassen, *Globalization*, p. xxi.

[24] "Subaltern Studies: Deconstructing Historiography," in Donna Landry and Gerald Maclean

(eds), *The Spivak Reader: Selected Works of Gayatri Chakaravorty Spivak* (New York, 1996), p. 214.

25 Spivak, "Subaltern Studies," in Landry and Maclean (eds), *Spivak Reader*, p. 214.

26 Donna Landry, *Muses of Resistance: Laboring-class Women's Poetry in Britain, 1739–1796* (Cambridge, 1990), pp. 246–7; Spivak, "Subaltern Studies," in Landry and Maclean (eds), *Spivak Reader*, p. 214.

27 Hortense Spillers, "Mama's Baby, Papa's Maybe: An American Grammar Book," *Diacritics*, 17/2 (Summer 1987): 65–81. This concept is extensively explored in Chapter 5.

28 Gayatri C. Spivak, "More on Power/Knowledge," in Landry and Maclean (eds), *Spivak Reader*, p. 157.

29 Spivak, "Subaltern Studies," in Landry and Maclean (eds), *Spivak Reader*, p. 216.

30 Spillers, "Mama's Baby."

31 For the most succinct enunciations see Gilroy, *The Black Atlantic*, and Stuart Hall, "Cultural Identity and Diaspora," in Patrick Williams and Laura Chrisman (eds), *Colonial Discourse and Postcolonial Theory: A Reader* (New York, 1994), pp. 392–403. On circumatlantic creolizations – new worlds made and born – see Blackburn, *Making of New World Slavery*, pp. 584–92.

32 Gilroy, *The Black Atlantic*, p. xi.

33 Bayly, *Birth of the Modern World*, p. 6.

34 Davies, *Black Women*, p. 11.

35 Richard Sheridan, "Resistance and Rebellion of African Captives in the Transatlantic Slave Trade Before becoming Seasoned Labourers in the British Caribbean, 1690–1807," in Verene Shepherd (ed.), *Working Slavery; Pricing Freedom* (New York, 2002), p. 202.

36 Bayly, *Birth of the Modern World*, p. 9; see also Sassen, *Guests and Aliens*, p. 9.

37 Ibid., pp. 8–9, 21–2.

38 Davies, *Black Women*, p. 36.

39 In conjunction with postcolonial critical and historical work, Carole Boyce Davies' (1994) analysis of black women's writing provides a preeminent theoretical anchor for the concept of "transnation," not only because I write about Phillis Wheatley – the literary sine qua non of early modern black female diasporic writing – but because Davies so aptly theorizes transnationality, foregrounds the experience of the oppressed in theorizing, and identifies theory's practical value. To summarize Davies, the "ability to locate in a variety of geographical and literary constituencies is peculiar to the migration that is fundamental to African experience as it is specific to the human experience as a whole ... The dynamics of location and re-connection offer a new and more contradictory set of questions and responses ... The dismantling of received geography is an important step ... critical work ... moves to redefine our geography, to re-create and remove the lines of impossibility in which we exist ... if we take any feminist issue and run it up the scale to its most radical possibility, its most clarifying illustration will be the experience of Black women ... we define theory as 'frames of intelligibility,' by which we understand the world, and not as reified discourse used to locate, identify and explain everything else ..." (*Black Women*, pp. 4–35).

40 From Spivak's extensive writings on the subaltern, I refer the reader especially to "Can the Subaltern Speak?," in Bill Ashcroft, Gareth Griffiths and Helen Tiffin (eds), *The Post-colonial Studies Reader* (London: New York, 1995), pp. 24–8; "Subaltern Studies: Deconstructing Historiography," in Landry and Maclean (eds), *Spivak Reader*, pp. 203–35,

especially pp. 212–13; "Cultural Talks in the Hot Peace: Revisiting the 'Global Village,'" in Robbins and Cheah (eds), *Cosmopolitics*, pp. 329–48, esp. p. 333; "Explanation and Culture: Marginalia," in Landry and Maclean (eds), *The Spivak Reader*, pp. 29–51. Also, in "More on Power/Knowledge," Spivak articulates once more the "subaltern" as the "space of the displacement of the colonization-decolonization reversal," in Landry and Maclean (eds), *Spivak Reader*, p. 164.

41 Spivak, "Subaltern Studies," Landry and Maclean (eds), *Spivak Reader*, p. 212.

42 Andrew Crehan, "*The Rape of the Lock* and the Economy of 'Trivial Things,'" *Eighteenth-century Studies*, 31/1 (Fall 1997): 45–68; Louis Landa, "Pope's Belinda, the General Emporie of the World, and the Wondrous Worm," *South Atlantic Quarterly* (1971): 215–35.

43 Gary Kelly, *Women, Writing and Revolution, 1790–1827* (Oxford; New York, 1993), p. 185.

44 Aravamudan, *Tropicopolitans*, pp. 2, 5, and see Spivak above on the subaltern.

45 Donna Landry, *The Invention of the Countryside : Hunting, Walking, and Ecology in English Literature, 1671–1831* (New York, 2001), pp. 24, 30.

46 Ibid., p. 8.

47 Ibid., pp. 35, 54, 115.

48 In my view, Landry somewhat inexplicably blurs this distinction by repeatedly juxtaposing the two as somewhat related in scope and motivation: "The discourse of sensibility and benevolence so important in anti-slavery debates and in legitimating the expansion of empire took a domestic form in British confidence regarding the proper treatment of animals. It became patriotic to be kind" (ibid., p. 118). Of course antislavery sentiment had its mawkish, ambivalent, and self-deluding side, as Charlotte Sussman has elaborated, but it still seems to be going too far to equate the impulses of anti-cruelty and antislavery movements, because the former was *not* based on principles of identification and empathy, while the latter at least attempted to be.

49 Ibid., pp. 74–5; see also p. 76.

50 On occasion, Landry veers close to such an acknowledgment, as in her brief discussion of Alexander Pope's "Windsor Forest" and its interleaving of the hunt and empire (ibid., pp. 117–18).

51 See James Walvin, "Black and White: Slaves, Slavery and British Society, 1600–1807," in Verene Shepherd (ed.), *Working Slavery*, pp. 304–5.

52 Ibid., p. 308.

53 Ibid., p. 309.

54 Blackburn, *Making of New World Slavery*, p. 4.

55 Paul Lovejoy and David Richardson, "Letters of the Old Calabar Slave Trade 1760–1789," in Vincent Carretta and Philip Gould (eds), *Genius in Bondage: Literature of the Early Black Atlantic* (Lexington, 2001), pp. 89, 96.

56 M. Kerr, *Reflections on the Present State of the Slaves in the British Plantations, and the Slave Trade from Africa* (York, 1789), p. 11.

57 Walter Benjamin, "The Work of Art in the Age of Mechanical Reproduction," in Leo Braudy and Marshall Cohen (eds), *Film Theory and Criticism* (New York, 1999), p. 751.

58 On hybridity and mimicry, see Homi Bhabha, "Signs Taken for Wonders: Questions of Ambivalence and Authority Under a Tree Outside Delhi, May 1817," *Critical Quarterly*, 12/1 (1985): 144–65, and "The Other Question – The Stereotype and Colonial Discourse," *Screen*, 24/2 (1983): 18–36; on the "negative consciousness" of the subaltern as the true

historical consciousness see Spivak, "Subaltern Studies," p. 2. Spivak's account of the subaltern's negative consciousness as the true consciousness of historical process can be usefully compared with Gilroy's concept of the negative consciousness of the plantation slave whose death wish disrupts the western Enlightenment project of reason and yet generates a voice, an identity, and an interpellant of modernity (*Black Atlantic*, pp. 60–69). Gilroy writes: "The repeated choice of death rather than bondage articulates a principle of negativity that is opposed to the formal logic and rational calculation characteristic of modern western thinking and expressed in the Hegelian slave's preference for bondage rather than death" (ibid., p. 68).

[59]　Walter Benjamin, "The Work of Art," pp. 732, 734, and this quotation p. 736.

[60]　See in particular his comments, ibid., p. 733.

[61]　Mita Choudhury has written about "interculturalism" on the British stage (*Interculturalism and Resistance in the London Theatre, 1660–1800* [Lewiston, 2000]). For comparative figures on importation, survival, and reproduction of slaves in the Caribbean and North American plantation systems see Curtin, *The Atlantic Slave Trade: A Census* (Madison, 1969); Wood, *Poetry of Slavery*, pp. xxxvi, xxxviii; Shepherd, *Working Slavery*, p. 22.

[62]　Fredric Jameson, "Third World Literature in the Era of Multinational Capitalism," *Social Text* (1986), pp. 65–88.

[63]　Indira Karamcheti, "Minor Pleasures," in Gita Rajan and Radhika Mohanram (eds), *Postcolonial Discourse and Changing Cultural Contexts: Theory and Criticism* (Westport, CN; London, 1995), pp. 59–68.

[64]　Benjamin, "Work of Art," pp. 735–6.

[65]　Even a selective list of major plays isolates George Colman the younger's *Inkle and Yarico* (1787); Thomas Bellamy's *The Benevolent Planters* (1789); Mariana Starke's *The Sword of Peace* (1789); John Fawcett's *Obi; or, Three Fingered Jack* (1800); Colman's *The Africans* (1808); the anonymous *Furibond; or, Harlequin Negro* and Saint-Pierre's *Paul and Virginie* (1808); and Thomas Morton's *The Slave* (1816) (Wood, *Poetry of Slavery*, p. xviii).

[66]　Benjamin, "Work of Art," p. 737.

[67]　See especially Chapter 2.

[68]　Thus Sussman writes, "the status of these objects is ambiguous … the ambiguous status of curiosities in early modern colonial discourse … makes visible the … imbrication of imperialism and the commodification of human bodies …" (*Consuming Anxieties*, pp. 60–61).

[69]　James Cook as quoted in Thomas, *Entangled Objects*, p. 128.

[70]　Ibid., pp. 126–8, 130–31.

[71]　Ibid., pp. 130–31.

[72]　Ibid., pp. 133–40.

[73]　Ibid., pp. 140–41.

[74]　Ann B. Shteir, *Cultivating Women, Cultivating Science: Flora's Daughters and Botany in England 1760–1860* (Baltimore and London, 1996), esp. pp. 174–5.

[75]　Homi Bhabha, "The Other Question: The Stereotype and Colonial Discourse," in K.M. Newton (ed.), *Twentieth-century Literary Theory: A Reader* (New York: St. Martin's Press, 1997), pp. 293–301; Bhabha, "Of Mimicry and Man: The Ambivalence of Colonial Discourse," in Philip Rice and Patricia Waugh (eds), *Modern Literary Theory: A Reader* (London, 1996), pp. 360–67; Robert J.C. Young, *Colonial Desire: Hybridity in Theory, Culture, and Race* (New York, 1995).

76 Charles Smith, *Auctions: The Social Construction of Value* (Berkeley, 1989), p. 31.

77 Ibid., pp. 32–3.

78 Thomas Krise (ed.), *Caribbeana* (Chicago, 1999), pp. 111–12.

79 There is, however, an anthropological literature on the ethnography of value in transnational trade that destabilizes any fixed system of classifications and equivalencies, or any fixed articulation of foreign or exotic objects as prized or despised, in metropoles or in peripheries (see Thomas, *Entangled Objects*). In sum, Thomas' argument foreshadows the argument I am making in this book about the entirely contextual, social, and relational valence of objects and peoples in transcontinental trade and exchange. It is far more common, however, to come across assessments of valuation in colonial or mercantile contexts as static and predictable (see Bayly, *The Birth of the Modern World*, p. 42). However, see also Bayly's concept of "bio-moral … consumption" (ibid., p. 44).

80 Homi Bhabha,"Of Mimicry," and "The Other Question." On the mutual hybridity generated by the east/west encounter in India, see William Dalrymple, *White Mughals: Love and Betrayal in Eighteenth-century India* (New York, 2003), pp. xliv–xlvii, 6–7, 12–15, 21–3, 26–7, 29–39. However, echoing Bayly and others, Dalrymple traces the demise of this hybridity or transnationalism in the nineteenth century and thereafter (pp. 38–43).

81 Aravamudan, *Tropicopolitans*, p. 281; see also p. 283.

82 Linda Colley, *Captives: Britain, Empire and the World, 1600–1850* (London, 2002); Aravamudan, *Tropicopolitans*; Felicity Nussbaum (ed.), *The Global Eighteenth Century* (Baltimore; London, 2003).

83 Aravamudan, *Tropicopolitans*, pp. 1–3.

84 See ibid., p. 4.

85 In Aravamudan's terms, "tension between representational surplus and referential lack" (ibid., p. 5).

86 Jeremy Rifkin, "The Biotech Century: Human Life as Intellectual Property," *The Nation* (April 13 1998), p. 12.

87 Ibid., p. 12.

88 Ibid., p. 18.

89 Blackburn, *Making of New World Slavery*, pp. 270–71.

90 Ibid., pp. 503, 543.

91 Bill Ashcroft, Gareth Griffiths and Helen Tiffin (eds), *The Empire Writes Back: Theory and Practice in Postcolonial Literature* (London; New York, 1989), pp. 45–52, 96.

92 Ibid., pp. 95–6.

93 Ibid., p. 96, italics mine.

94 See Aijaz, Ahmad, "In Theory: Classes, Nations, Literatures," in Bart Moore-Gilbert, Gareth Stanton and Willy Maley (eds), *Postcolonial Criticism* (London; New York, 1997), pp. 248–72; Mona Narain, "Shifting Locations: Third World Feminists and Institutional Aporias," in Devoney Looser and E. Ann Kaplan (eds), *Generations: Academic Feminists in Dialogue* (Minneapolis, 1997), pp. 159–60; also much of Spivak's works cited above. Of additional interest is Nandini Bhattacharya, *Reading the Splendid Body: Gender and Consumerism in Eighteenth-century British Writing on India* (Newark; London, 1998), pp. 13–22.

Chapter 2

Family Jewels: George Colman's *Inkle and Yarico* and Connoisseurship

I begin with a twentieth-century echo of an eighteenth-century conundrum. William Ivey, past chairman of the National Endowment for the Arts, gave a keynote speech in 1999 at the Chicago Center for Arts Policy. The panel he inaugurated was entitled "Beyond Survival: How the Arts will Serve our Democracy in the New Millennium." Ivey and the panelists were discussing value – aesthetic and commercial – and how to avoid their divorce in the new millennium. Ivey spoke about the value of art as a communally "useful" activity, which the public would pay for if they could see themselves bettered by it, and if it made them feel good.[1] The panel was being held at the Chicago Museum for Contemporary Art, and the museum's director was one of the panelists. The director, who had also led Euro-Disney once, contested Ivey's logic. The arts were not "Vitamin B" for community development, he said, but valuable for their own sake. The artists in the audience loudly applauded at this. But Ivey had surely bested the ex-Euro-Disney now Contemporary Art man: the former's argument that art be useful not autonomous, translatable not obscure, reassuring not avant-garde, would surely find more takers everywhere outside the hallowed walls of the museum. No one evoked Benjamin, or explicitly referenced the commodification of aura, but Ivey's supporters evoked art as public works treasure, not as solipsistic privilege, individual preoccupation, or private hoard. Their utilitarian argument about aesthetic value is not unlike that of George Colman Jr., who argued, as I hope to show, that art makes better homes and public gardens.

In 1787, Colman Jr.'s play *Inkle and Yarico* was first produced at the Haymarket Theatre. The popular story of Inkle and Yarico first appeared in Richard Ligon's *True and Exact History of the Island of Barbados* (London, 1657), revived in Steele's *Spectator* 11 in 1711, and was retold many times thereafter.[2] In the original versions, the young English merchant Inkle was rescued by an American woman named Yarico from shipwreck off the American coast. In return for her protection and love, Inkle promised to take her with him to England. However, when he was rescued by an European vessel, he brought Yarico to Barbados and sold her there with her unborn child.

To recapitulate briefly Colman's version of this oft-told eighteenth-century tale, Inkle in this play is an English city fellow, bred in the consideration of his "interest" above all else. He confesses: "Even so my father tutored me; from my infancy, bending my tender mind, like a young sapling, to his will – Interest was the grand prop round which he twined my pliant green affections …."[3] In Ligon's story, when

Yarico pleads her love and her pregnancy with Inkle, he increases her price because she carries valuable cargo, as one might say. The original and prior versions end thus, but Colman makes two changes in his ending: Yarico is not pregnant, and Inkle is persuaded not to sell her. Instead, Inkle's humanity is kindled by the benevolence of Sir Christopher Curry, governor of Jamaica. Curry's daughter Narcissa had been promised to Inkle, and Curry offers to make Yarico a foster-daughter from compassion at her plight: "I'll cherish her like my own daughter; and pour balm into the heart of a poor, innocent girl, that has been wounded by the artifices of a scoundrel."[4] Curry, the West Indian governor, the colonial Man of Feeling, is a humane paternalist, willing to allow his daughter to marry her poorer lover Campley instead of Inkle. Narcissa marries the man she loves, and Yarico gets her Inkle in the end. Until then, however, Inkle's avarice bankrupts his supposed Christian superiority, making him like the "savages" he condescends to: "we christians [sic], girl, hunt money; a thing unknown to you – but, here, tis money which brings us ease, plenty, command, power, every thing ...."[5]

Not insignificantly, 1787 was also the year of the ill-fated Sierra Leone resettlement expedition, engineered by Granville Sharp, and supervised in its early stages by Olaudah Equiano as commissary.[6] This expedition, which ended in horrific failure and loss of life, was hailed by abolitionists as reinstating ex-slaves in a just and ordered system of self-government, and perhaps welcomed by racialist thinkers as purifying Britain racially.[7] In April 1787, when the expedition left Plymouth, Colman's play would have been in rehearsal. By September 1787, even though the project's failure was public knowledge and the HMS *Nautilus* sailed back from Sierra Leone with 276 survivors left behind,[8] Colman's play had already earned its niche in theatrical repertoires.[9] The spectacle of ex-slave emancipation and the Haymarket play thus may have been functioning simultaneously, the former lending energy to the latter. The coincidence of the play and the expedition point to some crucial conjunctions of sentimental discourse in public life and in theater, conjunctions that affirm a collocation of value, taste, and virtue in English national consciousness. According to some accounts, Colman changed the ending of *Inkle and Yarico* because John Bannister, who was to play Inkle, just could not stomach the inhumanity of Inkle's character.[10] While this anecdote from Colman's own *Random Records* is compelling as an immediate cause for the changed ending,[11] contemporary culture suggests other powerful long-term tectonics and revaluations of morality and taste – and of a moral taste, or a taste for sentiment – that contributed to Colman's acceptance of Bannister's suggestion.

When Colman's play opens, we see Inkle planning the rounding up and transportation of the rich resources of the Americas; it is clear from the beginning that such "collection" of property might include humans: "I was thinking, too, if so many natives could be caught, how much they might fetch at the west-indian [sic] markets."[12] His servant, Trudge, fears instead that they themselves might become "collectibles," mummies or stuffed trophies for the American natives: "All that enter here [in Yarico's cave] appear to have their skins strip over their ears; and ours will be kept for curiosities – we shall stand here stuffed, for a couple of white wonders."[13] But this refiguration into non-European souvenirs, the ghostly mementoes of native consumption, is amply averted in the text in ways that indicate Colman's idea of "collection" and revaluation.

Yarico – first seen as a possible consumer of white collectibles like her compatriots – rapidly becomes an aestheticized commodity. Her cave is first compared to a warehouse in the Adelphi, thus allying her with London's art world.[14] Then she is likened to a Wedgwood teapot.[15] The teapot metaphor for Yarico is especially complex in its provenance. First, comparison with a teapot identifies her with theater actors like Henry Mossop, notorious for the satirized theatrical "teapot" posture. The actor Mossop would stand with an arm crooked on his waist, and the other held out in declamation. R.B. Peake, Colman's biographer, wrote: "As an actor, he [Mossop] was accused by the critics of too much mechanism in his action and delivery: his enemies censured the frequent resting of his left hand on the hip, with his right extended, which they ludicrously compared to the handle and spout of a tea-pot, whilst others called him the 'distiller of syllables.'"[16] Mossop, significantly, was also the first "husband" of George Jr.'s mother, Sarah Colman.[17] The theatrical and the genealogical converged, therefore, in Colman's imagination in this textual allusion to the teapot.

Already we begin to see an imbrication of transnational material transactions with a metropolitan genealogical imagination and familialization pursuits. For instance, what are the implications of Colman's mother herself having had an illegitimate child with Henry Mossop, of Colman himself being his parents' illegitimate child in the beginning, of Sarah Ford Colman having been born in Jamaica?[18] What impact might this have had on the creation and fortunes of *Inkle and Yarico*, with its own obsessions with colonial legitimacy or the lack thereof? Are Mossop, illegitimacy, and the theatre where they belonged evoked in this description of Yarico as a Wedgwood teapot? Material culture, exemplified in theatre or connoisseurship, had necessarily existed threatened with a taint of illegitimacy, and this particular metonymic allusion seems to drive in that reality. However, a Wedgwood teapot had other market and aesthetic associations in Colman's day that make this comparison yet more consequential.

The specific Wedgwood teapot that the play refers to may have been a glazed utensil colored red to look like antique classical coloring, called *rosso antico*, a very popular Wedgwood release.[19] The Wedgwood teapot was based upon older red Staffordshire stoneware made to emulate imported Chinese redware teapots, but Wedgwood refined the stoneware body during the early 1770s and named it *rosso antico*.[20] Admittedly the antiquity of this innovation referenced Chinese antiquity, but its redness is critical in relating Yarico to another racial other, and its pretensions to the classical antique relates it well to the cults of antiquity among connoisseurs.

Most later depictions of Yarico, like Colman's, are Americanized or Europeanized, while in the 1738 poem of her epistle to Inkle she is called both "negro" and Amerindian, and early illustrations in general make her darker-skinned. Yarico's Amerindian red skin, and her Amerindian "classicality" of character and mien are both captured in this fortuitous material metaphor of the teapot, important for our understanding of Yarico's suture in the play with the connoisseurial and collecting craze for real or fake antiquity, and with theatricality, racial otherness, and general iconic marketability. Many slaves in Jamaica were in fact given classical names – Diana, Psyche – and collectors at home often called their black or colored servants by classical names.[21] Wedgwood, a neoclassical enthusiast, was himself a committee member of the Society for the Abolition of the Slave Trade, and manufactured the famous black and white Jasper cameos of a slave kneeling in chains in 1787. Widely and often freely distributed, these cameos became signs of taste – mounted in rings, bracelets, hairpins, and snuffbox lids – as much as of abolitionist sentiment, as evident in the eminent abolitionist Thomas Clarkson's wry remark: "Thus a fashion was seen for once in the honorable office of promoting the cause of justice, humanity and freedom." [22]

Eighteenth-century racial theory would suggest that the Amerindian being closer to the European ethnically, interracial sex between European and Amerindian, or a lighter-skinned other was more acceptable than sex between European and African or black Caribs. As Robert Young shows,[23] eighteenth-century racial theory gradually formulated that different races were actually different species, and therefore sex with a significantly different race would lead to a monstrous hybrid. Peter Hulme has also argued that the yellow Caribs on St. Vincent were considered a purer race because they were more willing to accommodate the British, unlike the resisting black Caribs.[24] Other motives for Yarico's "Americanization" in Colman's play might have included the differential taxonomy of race and appearance noted as a "narrative avoidance" by Roxann Wheeler:

> In as much as enslaved Africans were crucial to bolstering the British economy, not to mention them being the other population with whom Britons were most likely to have sex, they were banished from the pages of novels that depicted romantic love between Englishmen and non-European women. The more acceptable racial others found in intermarriage novels embody and serve the narrative function of negotiating wider cultural anxieties aroused by a slave-based empire.[25]

Colman's *Inkle and Yarico* is also the only version of this story that I have found that does not in fact linger obsessively on the "contrast" in appearance between Inkle and Yarico. Numerous other versions document the two particular tropes of Inkle's fair flowing ringlets, and Yarico's fascination with the contrast of his hair against her own dark skin. These tropes, on the other hand, are matched by descriptions of Yarico's tawniness or darkness and her "African" hair and features, which seal her "difference."[26] In Colman's play, this chiaroscuro of racial contrasts in startlingly absent, though only to be displaced on to the conveniently darker Wowski, whose blackness is no problem, presumably because her suitor Trudge is a working-class Englishman.[27] That interracial romance was otherwise seen as scandalous is signified by two "scandal" prints of 1788, one titled "The Royal Captain" and the other simply "Wouski," which snare the royal princes in the scandal of interracial romance. "The Royal Captain" (see Figure 2.1) shows a captain (meant to be Prince William Henry)

The Royal Captain.

Figure 2.1   "The Royal Captain," 1 April 1788, published in *The Rambler's Magazine,* vol. 6, p. 104, British Library shelfmark Cup. 820. a.12 p. 104. By permission of the British Library.

embracing a black girl in the interior of a cabin; "Wouski" shows Prince William Henry embracing a mulatta (see Figure 2.2). Yarico's skin color also fluctuates to accommodate her moods of protest or submission, which identify her in turns with more militant and more comprador circumatlantic populations. In 1778, the relatively subjugated Amerindians were less threatening than Caribbean slaves becoming increasingly more rebellious. Thus, the language of late eighteenth-century racism encounters the sentimental civilizational discourse emboldened by abolitionism, and empowered by the notion of a vague civilizational and racial affinity with the "noble" and subjugated Amerindian.[28]

The colors of Yarico thus spread across discourses of race and politics as well as of aesthetics and domesticity. Antique red teapot thus fits Yarico most perfectly as a description, in ways that further her future revaluation and her assimilation on stage, in the market, and in the family. Both of these topical allusions – cave and teapot – are signs of Yarico's revaluation. Yarico is no mere savage; even the performative aspects of her apparent savagery are mediated by her multiple links with English popular and refined culture. She becomes the sign of refined consumerism and civilized domesticity, though in a more public sense she is also like actors who "re-present" life to English audiences. The images and stagings of Yarico, therefore, enable her simultaenous revaluation as artifact and as art.[29]

Again, racial darkness in Wowski, Yarico's darker-skinned companion invented and animated by Colman, provides another metaphoric link to material culture. Her skin color is comparable to theatrical blackface, but is in fact more salubrious because permanent and reliable, as well as a sign of a loving, "wifely" temperament:

> Trudge. black-a-moor ladies … are some of the very few whose complexions never rub off. 'Sbud, if they did, Wows and I should have changed faces by this time ….[30]

Trudge's lines combine references to a wide range of passional, aesthetic and transfiguring "performances": lovers of difference, eaters of difference, and actors of difference. Yarico and Wowski remain firmly objectified as well as other. One more instance of such rhetoric in the play will be useful: slaves are likened to commodities that drive the engines of European economy, like black coal in a ship's hold, as a planter says when the rescued triad arrives in Barbados,[31] once again reminding viewers of "human cargo" driving the engines of English civilization and commerce.

I juxtapose the activities of commerce, collecting and connoisseurship with traffic in nonwhite women because these activities and their attendant flow of commodities and people raise important and abiding questions about the measures and character of value in late eighteenth-century English society. Luce Irigaray has succinctly summarized the imbrication of women, exchange, and value in a patriarchal society: *"what is required of a 'normal' feminine sexuality is oddly evocative of the characteristics of the status of a commodity.* With references to and rejections of the 'natural' – physiological and organic nature, and so on – that are equally ambiguous … trans-formation of women's bodies into use values and exchange values inaugurates the symbolic order."[32] The aspect in which I differ from Irigaray on this idea is that I

Figure 2.2   *Wouski*, by James Gillray. London, 23 January 1788, published by H. Humphrey. British Museum of Prints and Drawings 7260. Copyright The Trustees of the British Museum. Produced by permission.

believe use value may, in certain instances, have as much labor added to it as exchange value does.[33] Irigaray argues primarily that commodities acquire exchange value from the labor that men lavish on them.[34] While this is true where there is a strict division of market and home, in a connoisseurial society such a division becomes blurred. I believe that Colman's symbolic economy assumes that it is not only the object of exchange that is labored over. Colman's exchangeable value is sometimes raw nature and sometimes the product of labor, but it is not "cultivated" in the sense that would make it valuable for the home. It is, instead, bearer of tainted value when its labor is valuable only on the market. This exchangeable commodity must be further "cultivated" and "improved" with an eye to use value for home improvement, and becomes neither physical substance nor exchangeable value but symbolic capital. Hence in his case labor and cultivation also produce use value that is traded in the market but becomes transcendent at home: art, *objets*, and women.

Srinivasan Aravamudan also writes of the value of non-western others in an essay on *Oroonoko* of "the status of … Africans not only as pets but as commodities that could, at any time, be converted to cash."[35] If slave equaled commodity, and an African/American like Yarico because of her lack of "whiteness" and "civilization" was essentially a slave, then she was also consigned to a commodity by nature.[36] As in the case of pets, so in the case of Oroonoko and of other classicized chattel humans, Aravamudan writes, "The owner's disinvestment returns ... [them] to the identity of an objectified commodity on the martketplace ...,"[37] clearly an exact description of Yarico's defetishization. Thus, treasure becomes commodity in a rather simple course of psychological disinvestment by the white owner. Moreover, Aravamudan seems also to suggest that such a logic of investment and disinvestment, or "personalized fetish" and "transactional fetish" as he terms it, is articulated by slaves' reflections upon their condition.[38] Indeed, Yarico herself frequently laments her necessary recognition that what has happened to her is devaluation from treasure to commodity, from flesh to body (in Hortense Spillers' terms), the "modern Janus-like composite of personal fetish and transactional fetish, two faces that together make up the world of affect and economics."[39] From an object of personal use she has become a marketed commodity.

It is instructive then to turn to the history of attitudes in the Colman family vis-à-vis transnational connoisseurship, race, and gender, all contexts of valuation. The Colmans were involved with British interests and activities abroad since the reign of George II. Francis Colman served as British envoy in the courts of Vienna and Florence in the 1720s and 1730s.[40] He also served English friends as buyer of Italian antiques, luxury exports, as well as singers for the Italian opera in England. His son George Colman the elder published a satirical weekly called *The Connoisseur* in 1754, soon after Samuel Foote's play *Taste* was performed in 1752. In this journal, uninformed connoisseurs were the targets of satire. The journal also spelled out the link between connoisseurship and plunder: "If the libraries and cabinets of the curious were, like the daw in the fable, to be stripped of their borrowed ornaments, we should in many see nothing but bare shelves and empty drawers."[41] The Colmans' involvement with connoisseurial discourse was a family tradition, therefore.

Colman the younger inherited his family's skepticism about motley collectors. During a tour to the North of England in 1775, he wrote derisively of his father's friend Joseph Banks, the naturalist of Captain Cook's voyages and a president of the Royal Society:

> Our progress, under all its cumbrous circumstances, was still further retarded by Sir Joseph's indefatigable propensity for botany. We never saw a tree with an unusual branch, or a strange weed, or anything singular in the vegetable world, but a halt was immediately ordered, out jumped Sir Joseph ... Many articles, "all a growing, and a growing," which seemed to me no better than thistles, and which would not have sold for a farthing in Covent Garden Market, were pulled up by the roots, and stowed carefully in the coach as rarities.[42]

Banks is defined as an indiscriminate collector in these remarks. In Nicholas Thomas' description of Banks, Thomas too stresses the assemblage of various objects and ornaments, not neatly classifiable, surrounding Banks in his portrait. Banks' portrait, Thomas suggests, denotes mastery over nature, and over certain scientific pursuits, but he is far from being a connoisseur in the socially privileged sense of the term.[43] Colman therefore criticizes Banks' virtuoso "spirit of research," and rebels against this tediousness by foregrounding "the novelty of the thing, and rambling through wild sylvan tracts of peculiarly romantic beauty, [which] counteracted all notions of studious drudgery, and turned science into a sport."[44] Institutionalized science was not to be the entertainment industry that Romantic or Picturesque tourism – both refiguring nature and sport – were becoming. [45]

Banks had also brought along with him Omai, the famed Polynesian "savage."[46] When Banks was droning on about scientific minutiae, explaining to his party the "rudiments of the Linnaean system," he "entertained the adults, Omai excepted."[47] The bored savage had an apparent bond with Colman in their mutual disdain for scientific pedantry. Colman Jr.'s observations on human and botanical collectibles in 1775 and his celebrated play upon England's collections abroad in 1787 are connected by a crucial distinction he too made between true and false connoisseurs: *mere* collectors like Banks, and antiquaries, were false connoisseurs. Another example illustrates the application of this distinction between science and connoisseurship. Colman remarked copiously, even obsessively, on Omai the "savage."[48] These remarks tend to re-evaluate and re-present Omai. Colman takes a swim in the Scarborough sea on the back of the obliging savage; Omai becomes here a merman, Arion's dolphin, or a triton, descriptions that classicize him, adding exchange value to his already "valuable" initial appearance as "pale moving mahogany, highly varnished …."[49] Somewhat upon the analogy of Charlotte Sussman's reading of Swift's Gulliver's voyage to Houyhnhnmland, I read this refiguration of Omai as treating "bodies as raw materials to be transformed … At its most extreme, such objectification is shown to lead to the possibility of valuing the bodies of cultural others simply as the raw material for interesting … or useful objects …."[50]

This refiguration of Omai echoes Johann Reinhold Forster, another noted traveler, who compared the Tahitians and Tongans to the ancient Greeks. As Thomas writes, "Descriptions of other people always embody some commentary … on home … The voyage literature of the late eighteenth century at once affirms the distance between European civilization and the social condition of Pacific islanders and – to a varying degree – relativizes the advancement of the former."[51] Omai's presence beautifies nature from raw material to culture while retaining traces of the foreign and the bestial.

In another context, the advent of Omai the polynesian on English cultural consciousness coincided with or triggered the marshalling of artistic and artisanal resources to improve and enhance public pleasure on the stage. As Edgar Wind has written, "The climax of Loutherbourg's theatrical career was his production (at Covent Garden in 1785) of the exotic pantomime *Omai; Or, a Trip Around the World*, 'the costumes being designed from studies made by John Webber, RA, the painter who was with Captain Cook on his last voyage ….'"[52] Figuring the savage thus involved a whole array of aesthetic innovations to satisfy the craving for appropriating exotic "treasures." If, "to a large extent, the movement of all these articles from indigenous to European exchange circuits was a movement of commoditization,"[53] Omai's classicization is evidence of a particularly rich tension in the shifting and evolving discourse of material culture. In the narrative of Colman's tour, Omai too becomes a trope of refigured value in a nexus of scientific, cultural, and fiscal discourses. He experiences a reversal of Yarico's fate, turning into treasure from commodity.

Later during the tour, Colman's contempt for Banks' indiscriminate collecting bursts forth again in a long invective upon living versus dead value, or connoisseurship versus antiquarianism or academicism, in the context of fiscal value figured as currency. Banks has just excavated an archaeological site:

> As to the products of the *Tumuli*, which were to reward our toils, they consisted of a few crumbling pots, dignified by the name of urns, of less intrinsic value, than a Staffordshire pipkin:[54] and some small pieces of copper money, with which it was impossible to toss up, for they boasted neither heads nor tails; whatever had been stamped upon them was either quite obliterated, or inexplicable. Two or three of them came into my possession, from my being one of the researching party, but I did not keep them long; and, from that time to this, I have evinced no talents as a hoarder of coin. My attempts, indeed, in this way, have been generally made with a view to modern English specimens, stamped with the King's head of the Brunswick line; many of these have, at different times, been in my hands; but somehow or other, they have soon passed out of them again, and I have never been able to succeed as a collector.[55]

This, then, is Colman's joke upon his own unthrifty nature, gaining point from Banks' antiquarian coin-collecting as direct target.[56] His joking distinction above between dead money and live money refers explicitly to coins with a face value to them and those without. The distinction between "face" and "faceless" refers to the eighteenth-century change in the concept of coin value from weight to circulation, from absolute or static value to relative or exchange value, or as James Thompson has defined it, from name to face.[57]

Thompson argues that the late seventeenth-century devaluation of coinage in England led to the revaluation of coin by face value and exchangeability, not by kingly name or origin as the source of absolute value. This displacement of absolute value by exchange or relative value both created and was created by a flourishing exchange economy. Thompson, however, goes further to show that in the later eighteenth century, sentimental critiques of commercial excesses led to a gradual dissociation of value from trade, colonialism or slavery: face then became name, as value was cleansed and redomesticated through sensibility, empathy and femininity. A private space analogous to that previously signified by monarchy was needed to "rename" this new "face" of value, and women, home, and the family became these new repositories of intrinsic value, the cleansed coinage. What started, therefore, as a replacement of "name" by "face" value, ended, under moral pressure to reform inhumane commerce and greed, in re-presenting "face" as "name."

This history of coinage and the moral shift accompanying its valuations shed further light on Colman's expressions of disdain for live versus dead coinage. Though George Jr. bragged about getting a lot of money and spending it fast, in *Inkle and Yarico* the adult George returned to sentimental practices of privileging intrinsic or absolute value, and thereby distinguishing true collectibles – true appendages of the material self – from lucre, trash, or fakes. At the end of the passage quoted just above, Colman is still opposing exchange value to intrinsic value, joking about not saving enough money to be rich. But by the later date of *Inkle and Yarico*, he will have indeed stopped extolling the "collection" of this morally worthless coin, and praise instead the true "worth" of domesticated female virtue and affection. Unlike the shameless merchant who "hunts" or "collects" money as a hoard, not a national treasure, Colman's refined "connoisseurship" thus gives him a new perspective on "intrinsic" value, causing his dramatic characters to treasure Yarico for what she might symbolize, and not for what she can fetch. By 1787, he has ostensibly outgrown an earlier currency or transactional fetish.

Omai is not directly present in the above discussion of coinage, but he was, again, part of a larger scheme of exchange and exploration, and an object of valuation thereby. Among other contexts of value in which Omai is imbricated, we come upon mineralogy, vulcanism, and other disembowelings of the earth. The travelers visited the Alum Works on the Mulgrave estate, the possession of Captain Phipps, later Lord Mulgrave.[58] From the excavation and disturbance of the earth's crust and ores, Colman soon moves to a different excavation of the earth, that of earth ovens, wherein Omai proves an expert. Describing Omai's Otaheitian cuisine, Colman quotes a passage about south sea clay oven cookery from Cook's *System of Universal Geography*, which describes Otaheitian ovens as semi-volcanic structures, with stratified layers of thermal activity: "it appears that the cooks of the Society Islands are, in fact, bakers, whose ovens are underground, with mouths at the top."[59] Not only is the volcano, a much-discussed natural phenomenon after the publication of William Hamilton's *Campi Phlegraei*,[60] socialized here into the baker's oven, but the misguided scientific collector's habit of over-reading the sites of national geological memory is opposed by a nice, warm meal produced by a savage but priceless cook. Comfort arrives unexpectedly in the midst of feverish antiquity- and novelty-searching in the form of this domesticated, classicized novelty, whose culinary frolics dispel the plutonic gloom of digging up national and geological history. The refiguration of value heralds the triumph of pleasure and utility rather than antiquarian collection or soulless commerce.

Colman's strong preference for living and pleasing artifacts over merely old or merely new things also fits nicely into the contemporary debate over antiquarianism and connoisseurship. Antiquarians were considered by some to be fusty collectors of old things merely for their antiquity;[61] connoisseurs, on the other hand, valued appearance combined with intrinsic worth, perhaps even uniqueness or "one-of-a-kind-ness," to quote Charles Smith.[62] Unique and lasting value were greater attractions for connoisseurs than mere antiquity or mere academic interest. Often a grand tourist, the connoisseur joined the Society of the Dilettanti, while the antiquary joined the Society of the Antiquaries.[63]

In 1628 John Earle, Bishop of Salisbury, wrote of an antiquary: "he is one that hath the unnatural disease to be enamoured of old age and wrinkles, and loves all things ... the better for being mouldy and worm-eaten."[64] And in the late eighteenth century Francis Grose wrote: "Among the numerous purchasers of coins, marbles, bronzes, antiquities and natural history, how few of them have their pursuits directed to any rational object ... I fear the majority of our present collectors ... rather hope that being possessed of rare and costly articles will serve for their passport to fame, be admitted as proof of their learning and love of the sciences, and at the same time obliquely insinuating some idea of their riches."[65] Colman too was thus offering fine distinctions about the art of collecting, distinctions more in favor of utility than mere antiquity, of rational yet refined enjoyment rather than covetousness and mere erudition. The antiquarian obsessions of the later eighteenth century, as Trumpener shows, are excessively discursive and surreal: "The world of the living is overwhelmed by antiquarian conjectures about the dead; the natural world is overwhelmed by the library, by an ongoing discourse of place, and by previous scholarly debates."[66] Places and things are overshadowed by studies, analyses and debates, including culturally imperialist ones. Colman resists this hyperdiscursivity with attempts to reanimate the seemingly dead, remote, or purely theoretical.[67]

Colman's critique of Banks targets both Banks' interest in material trivia and antiquarians' hyper-discursivity as explicated by Trumpener:

> Antiquarians' work is attacked both for the ostensible baseness of its objects of study and for the literal-mindedness of its belief that it can deduce civilizational forms from physical remnants: antiquarians proverbially mistake the discarded chamber pot or the cooking pot found in the bog for an antique urn, postholes dug thirty years ago for the traces of ancient buildings, and on this basis misdeduce the local course of Roman conquest ... In attempting to interpret the evidence of the world, antiquarians enter unknowingly into an epistemological quagmire, in which they successively lose all sense of direction and all sense of perspective.[68]

Antiquarianism joined with cultural nationalism on the peripheries of Britain seemed ridiculous to dominant culture: "When eighteenth- and early-nineteenth-century intellectuals tried to mock or discredit antiquarian theories, they attacked with particular vehemence the antiquaries' founding premise: the belief in the reconcilability of material and linguistic sources and the elevation of the physical fragment, the worn or broken artifact of everyday life, to the same status as written records."[69] Colman sees both antiquaries' hyper-discursivity and hyper-materialism – existing in tension in both imperialist and nationalist antiquarianisms – as a veneration of mortiferous uselessness. Antiquaries' discomfiture, in such cases, serves to entrench cultural imperialism, not to enhance deeper understanding of the other. It is more than ironic that analogous indiscriminate collecting within the quasi-scientific sphere, such as Joseph Banks', in fact foreshadowed the material entrenchment of future imperialism.[70]

At the opposite end of the spectrum from antiquarianism and culturally unusable collecting, there were attempts in eighteenth-century Britain to revive and use other cultures' historical alterity to suit English Enlightenment needs for improvement, consolidation, modernization. The "foreign" objects so transvalued range from the Celtic bard to architectural monuments in Kew gardens. Kew gardens' architecture serves as an instance of imperialist expropriation.[71] As the architect William Chambers' commentary showed, the monuments at Kew rang every note in the score of British expansionist paeans: Spain, France, the Mediterranean, and the Islamic and oriental worlds. The project at Kew, meant not only as a royal pleasure ground, but as a monument to English victories over the French and the Spanish, shows the range of British ambitions abroad. Thus it contains an antique gallery, an Alhambra, a Turkish mosque and various Pagodas, a Gothic cathedral, a Temple of Victory to commemorate the Minden victory in the Seven Years War (1759), and a Temple of Peace to commemorate the Paris peace of 1763.[72] The forty-third plate in William Chambers' *Plans, Elevations, Sections, and Perspective Views of the Gardens ... at Kew in Surrey* shows "a view of the Wilderness, with the Alhambra, the Pagoda, and Mosque."[73]

As this description shows, the monuments symbolizing England's expropriation of Spanish, Oriental and Islamic cultures are juxtaposed with wilderness in Kew's public spectacle. *Plans, Elevations, Sections* is thus an omnibus of arts as well as political triumphs, and Chambers' actual text is a commemorative portable miniature of this omnibus public project. The classical temples and Roman ruins at Kew are further symptoms of the project of aestheticizing foreign antiquity. Anne Janowitz has shown the eighteenth-century preoccupation with ruins as a marker of British imperialism, "while also indexing an imperial anxiety … Though the spectacle of ruins in the landscape offers evidence of a nation possessed by a long history, the material that ruinists draw on to make figures may produce different meaning within some other group's imagination."[74] Greek and Roman ruins could simultaneously signal England as the new Rome and the impermanence of empire, thus uniting triumph and worry. Since the appropriated, reconstituted "treasure" never lost its association with the plunder of other cultures, the gesture of transplanting cultural treasures is always fraught with ambivalence.[75]

Chambers' transvaluation of alterity and antiquity at Kew, complete with the improver William Kent's contributions, seems to have succeeded in burying the anxiety of these transplantations, but the anxiety resurfaces decade after decade. Connoisseurship as a discursive institution tried to disregard the material singularity of its subject to enfold it within a self-referential aesthetic, an aesthetic that is often also represented as genealogical and domestic. Trumpener offers the bard as a prime example of English imperialists' appropriation of the antiquity and cultural traditions of Ireland, Scotland and Wales for an enlightenment project of modernity and utility.[76] For non-English Britons the bard symbolizes a communal, cultural voice, but to the English he (and it is generally a he) symbolizes an individualistic, romantic ethos of expressive freedom. The English appropriation of Bardic song – its enclosure within a self-referential English aesthetic – is an example of unease with radical antiquity and alterity in English national consciousness and imperialist memory.[77]

A similar form of anxiety surfaced in the project of classicizing the foreign when slaveowners gave their slaves pompous classical names: "Whether Caesar, Pompey, or Cato, classical names were used to personalize pets and rename slaves, fulfilling a range of comic functions for the owners."[78] The doubleness of the slave body that was used to reproduce both commercial profit and classical traditions (in a hybrid sense) led to an uneasy reminder of the irreducible remainder of colonial and slaveowning transactions underwritten by middle-class or aristocratic domesticity.

Peripheries struggled to retain their chronotopic and cultural uniqueness and continuity though enlightenment metanarratives confronted them with universalism, temporal succession, economism, and other institutions of improvement.[79] These cultural preoccupations of Colman's day evidently stamped his cultural projects with their own impress. In Omai's case as in *Inkle and Yarico*, too, Colman appropriates an alien history and identity not to empower the other, but to make the other the imperialist's commodity fetish.[80] Yet the indubitable reality of a continuous practical and discursive slippage between connoisseurship and indiscriminate collecting cultures could never be totally set aside. Despite the worrisome erasure necessary to sustain connoisseurial culture and colonization, the irrepressibility of material practices and ideologies emerged. The very method of acquisition of connoisseurial objects – a grab and run technique – often resembled too closely the hit or miss, accidental techniques of antiquarianism, collecting, slave-trading, and colonialism. In the recontextualizaiton of objects like Yarico – objects acquired accidentally or hurriedly[81] – for instance, the revaluation naturally had to occur not at the moment of acquisition but at the moment of symbolic consumption. Thus, only when in Jamaica, beyond the pales of pure or raw nature, Yarico's commodity fetish status as woman or slave surfaced fully.

Under such circumstances, given the lack of any teleological or genealogical certainties, ontological leanings resurfaced, meeting unrefined curiosity and, in some instances, greed. Many connoisseurs showed disturbing signs of acting like antiquaries, valuing the rare and the fusty over the beautiful and the strange.[82] Clive Wainwright thus anatomizes collectors' apparent disorderliness: "each object fitted into the collector's mental model of his collection, which may or may not have been based upon intellectually sound principles. His brain alone stored the invisible yet vital cross-references that linked one object or group of objects with another. Their disappearance on the death of the collector frequently meant that what to him was a supremely logical assemblage of objects seemed to the next generation a chaotic jumble of curiosities."[83] Such had been some real seventeenth-century collectors, and characters like Gimcrack in Thomas Shadwell's *The Virtuoso* (1676), who collected for knowledge and curiosity, not for refined yet rational enjoyment.[84] Such collectors will be revisited in chapter four, but the "mixed collections" of indiscriminate collectors – who seemed to combine naturalistic and artistic antiquities pell-mell[85] – had to be met head on with a connoisseurship valuing the right thing for the right reason.

Some of Colman's contemporaries did show a desire for authenticity, unbounded immediacy, resembling Colman's own aspirations of familializing the exotic. Thus, British grand tourists in Italy from Addison on tried to appropriate Italian antiquity into self-consolidating cultural capital for themselves while treading Italian ground. They experienced what they saw in their own time through the lens of an inner eye tinctured by Virgil, Horace, Pliny, Lucan, Strabo, and Livy.[86] Their desire to reanimate the exotic dead is to be traced in Colman's aspirations for his dramatic "objects" too.

Such expropriations were redeemed by presenting them as public-spirited, civic acts by wealthy men. Like David Hume, who wrote of the salutary transformation of hoard into treasure by its rechanneling into public works,[87] Edward Southwell had written in 1726 of the wonderful public works of Rome as "the expence of one private man ... noble monuments of a publick spirit and disinterested regard to the good of one's country ...."[88]

John Soane wrote in the introduction to his *Plans Elevations and Sections of Buildings* (1788):

> In ancient times it was great and meritorious to raise the temple, the portico, and other public edifice. How great the advantage and glory that accrued to the Roman name and empire from their buildings, the amphitheatres, triumphal arches, baths, aqueducts and other remains of ancient magnificence abundantly testify. The monuments and trophies that were raised at the public expence to perpetuate the memory of great atchievements [sic], at the same time that they immortalized the fame of individuals, were lasting proofs of the justice and liberality of the people ....[89]

The expropriation of Rome and Roman antiquity, while it allowed taste and private magnificence to be re-invented in England, could also be fitted into a Humean rhetoric idealizing civil humanism. In an essay titled "Of the Rise and Progress of the Arts and Sciences," David Hume compared Europe to a copy at large of what Greece was in miniature.[90] Hume too praised the refinement and rise of classical arts and projects of taste, and distinguished the living arts and indeed the trades that distinguished public good and spending from vicious accumulation and self-indulgence.[91] Hume anticipates Colman's redefinition of wealth as treasure, not hoard. The civil arts of a country can strengthen and revitalize its bourgeois public. Hume writes:

> industry, knowledge, and humanity are not advantages in private life alone; they diffuse their beneficial influence on the *public*, and render the government as great and flourishing as they make individuals happy and prosperous. The increase and consumption of all the commodities, which serve to the ornament and pleasure of life, are advantages to society; because, at the same time that they multiply those innocent gratifications to individuals, they are a kind of *storehouse* of labor, which, in the exigencies of state, may be turned to the public service.[92]

Exemplary live collectors, such as William Beckford, contributed to this cultural trend of transvaluing the commodity by domesticating it. Beckford earned the respect of contemporary as well as future cognoscenti for his taste, scholarship, and pursuit of antiques that he then domiciled in his famed private residence, Fonthill Abbey.[93] Not only did Beckford transvalue the foreign by collecting foreign cultural treasures and making Fonthill a repository for them, but he also endowed them with metropolitan symbolic and genealogical dimensions, by making his great house and its artistic treasures a studio and a study for living artists.[94] Beckford might have been Colman's model of the true connoisseur, who collects and values antiquity but uses it as living treasure; as Wainwright has shown, in his blend of medievalia with sixteenth- and seventeenth-century *wunderkammer* style, in his appreciation of "works of art" as "virtuoso craftsmanship in precious and exotic materials," Beckford the gothic revivalist was a connoisseur ahead of his time.[95] Not insignificantly for this discussion, a vast part of Beckford's wealth was based on his West Indian plantations, whose dwindling profits led to the declined income that caused Beckford to sell off his treasured hoard in 1822.[96]

Enthusiasts of neoclassicism and classical antiquity also exemplified the emerging consensus on value in trade and connoisseurship. Admiration of Greek and Roman civil culture led Richard Bromley to defend the Athenian Pericles despite his military downfall: "the result ... of such a system as that which was pursued by Pericles, so far I mean, as ingenious merit, unconnected with what was dissolute or vicious, was patronized and reared ... was but a *circular rotation of treasure*, which when it had run through ever so many hands came back by one means or another to the public account, without tainting the public in it's [sic] course. If the ocean feeds from it's [sic] great plenitude the lesser rivulets, they all run back to pay their tribute to the sea again."[97] The "good" hellenic projects of taste, Bromley argued, turned wealth into treasure, and exchange into use. The same for the Romans: the earlier Romans "collected" or "plundered," and then hoarded; but Agrippa "recommended ... that the works of art possessed by individuals should be devoted to the public use in some public repositories, for the improvement of those who meant to prosecute the arts, and for the admiration and pleasure of all."[98] Luxury was *good* for a nation in this way, and had not undergone the "pernicious" change that Hume cautioned against in "Of Refinement in the Arts." He argued there that projects of taste, which in Hume's and Bromley's day would include connoisseurship, could be harmful if they remained unrealizable as treasure, or stagnated undemocratically as wealth only.[99] Luxury and taste were forms of wealth not to be hoarded, but to be held in readiness for public benefit. Exchange thus gave way to use as value solidified into monuments of national taste. If, in Hume, value as treasure, not hoard, animated public existence, in *Inkle and Yarico*, value as treasure, not exchange or hoard, animated domestic life; both use and exchange value were thus animated by reserve labor.

Foreign "parts" were early figured as collectibles of unstable psychic or material signification in the Colman familial discourse. Thus, David Garrick wrote to George Colman the elder from Rome in 1764: "I am antiquity-hunting from morning till night, and my poor wife drags her lame leg after me."[100] In the early eighteenth century, Colman the elder's father Francis Colman had been involved in a number of informal exchanges of damasks and Florentine marble furniture with various friends and acquaintances in England and abroad.[101] At this time, one of his diplomatic endeavors generated a joke about his handling of "foreign parts." Francis Colman had to ascertain the dowager Duchess of Parma's supposed pregnancy, which would determine the balance of power between England, France, and Spain. William Pulteney, Lord Bath, wrote thus jocosely to Colman during the controversy over this: "By the bye, I am told that you, among others, are one appointed to peep into the lady's privities, and watch narrowly that no pretender be imposed upon the world ... I wish you could have got an article inserted ... whereby the Venus of Medicis, and half-a-dozen other of the best statues and curiosities of the gallery should be given and yielded to us, by way of acknowledgement for the services done to Don Carlos ...."[102] The joke contains two important connoisseurial subtexts. First, the Duchess' private parts are linked with Italian art. Second, connoisseurship is analogous to scrutiny and censorship of cultural and political genealogies.

A prevailingly familial discourse, this also resolutely feminizes the foreign and underscores the bent of the Colman family's interchanges about travel, tourism, and exchange. Foreign things – "parts" – are fetishized and feminized, and familial structures are imposed on the fetish perforce inserted into the exchange nexus. The foreign as an object of virtu, or taste, becomes a household thing once it has been stripped of its threatening, defamiliarizing alterity by the evaluating gaze. The lifestyles of Britishers with a record of "foreign" connections – artists, connoisseurs, ambassadors, and their mistresses – also demonstrated the multiple juxtapositions of women, sex, collectible exotica, and connoisseurship, as evident in the career of the infamous Emma Hamilton.[103]

Other connoisseurial rhetoric on woman as other is found in Colman's *Eccentricities for Edinburgh*, in the poem entitled "Fire! or the Sun-poker." Of the Gods' reception of Pandora, the "made" woman who disperses Prometheus' human community, Colman speaks in terms that evoke the commodity and the fetish, the collectible and the saleable:

> So, – when the Fair One was announc'd,–
> Up their Immortalships all bounc'd,
>   Without the least decorum;
> And all the *Cognoscenti* of the Skies
> Popp'd up their spying-glasses to their eyes,
>   To pass their judgment on the Piece before 'em;
>   Peeping, and peering,
>   Praising, or jeering;
> Spluttering encomium, and stricture;
>   As purchasers, and puffers, auctioneering,
>   Cry up, or down, a Statue, or a Picture.[104]

Like a group of dilettanti – self-appointed cultural elites – the gods here behave like false connoisseurs whose acumen is befogged by their acrimony, whose skill is overshadowed by their superficiality. Colman further writes: "The Gods and Goddesses had firm reliance/ On their own skill, in every Art, and Science;/ Each was a *Connoisseur*, or *Connoisseuse*; – That is, they had a general smattering,/ Enough to set them, on all subjects, chattering,/ Like sundry Gentlemen who write *Reviews*; –."[105] Once more, being a good connoisseur is a high, almost Olympian achievement, and definitely a male-dominated enterprise.

Another example of revaluation tied to paternalist familialism is to be found in comments in George Colman the senior's correspondence with Elizabeth Inchbald, the budding playwright, in the 1780s. Colman senior's letters to Inchbald are avuncular at best, and proprietory at worst. He decides the value and marketability of her writing for her in the following words:

> I hope & believe that the farce you have finished is not, as you say, extremely nonsensical. Nonsense is not your talent; but if I can, by any dramatick or theatrical alchymy transmute what you call Nonsense into any thing like I'll tell you What, or the Mogul Tale, I think it may, like them, support itself without Songs, which will put you to a certain expence, without a certainty of repaying you. Whatever it is, I shall be glad to see it, & will, as I ever have done, tell you my real thoughts on it, & give you all the assistance in my power.[106]

The message is clear: it is Colman senior the manager who can truly appraise Inchbald's dramatic writing, and she should leave it to him to assign and extract a value for it in the theatre market. Meanwhile she can be a member of the Colman dramatic family or repertoire, and forget about owning her own plays: both Inchbald and her play are to be reanimated, domesticated, transvalued, and recirculated by Colman, an idea captured in his phrase "alchemy."[107]

The debate between Inchbald and Colman about who owns her plays sounds a familiar theme. This and the Duchess of Parma incident foreshadows a theme of commodifying and revaluating femininity that reappears in Colman's *Inkle and Yarico*. Colman's Yarico is a commodity who is threatening as long as she remains unfamiliar, unclaimed, and unsubordinated to the patriarchal family. She triggers collective male anxiety by being desirable, feminine, and unclaimed, unstable value. Commercial exploitation, or selling her into slavery, will realize a certain crude economic value, but this is not Colman's social objective. As a connoisseur, he desires to domesticate the value Yarico embodies, to have her adorn a so-called moral, semi-private economy. As a descendant of connoisseurs and a member of a society priding itself on connoisseurial taste, Colman indicates a sentimental aesthetic solution to his society's moral puzzle of profitable but reprehensible commerce. Male anxiety and male guilt are allayed, yet male power is reasserted by withdrawing Yarico from the public exchange economy and familializing her within a more subtle traffic in women, that of marriage and inheritance.

In his ending of the play, when Yarico becomes a foster-daughter of Christopher Curry, the British Governor of Jamaica, Colman effects a revaluation of the foreign woman from market capital to symbolic capital. This revaluation bestows on her a reassuring genealogy, one that Curry's real daughter Narcissa would already have by virtue of Britishness. Yarico does not thereby merely recover a lost identity. She is in fact remade thereby, given a whole new identity and value, made domestic and demystified, but still owned. This sort of ownership can be seen as a mark of taste, as in owning greco-roman antique collectibles, not of naked acquisitiveness, as in trading in slaves. Symbolizing human traffic assuages guilt for commercial exploitation of other races, but subtends the masculine orders of value and exchange.

The above discourses of connoisseurship, tourism, and public works projects refocus our view of *Inkle and Yarico* upon the problematic but critical recontextualization of the foreign in the intercultural zone, as Charlotte Sussman has suggested.[108] Dabbling in difference had some adverse consequences; the very same Italy that yielded objects of connoisseurial taste and virtue – "music and painting ... statuary and architecture ... cabinets of rarities ... and collections of all kinds of antiquities" – could give Englishmen venereal disease.[109] The proverb "See Rome and Die" also had a double meaning, as in the case of travelers contracting the infamous Roman fever.[110] The joys of the foreign could be thrilling as well as killing, as Inkle and Trudge speculate in the cave scene.[111] Thus, finding and assuming the right attitude towards foreignness in the intercultural zone becomes crucial. At the beginning, Colman's Inkle's attitude to travel seems consciously defined in opposition to all aestheticized travel altogether. His language upon shipwreck on the American shores would seem to yield a reading of only commercial interests and values. Thus he speaks to his uncle, Mr. Medium, lost with him, about traveling and collecting versus profit-making:

> Inkle. What, would you have a man of business come abroad, scamper extravagantly here and there and every where, then return home, and have nothing to tell, but that he has been here and there and every where? s'death, sir, would you have me travel like a lord?
>   Med. No, the lord forbid.
>   Inkle. Travelling [sic], uncle, was always intended for improvement; and improvement is an advantage; and advantage is profit, and profit is gain. Which in the travelling [sic] translation of a trader, means, that you should gain every advantage of improving your profit.[112]

Profit-making and book-keeping are Inkle's obsessions, and the play makes capital of them.[113] However, he also parodies, albeit unconsciously, the language of "true" connoisseurs who mocked callow and untrained aristocrats for going abroad on the tour and for seeing foreign parts without really recognizing their true value. Inkle's apparent mercantilist singlemindedness is fraught with the potential for connoisseurial double meanings. On the one hand, Inkle, with his eye on "interest" defines "improvement" as augmentation of financial capital, a definition with which his punning emphasis on "interest" is compatible,[114] thus refuting dilettanti and connoisseurs who would define improvement as producing psycho-aesthetic capital. Yet, on closer look, he and the true connoisseurs are not unalike. He revises, not refutes, the grand tour ideology of collecting. The reference to the shallow Lord especially sharpens the possibility that Inkle challenges those grand tourists who travel aimlessly or obsessively, not knowing the true value of what they see. The play is about his humanitarian re-education in connoisseurial art and science, and this play on words anticipates his potential. The "lords" collect valuable art objects and prestige; Inkle collects slaves and commercial fortune. The lords need to appreciate the humanizing value of their property as treasure;

Inkle needs to revise his theory of "improvement" to appreciate the female slave he picks up as treasure, not commodity.

Throughout the play, as we have seen, Yarico is defined in terms of many kinds of valuable commodities: theatrical, commercial, or familial. Her value is constantly shifting, too, until it comes to rest in the family. As Irigaray writes, "In order for a product – a woman? – to have value, two men, at least, have to invest (in) her."[115] Incidentally, while the original stories generally depict Yarico and Inkle meeting alone, or even Yarico rushing in upon Inkle,[116] in Colman's play the moment of encounter is staged rather differently. Inkle and Trudge break in on Yarico and Wowski, and proceed to categorize and evaluate the cave, the objects, and the women in its inmost recess.[117] Again, when Yarico is next evaluated, Sir Christopher Curry and Inkle are the speakers and subjects of the transaction. Curry makes a remark that can be read in more ways than one: "I can't help thinking the only excuse for buying our fellow creatures, is to rescue them from the hands of those who are unfeeling enough to bring them to market."[118] Whatever the play protests, Curry's words bear out that two men must join to give value to a woman and a commodity. However, Curry's stated expectations also make it very clear that the sort of fellow creature in whom he is interested is an aesthetically pleasing one: "as you say she is a delicate girl, above the common run, and none of your thick-lipped, flat-nosed, squabby, dumpling dowdies ...."[119]

In terms of looking at women and racial others, therefore, Colman brought to bear the connoisseurial rather than the collector or antiquarian attitude to collecting, which led him to represent slavery as tasteless as much as wrong. In preferring connoisseurship over antiquarianism, Colman entered a long-running aesthetic debate about the true purpose of collection and exchange, and furthered a larger project of re-presenting marketable value apotheosized as virtue. Value or virtue had to be cleansed of the commercial taint, and repossessed on different claims; face had to become name. One topical way to do this was to feminize value and sentimentalize exchange.

Nationwide, commercial exchanges were masked by sentimental rhetoric, as Peter Hulme has documented, to soften criticism of colonial practices.[120] From Hulme's demonstrations of sentimental evasions of political responsibility, it could be inferred that Colman's Yarico's sentimentalized "daughterliness" and tawniness suggest her absorption into interstitial "yellow carib"-ness – the kind of Carib identity the British favored in the Carib wars of the 1770s and 1790s – enabling Colman to tread a middle path between planter hostility and sentimental metropolitan anti-abolitionism. Yarico's color and sentimental future could, according to Hulme, reflect a primarily political unconscious.[121] However, it is also possible that Yarico's color and revised fate reflect an aesthetic imaginary as well as the manipulation of radical or libertarian protest, much as the rhetoric of "family values" does today.

This sentimental aesthetic of (family) value, which cheers the British hearth while allowing British trafficking to run otherwise unchecked, parallels the connoisseur's view that the "valuable" is the "tasteful" and the "useful," the commodity transformed into treasure. Thus, for instance, Maxine Berg and Helen Clifford have examined the iconography of trade cards around the 1780s to conclude similarly that the icons of trade and taste deployed femininity and classical antiquity inseparably:

> By the 1780s the profusion of objects so typical of the trade cards up to the 1760s have been replaced by classical imagery … Classical references take two forms, either elegant ladies in billowing 'antique' dresses that waft scrolls of descriptive text before the viewer, or slightly later the appearance of classical urns and vases, some of which are recognisable [sic] artifacts like the Warwick Vase. The latter category relies on the creation of identifiable icons, whose presence transcends any particular material … it is not the purchasable goods that are important, but the transcending association with a particular idea of the classical.[122]

Yarico, as the discussion of the antique red teapot image has shown, was clearly such an identifiable icon, whose iconicity foregrounded precisely the intersections of commerce and taste the tradecards so overtly connote. Sentimentalizing and domesticating value helped Colman and his contemporaries to defuse the social tensions generated in exploration and exploitation of other cultures. British collectibles could seem from this viewpoint not violent appropriations of other national histories, but a tastefully naturalized part of England. Idealized connoisseurship, in this extended sense, humanized market practices in an age worried about the excesses of commerce and the attendant devaluation of art and people, but nevertheless unwilling to leave off traffic in either. By collecting "living" value, British connoisseurs argued that they provided a viable soil for such value to flourish, while the soil itself was "improved" by this transplantation.

Colman's project of transvaluation shows that like so many of his contemporaries he had difficulty acknowledging Britain's political excesses. Antiquarianism and the slave trade, two institutions that forthrightly express the radical alterity of history and humanity, unnerve his writing. On the other hand, the project of "taste" that he adopts sanctions the erasure of radical alterities and specificities, and tames these radically other entities into lovable ones. The rhetoric of "taste" infuses Colman's language, allowing us nevertheless to glimpse the crude underbelly of this supposedly pure aesthetic. As a contemporary of Colman wrote about the latter's *John Bull*,

> there is one striking peculiarity of modern comedy which, it is to be feared, is derived from our Manners. The sole interest now turns on poverty and wealth. We are no longer agitated by the various distresses and final successes of a generous passion … the distress arises from urgent creditors and sheriffs; and the happy catastrophe, from the intervention of fortune (like a god in some of the Greek tragedies) in the shape of an unexpected bequest or the detection of a forged will.[123]

Though the review was written sixteen years after *Inkle and Yarico*'s publication, this reviewer's fear and his insight clearly foreground an important, enduring dialectic of Colman's age: virtue versus commerce. This dialectic is an endlessly fruitful problem for Colman, who frequently takes material culture on board to produce cultural material from it.[124] As with *Inkle and Yarico*, Colman's plays and their characters wish to reconcile virtue with a cleaner, that is familialized, commerce.

That commercial underbelly of virtue can be resolved quite simply into a picture of class differences. Inkle is a "cit," a member of the aspiring bourgeoisie, as his upwardly mobile marriage to Narcissa would have confirmed. The preference Colman and Hume show for wealth defined as treasure – not hoard or commodity – marks their discourse as that of the bourgeoisie, as opposed to the hoarding aristocrats, or the trading classes. Once again, the domestication of enterprise goes hand in hand with the bourgeoisification of value, private aspirations fueling a public discourse. The surge in collectors of British antiquities, as Wainwright has shown, can be traced, like domestic tourism, to structures of class and relative spending power.[125] People who confined their interests to British antiquities rather than classical ones, and those who confined their traveling to Britain rather than the continent, were often middle-class, and a growing group. The nationalistic culture of connoisseurship espoused by Colman, and its middle-class characteristics, were a feature of the times. Public, middle-class culture particularly required the appropriation and sanitization of alterity as publicly displayed treasure. As Joshua Reynolds saw it, and as John Brewer has described it, "the owners of major collections were encouraged to make their treasures available to interested connoisseurs and painters … painters were [otherwise] never certain of securing entry into the houses of the grand connoisseurs."[126]

Indeed, the first attempt to found the Royal Academy of Arts (1755) floundered because artists would not accept the tyranny of gentlemen connoisseurs, and the Dilettanti Society, composed of such, would not lend their imprimatur to artists who wouldn't take their verdicts as binding.[127] And, the Royal Academy itself stood testimony to the idea that "the activities of a private man of taste are subordinate to the higher aim of helping … to create a distinguished national school of art. The connoisseur is made the servant of the artist … The links with commerce and cash were glossed over."[128] Such public artistic treasures were inevitably further commercially inclined, of course; for instance, British artists who trained and practiced in the homes of the rich such as the Duke of Richmond, were converting artistic treasure to art with a marketable future. As we have seen, in *Inkle and Yarico* too bourgeois familial rhetoric conceals commercial infrastructures.

Thus, in Colman's *John Bull*, the virtue of the tender-hearted though fallen Mary Thornberry, Job Thornberry's daughter, is redeemed by marriage to her aristocratic seducer. The match, though, comes about through the efforts of the mysterious East-India merchant, Mr Peregrine. His deeds are buttressed by the bluff bourgeois rhetoric of Thornberry himself, who takes on the establishment embodied in Sir Simon Rochdale, the local Justice of the Peace as well as Mary's seducer's father. Not only does East-Indian commerce supply Mary's dowry, but it is in fact expropriated to redeem England's declining aristocracy, as Peregrine turns out to be Sir Simon's older brother, and his immense wealth is harnessed to English families, homegrown virtue and philanthropy. Nobleman, honest tradesman, and aristocrat disguised as merchant are links in a chain of deference and obligation, creating the illusion of class harmony and redeemed female virtue.[129] Keeping Colman's longstanding preoccupation with transvaluation in mind, we can return to the oscillating public and private cultures of *Inkle and Yarico* to find profit alchemized into use-value, goods into property, slave into daughter, commodity into treasure.

The play concludes by repressing the memorable and anxiety-producing reality of traffic in slaves, women, and other commodities, to present a lighter view of public confraternity. Male "understandings," about daughters and female slaves, leads to the humorous reassignment of commodity values, denouncing the fatuously singleminded collector who would commodify an exotic female, or the rake at home who would ruin the virtue of a woman or the sanctity of home. The family romance sports a father-daughter-suitor plot involving a fungible female.[130]

Is the story of *Inkle and Yarico* partial evidence, then, of the finally successful separation of male and female, public and private spheres, a transformation that James Thompson traces in his analysis of political economy and the novel? Or is it a particular historical negotiation of the inevitable moral and ethical conflicts daily confronting a culture profiting from plantocracy and slavery? The answer maybe that Colman's *Inkle and Yarico* helps moderate rising anti-slavery critiques fretted with debates on gender.[131] But *Inkle and Yarico*'s resolution of England's ethical crisis attendant upon plantocracy and slave-trading cannot be completely grasped without investigating the related debates on taste, connoisseurship, and gender. Evidently, Colman is aware of the issues, indices and tropes of abolitionist discourse. However, it is also the case that the hymeneal conclusion of *Inkle and Yarico* re-inscribes, while seeming to critique, the benefits of the global flow of people and things. Domestic and imperial ideologies must be read against each other. The play that Elizabeth Inchbald said would forever silence the objections of abolitionists like Wilberforce to the theater[132] provides another example of drama wherein global exchanges in women, slaves, collectibles, and commodities still shore up Englishmen's identity.

As Charlotte Sussman has perceptively remarked:

> the antislavery movement was inflected by gender ideologies … the lives of white women living in Britain during the eighteenth century were to some degree structured by the dynamics of colonialism and race … Seeing the allegiances of female antislavery activists bisected by the bonds of class and sex helps explicate the contradiction between their identification with West Indian slave women, and their denial of alternative forms of agency or subjectivity to such women.[133]

The elision of Yarico's harsh realities by the reinscription of that story within Narcissa's underscores Sussman's insight.

According to Catherine Moore, in the *Spectator* version of *Inkle and Yarico*, gender conflict was more topical than racial conflict. The faithlessness of women was the issue under debate, not the promise-breaking of Europeans towards other races.[134] In Martin Wechselblatt's view, earlier versions of *Inkle and Yarico* – from 1711 to 1738 – emphasize commercial England breaking its promise to subject races and betraying them into slavery, particularized in Inkle's betrayal of Yarico, but mid-century versions of *Inkle and Yarico* mask the excesses of commerce by criticizing the passionate excesses of other races. Wechselblatt argues, therefore, that in earlier versions there is a dominant though muted sentimental mode. In the later versions, the subject races betray one another and themselves into slavery, the cause being their own ungovernable passions, especially if they are black, like Yarico (or Dido).[135] The use of the heroic epistle in eighteenth-century tellings of this story is meant to foreground, in Wechselblatt's view, a basic story of a promise not kept to oneself, an act by non-western cultures frowned upon by western credit-based commercial society.[136]

Wechselblatt finds, therefore, that while sentimental and gender discourse had been dominant in interpreting the Inkle and Yarico story in the early eighteenth century, in the mid-century the focus had shifted to race, as commerce and colonialism flourished. In this chapter I have argued that this mid-century preoccupation with race – whether imperialist or plain curious – provoked a reaction later in the century in the form of a shift to an earlier focus on women and the family. Late eighteenth-century versions of *Inkle and Yarico* denote both a return to gender politics and an emphasis upon the west's inhumanity. These two changes reflect a real and troubling crisis in commerce and imperialism.[137] We are well into the era of sentimental literature on slavery and colonialism via connoisseurship.

The modified ending of Colman's *Inkle and Yarico* is only one signal of the later eighteenth century's ambivalence about race and commerce; it retreats from the risks of encountering racial difference to the containing and controlling frames of gender relations and family ideology. Race had become a more inflammatory concept as enlightenment science and philosophy were stripping it of its cultural and civilizational emphasis and endowing it with a biological determination.[138] Once race was determined to be biological, the only way to justify continuing involvement with other races was to resurrect civilizational constructs like the bourgeois heterosexual family and select certain races to be members of it. Race is largely figured through and as gender, therefore, before Colman writes his play.

Wechselblatt's argument further converges with mine as we explore the outcome of two frightening slave rebellions in Jamaica in 1772–73 and 1795–96. Politically, the rise of slave rebellions made slavery more and more present and distasteful in the metropolis. Therefore, blaming the exploited for their own plight, and continuing commerce on widely denounced principles no longer adequately coped with "the increasing frequency and violence of slave revolts ...."[139] Granville Sharp, among others, sounded a trenchant criticism of Jamaican plantocracy. The Somerset case (1773) also inaugurated the dawn of a new debate over slaves' humanity and legal status.[140] Teresa Michals writes that the preference for inalienable, that is immoveable, property manifested itself most strongly after the Somerset case, with direct consequence for the status of slaves in England, who thereby came to be theoretically defined as inalienable not exchangeable property. Though this did not legally free British slaves,[141] such a widely held perception appears in prominent poetic utterances such as Cowper's *The Task*, Book II, wherein he writes:

We have no slaves at home. – Then why abroad?
And they themselves once ferried o'er the wave
That parts us, are emancipated and loos'd.
Slaves cannot breathe in England; if their lungs
Receive our air, that moment they are free:
They touch our country and their shackles fall.
That's noble, and bespeaks a nation proud
And jealous of the blessing. Spread it then,
And let it circulate through every vein
Of all your empire; that where Britain's power
Is felt, mankind may feel her mercy too.[142]

The links between all these changes and the transformation and immobilization of value in a familial context in *Inkle and Yarico* are evident. In an age of sensibility dominated by Cowper, readers may have lost interest in real women's amorous perfidy – exemplified in the story of the Widow of Ephesus in the *Spectator* – and empathized instead with feminized victims of racial perfidy and exploitation, and their apparent redeemers.[143] One might say, gender now becomes the expressive mode for sentimental discourse on race and slavery.

Culturally, the carnivalesque images of other cultures made association with them more and more culturally threatening. Scientifically and philosophically, the reduction of "other" cultures to their racial attributes made association with them biologically grotesque. Finally, and in Colman's case most pertinently, the scandalous brew of commerce and slavery made a transvaluation and "civilization" of value acquired in intercultural settings imperative. To rescue the west from self-mutilation for its traffic with the non-western or the slave, gender discourses and the familial exchange of affect and women provided a meliorating device, not unlike the enshrining of "family values" and the "human family" to counteract the perceived dangers of radical, multicultural "difference" at the sentimental end of the ferocious twentieth century. Simultaneously, the representation of commodity as feminine masked how femininity was commodified. Representing purchase as familialization masked control of wives, daughters and commodities. Commodity fetishism figured as the sentimental ascendancy of daughters and wives. Commercial concepts of value were thus purified and privatized by the triad of home, refinement, and women.

Colman's Narcissa and Yarico are thus imbricated in global commodity flows. In Irigaray's words: "*As commodities, women are thus two things at once: utilitarian objects and bearers of value.*"[144] In fact, when Inkle learns of the ship containing Narcissa having sailed without him, he exclaims: "My property carried off in the vessel."[145] In the chaotic world of traffic, Narcissa's transformation from fixed to movable property in Inkle's eyes hints at her identification with that other movable property, Yarico. In the end, Yarico's humanization accommodates romantic love within this sordid commodity nexus. But this humanization is also a surrogation, in Joseph Roach's sense; it helps culture to come to terms with unbearable memory.[146] Yarico becomes Sir Christopher's surrogate daughter by purchase, at the moment that he is about to lose his real one by marriage, before she can be Inkle's wife. The interchangeability of daughters or wives and slaves makes their commodification indistinguishable.

Bryan Edwards, a west India Merchant and Member of Parliament, provides one instance of this linked commodification. In his *History, Civil and Commercial, of the British Colonies in the West Indies* (1793), Edwards incorporates Isaac Teale's poem, "The Sable Venus: An Ode" (1765), in which "apparently without any self-consciousness ... [he] follows this fantasy of a Black Botticellian Venus, triumphantly riding in her chariot from Angola to Jamaica to be enthroned by enraptured, desiring colonists, with an ahistorical account of the slave trade, giving detailed figures for the numbers of Africans transported across the Atlantic each year."[147] Yarico's surrogacy consists of the fact that as a slave but also a woman, her pure exchangeability must be masked by the sentimental strategy of familializing her. It was as a woman yet unowned that she was pure exchange value. Once she is owned, and the fate of maternity hangs over her – though Colman excises the historical detail of Yarico's pregnancy from his sanitized sentimentality – she is fixed property, use value. When Inkle thinks he has almost concluded his sale of her, he says: "my labor now is paid."[148]

It is his laboring for her "good"[149] that has brought her to the market as a commodity. But a different sort of labor – perhaps that of legitimate childbearing, that will domesticate her as use value yet psycho-aesthetic capital – ends this play, to convince viewers of its reformism. Restored from market to home, commodity becomes treasure, slave becomes daughter and wife. If she is the mother of a new race, society will at least not have to witness a monstrous birth: "man begets man as his own likeness, wives, daughters, and sisters have value only in that they serve as the possibility of, and potential benefit in, relations among men. The use of and traffic in women subtend and uphold the reign of masculine hom(m)o-sexuality, even while they maintain that hom(m)o-sexuality in speculations, mirror games, identifications, and more or less rivalrous appropriations ...."[150]

In essence, then, Colman's play is a signpost of a tripping of an ideological discourse. Eighteenth- and nineteenth-century debate over connoisseurial taste and its social utility was complex and rapidly changing. Colman's brand of refined connoisseurship displaced a previous, more elitist connoisseurship. Colman was in the business of pleasing audiences who liked to feel good about themselves.[151] As John Brewer has detailed it, later eighteenth-century connoisseurs like William Hamilton, Richard Payne Knight, and Charles Towneley had spearheaded the obsolescence of the virtuoso. On the one hand, the virtuoso's enchantment with antiquity for its own sake had been replaced by connoisseurs' preference for objects that were not merely old but tasteful, enjoyable, a preference shared by Colman. Second, this enjoyment had to have the approval of aesthetic merit in the object, and could not be mere hyper-materialism. The virtuoso's love for a ragbag of "natural wonders" was replaced by the connoisseurs' critical preference for objects of culture, not merely natural curiosity. Analogously, Colman's Yarico and Omai, from being natural wonders, turn into human-made works of artistry, susceptible to rules of taste and criticism.

Taken together, connoisseurial virtue, as it evolved through the Colmans' century, displaced indiscriminate antiquarianism and the cabinet of any and all curiosities with a taste that was also utilitarian. Even when the connoisseurs prepared for their own obsolescence, their values remained in public culture. Conflicts developed between connoisseurial rules and the public artist's taste in the revolutionary era. The connoisseurs rejected the artists' claim to authority in matters of taste, to begin with. The artists in turn rejected the connoisseurs' project of taste, based as it seemed on patrician travel and cultural and sexual appropriations of the other. The artists argued for a public, moral project of national taste. To early nineteenth-century artists, while it remained important that taste be a matter of "intrinsic" worth, aesthetic value and critical transcendence over nature, some connoisseurs' relationship to their "valuable" collectibles threatened to transform public treasure into private hoard. As Brewer writes, the Elgin Marbles Select Committee hearings settled the "value" of collectible antiquity as intrinsic, not commercial or commodified, but also as national, not private.[152] Artists were also alchemists of raw antiquity into objects of contemporary, tasteful appreciation, but they intended these transformed "valuables" for public use. Thus, the refined connoisseurs of Colman Jr.'s generation paved the way for their own demise, but they had popularized their aesthetic project for generations to follow.

Having begun with a general discussion of value in our culture as arts discourse defines it, I would like to conclude with a recounting of the debate on value in the arts discourse of Colman's day. The imbrications of gender, value, and taste in *Inkle and Yarico* can be almost exactly applied to Frances Burney's *Camilla*, published five years later.[153] In *Camilla*, the heroine finds herself in a male economy wherein she is a commodity to be evaluated, and then possessed by Edgar Mandeville if she passes the value test. Camilla is desirable, otherwise there would be no point to the story, but being desirable does not endow her with choice. Instead, she is to be chosen. Her lover Edgar Mandeville and his bearleader Dr. Marchmont the misogynist conduct a voyeuristic trial of Camilla from which she emerges singed but not consumed, and apprised of the "moral" rule that she must withdraw from public society and an active economy of desire. The evaluation of Camilla proceeds on three basic premises. First, men are understood to be consumers and controllers of exchange; second, women are understood to be the symbolic commodities of this traffic; and third, evaluation of commodities implies the *a priori* right to unimpeded scrutiny of the commodities by the consumers. Thus are established the conditions for what Gayle Rubin has called the "traffic in women."[154] It is nearly a critical commonplace now to argue that this model of gender, power and exchange obtains in Burney's novel. Claudia Johnson and James Thompson have recently described these dynamics. Thompson writes about Camilla's extravagance, both emotional and financial, as impeding her familialization as Edgar's wife.[155] Johnson demonstrates that men's emotional extravagance shapes *Camilla*'s sentimental economy; in it women are instruments and mediums, but not self-realized subjects.[156] Both these critics help us understand the discourses of gender, value, and taste operative in Colman's and Burney's work and society, wherein "the fact that women are branded with the proper name – of the 'father' – should be viewed as the symbolic payment awarded them for sustaining the social order with their bodies ...."[157]

Notes

1   Peter Tasch remarks on a similar motive underlying George Colman Jr.'s aesthetics and his audience's taste (Peter A. Tasch [ed.], *The Plays of George Colman the Younger* [New York, 1981], vol. 1, pp. xviii–xix, xxxi, xxxix).

2   *Inkle and Yarico*, acted 164 times until 1800, was the second most frequently produced play of the late eighteenth century, following Sheridan's *School for Scandal* (Barry Sutcliffe, [ed.], *Plays by George Colman the Younger and Thomas Morton* [Cambridge; New York, 1983], pp. 24–5).

3   George Colman Jr., *Inkle and Yarico, an Opera in Three Acts*, with remarks by Mrs. Inchbald (New York, 1806), pp. 55–6. All further references to the text will be to this edition unless otherwise specified. Rational "self-interest" in the sense of *amour-propre* was propagated as the glue of social existence by various enlightenment "philosophes," but derided and rejected as nothing but self-love or *amour-de-soi* by Rousseau, who saw it as the obstacle to all meaningful natural intercourse between individuals. See Mark Hulliung, *The Autocritique of Enlightenment* (Cambridge, 1994). In the *Interesting Narrative of Olaudah Equiano* (*Interesting Narrative and Other Writings*, ed. Vincent Carretta [New York, 1995]), "interest" is reconciled by the narrator with Hutchesonian benevolence conducive to rational economic existence as well as philanthropy. While Equiano strategically adopts the "philosophical" position on this question, Colman's debunking of strategic "interest" in *Inkle and Yarico* demonstrates Colman's also strategically "sentimental" attitude.

4   Colman, *Inkle and Yarico*, p. 52.

5   Ibid., p. 52.

6   Aravamudan, *Tropicopolitans*, p. 256; Olaudah Equiano, *The Interesting Narrative* (1789), cited in Aravamudan, *Tropicopolitans*, p. 396, n. 41.

7   Ibid., p. 254.

8   Ibid., p. 258.

9   The play was first performed at the Haymarket Theatre on 4 August 1787 (Sutcliffe, *Plays*, p. 262).

10   Ibid., pp. 22–4.

11   George Colman Jr., *Random Records* (2 vols, Huntington Library 110464), vol. 2, p. 180.

12   Colman, *Inkle and Yarico*, p. 8.

13   Ibid., p. 14.

14   The Adelphi was the site of the offices of the Society of the Arts, and also the site of merchants' warehouses as rebuilt by William Chambers, the royal architect.

15   Colman, *Inkle and Yarico*, pp. 40–41.

16   Richard Brinsley Peake, *Memoirs of the Colman Family, Including their Correspondence with the Most Distinguished Personages of their Time,* originally published in 1841 (2 vols, New York, 1972), vol. 1, pp. 331–2.

17   Jeremy F. Bagster-Collins, *George Colman, the Younger* (New York, 1946), p. 2.

18   Ibid., p. 2.

19 Sutcliffe, *Plays*, p. 98; Carol Macht, *Classical Wedgwood Designs* (New York, 1957), pp. 7–9, 37; Hilary Young (ed.), *The Genius of Wedgwood* (London, 1995), p. 23. Susan Lambert mentions a type of frame produced for their prints by the early twentieth-century Medici society, "described by the Society as 'a fine reproduction of an early tortoiseshell and ebony model' … handmade in 'red imitation tortoiseshell, with black and wood beading'" (*The Image Multiplied: Five Centuries of Printed Reproductions of Paintings and Drawings* [New York, 1987], p. 191). This frame clearly reproduces some of the visual impact of an "antique," classical object, of *antico rosso*.

20 Hilary Young produces the Staffordshire model for this teapot (Young, *Genius*, p. 23).

21 Carol Barash, "The Character of Difference: The Creole Woman as Cultural Mediator in Narratives about Jamaica," *Eighteenth-century Studies*, 23/4 (1990): 407–24.

22 Quoted in Robin Reilly, "Josiah Wedgwood," in Young, *Genius*, p. 56; see also Sussman, *Consuming Anxieties*, p. 127. However, we must also take note of a reverse flow of consumer goods and their self-producing capacities. James Walvin writes that according to Bryan Edwards, "some Jamaican slaves 'have larger houses with boarded floors … a few even have good beds, linen sheets, and mosquito nets, and display *a shelf or two of plates and dishes of queens or Staffordshire ware*'" (Walvin, "Black and White," p. 310).

23 Young, *Colonial Desire*, pp. 29–54.

24 Peter Hulme, *Colonial Encounter: Europe and the Native Caribbean, 1492–1797* (London, 1986), p. 226.

25 Roxann Wheeler, "The Complexion of Desire: Racial Ideology and Mid-eighteenth-century British Novels," *Eighteenth-century Studies*, 32/3 (1999): 313–14.

26 As in Frances Seymour, the Countess of Hertford's "The Story of Inkle and Yarico" (1738, ll. 26–30, in Krise, *Caribbeana*, p. 142); Steele's *Spectator* 11 (1711, in Frank Felsenstein, [ed.], *English Trader, Indian Maid* [Baltimore, 1999], p. 87); Anonymous, "The Story of Inkle and Yarico, from the Eleventh *Spectator*" (*London Magazine* 1734, in Felsenstein, *English Trader*, pp. 103–4); Anonymous, *Yarico to Inkle: An Epistle* (1736, in ibid., p. 115); Stephen Duck's "Avaro and Amanda: A Poem in Four Canto's," Taken from *The Spectator*, vol. I, No. XI (1736, in ibid., pp. 127, 133); and in the anonymous "Inkle and Yarico," in the *New Novelist's Magazine*, vol. 2 (London, 1787), pp. 116–17.

27 As Wheeler has reminded us, "there was a more tolerant attitude in Britain than in the colonies in regard to interracial liaisons, especially among the serving classes" ("Complexion of Desire," p. 314).

28 For the latter notion articulated see Wheeler "Complexion of Desire," p. 325.

29 At the McMaster University Taylor conference, 1999, where this essay was first presented, several members of the audience offered cognate explications of Yarico's receptacle status. Among these were mentioned the childbearing capacity of women which, some suggested, would argue that Yarico was not being commodified, but embraced into the family. I would like to thank Emily Haddad especially for her comments. However, I submit that Yarico's receptacle form in this play connotes not her humanity, but her commodification, even (or especially) if the vessel she signifies is that of the mother. The play locates her between human and thing just as slaves were, and reconfers her humanity only in terms convenient to sentimental rhetoric, just as Colman's society did to actual slaves in sentimental fashion. Sentimental exaltation does not change the market reality of slaves' commodification and exchange.

30 Colman, *Inkle and Yarico*, p. 41.

31 Ibid., p. 21

32   Luce Irigaray, "Women on the Market," in Catherine Porter (trans.), *This Sex Which is Not One* (Ithaca, 1986), p. 187; original emphasis. I am indebted to Maire Mullens for redirecting me to Irigaray's article.

33   I discuss this below with reference to David Hume's work; see Hume below on "labor" being a potential resource to transcend private hoarding.

34   Irigaray, "Women on the Market," pp. 173, 175.

35   Aravamudan, *Tropicopolitans*, p. 39.

36   H.L. Gates Jr., "Phillis Wheatley and the Nature of the Negro," in *The Idea of Blackness in Western Discourse* (New York, 1982); reprinted in William Robinson, *Critical Essays on Phillis Wheatley* (Boston, 1982), pp. 215–30; this quotation p. 217.

37   Aravamudan, *Tropicopolitans*, p. 44.

38   Ibid., pp. 277–8, on Olaudah Equiano.

39   Ibid., p. 278.

40   Peake, *Memoirs*, vol. 1, pp. 1–10.

41   George Colman Sr. and Bonnell Thornton (eds), *The Connoisseur: by Mr. Town, Critic and Censor-General* (London 1754–56), vol. 1, pp. 140–43.

42   Peake, *Memoirs*, vol. 1, p. 357.

43   Thomas, *Entangled Objects*, p. 143.

44   Peake, *Memoirs*, vol. 1, p. 366.

45   Landry, *Invention of the Countryside*, pp. 22–5, 30, and 113–42.

46   Peake, *Memoirs*, vol. 1, p. 355. Peake's use of the term "bearleader" to describe Banks' role suggests an interchangeability between English "milords" on the grand tour and "noble savages" in England.

47   Ibid., vol. 1, p. 366.

48   Ibid., vol. 1, p. 358.

49   Ibid., vol. 1, pp. 360, 362–3. See Katie Trumpener on the enlightenment's tendency to classicize antiquity (Katie Trumpener, *Bardic Nationalism: The Romantic Novel and the British Empire* [Princeton, 1997], pp. 116–17).

50   Sussman, *Consuming Anxieties*, pp. 63–5; see also pp. 72–5, on people as portable goods, etc.

51   Thomas, *Entangled Objects*, pp. 144–5.

52   Edgar Wind, *Hume and the Heroic Portrait: Studies in Eighteenth Century Imagery*, ed. Jaynie Anderson (Oxford, 1986), p. 91.

53   Thomas, *Entangled Objects*, p. 150.

54   As I have noted above, the Wedgwood teapot to which Trudge compares Yarico in the play imitated earlier Staffordshire red stoneware teapots. Colman's persistence with the changing valuation of Staffordshire ware runs parallel to Josiah Wedgwood's own view that his "antique" teapot was somewhat vulgarized by association with these common Staffordshire potteries (Young, *Genius*, p. 23). Clearly, value makes its ghostly appearance in various discussions of material culture by Colman, and while antiquity is valued by Colman as well as Wedgwood, the "commonness" of contemporary Staffordshire red stoneware product brings upon it contempt for its mundane ordinariness when compared to Wedgwood's Staffordshire line.

55   Peake, *Memoirs*, vol. 1, p. 367.

56   Banks' collecting was also lampooned by Colman in his play *A Turk and No Turk* (1785), wherein eccentric collecting and worthless or spurious objects – including humans – meet in Sir Simon Simple's desire to "collect" as his son-in-law a Turk, actually a penniless

young man in disguise who loves Sir Simon's daughter. Peter Tasch comments that Sir Simon Simple may have been based on Joseph Banks (Tasch, *Plays*, vol. 1, p. xvi). For extensive satire on Simple's alias Banks' faddish fascination with the foreign see *Turk and No Turk* (Tasch, *Plays*, vol. 1, pp. 18–19, 57).

57   James Thompson, "'Sure I have seen that face before': Representation and Value in Eighteenth-century Drama," in J. Douglas Canfield and Deborah Payne (eds), *Cultural Readings of Restoration and Eighteenth-century Theater* (Athens, GA, 1996), pp. 281–308.

58   Peake, *Memoirs*, vol. 1, p. 365.

59   Ibid., vol. 1, p. 370.

60   Richard Hamblyn, "Private Cabinets and Popular Geography: British Audiences for Volcanoes in the Eighteenth Century," in Chloe Chard and Helen Langdon (eds), *Transports: Travel, Pleasure, and Imaginative Geography, 1660–1830* (New Haven, 1996), p. 179.

61   In the preface to his own play, *Feudal Times; or, the Banquet-Gallery* (1799), Colman mocked fusty antiquaries thus: "Black-Letter Gentlemen … may cavil at the term, *Banquet-Gallery* … I leave the discussion to Antiquaries, and Nomenclators; – whose attention … has often been sedulously employed upon a subject of as little importance" (Tasch, *Plays*, vol. 2, pp. v–vi).

62   Smith, *Auctions*, p. 31.

63   Clive Wainwright, *The Romantic Interior: The British Collector at Home 1750–1850* (New Haven; London, 1989), p. 5.

64   Quoted in Wainwright, *Romantic Interiors*, pp. 5–6.

65   "On the Irrational Pursuits of Virtue," quoted ibid., p. 61.

66   Trumpener, *Bardic Nationalism*, p. 107.

67   I have shown in the next chapter on the dramatist James Cobb the eighteenth-century English propensity to people the cultural imaginary with the revived real and symbolic exotic dead: the mummy, the slave, the antique. There, as in this chapter, my analysis is heavily indebted to Joseph Roach's pathbreaking *Cities of the Dead: Circum-Atlantic Performance* (New York, 1996).

   Regarding the animation of the dead female antiquity, moreover, the work of Chloe Chard has been very helpful to me; see especially her "Grand and Ghostly Tours: The Topography of Memory," *Eighteenth-century Studies,* 31/1 (1997): 101–108. See also John Brewer on the Dilettanti (*The Pleasures of the Imagination: English Culture in the Eighteenth Century* [New York, 1997]). A horrific conflation of women, commodification and antiquity might, however, be found in James Boswell's pro-slavery poem "No Abolition of Slavery; or, The Universal Empire of Love: A Poem":

> Try what th'accurs'd Short's Garden yields,
> His bludgeon where the Flash-man wields;
> Where female votaries of sin,
> With fetid rags and breath of gin,
> Like antique statues stand in rows,
> Fine fragments sure, but ne-er a nose (1791, in Wood, *Poetry of Slavery*, p. 192).

68   Trumpener, *Bardic Nationalism*, pp. 27–8.

69   Ibid., p. 27.

70   Thomas, *Entangled Objects*, p. 143.

71   Not only architecture, but botany was another of the imperial projects enshrined at Kew
     (Shteir, *Cultivating Women*, p. 11).

72   Under construction in 1766, when Chambers' *Plans* was published.

73   William Chambers, *Plans, Elevations, Sections, and Perspective Views of the Gardens
     and Buildings at Kew in Surry, the Seat of her Royal Highness the Princess Dowager of
     Wales* (London, 1763; repr. 1966), p. 7.

74   Anne Janowitz, *England's Ruins: Poetic Purpose and National Landscape* (Cambridge,
     1990), pp. 2–3. In his *Salon de 1767*, Diderot criticized paintings of ruins by Hubert
     Robert for being too crowded with human figures, thus disallowing Diderot the sublime
     experience he always sought, that of entering the paintings though a beholder (Michael
     Fried, *Absorption and Theatricality: Painting and Beholder in the Age of Diderot* [Berkeley,
     1980], pp. 128–30). This desire seems not unrelated to the imperial desire to eviscerate
     ruin landscapes of local human presence mentioned by Janowitz, and by Mary Louise
     Pratt, *Imperial Eyes: Travel Writing and Transculturation* (London; New York, 1992).

75   Janowitz, *England's Ruins*, pp. 2–3, 14–15.

76   Trumpener, *Bardic Nationalism*, pp. 29–30.

77   Ibid., pp. xv, 4, 6; Brewer, *Pleasures*, p. 636.

78   Aravdamudan, *Tropicopolitans*, p. 64.

79   Trumpener, *Bardic Nationalism*, pp. 21–3, 29–30.

80   Peter Hulme has written of *Inkle and Yarico*, however, that "'Inkle and Yarico', the
     product of no single authorial consciousness but rather a story that (English and European)
     society chose persistently, over a period of seventy years, to tell itself, has the advantage
     of providing a narrative that changes over time so that it is possible, at least in theory, to
     produce a time-length equivalent to that revealed in analysis, laying bare something of
     the story's political aetiology" (*Colonial Encounters*, p. 228).

81   The accidental or hurried nature of much colonial enterprise is also explored in Chapter
     3, but also see Thomas, *Entangled Objects*, and Dalrymple, *White Mughals*, for wider
     eighteenth-century phenomena in colonial and peripheral realms.

82   Brewer, *Pleasures*, p. 253.

83   Wainwright, *Romantic Interior*, p. 8.

84   Brewer, *Pleasures*, pp. 253–4.

85   Wainwright, *Romantic Interior*, p. 9.

86   Jeremy Black, *The British Abroad: The Grand Tour in the Eighteenth Century* (New York,
     1992), pp. 279–80.

87   David Hume, *Of the Standard of Taste and Other Essays*, ed. John W. Lenz, (Indianapolis,
     1965).

88   Quoted in Black, *British Abroad*, p. 279.

89   Sir John Soane, *Plans, Elevations, and Sections of Buildings Erected in the Counties of
     Norfolk, Suffolk ...* (1788), p. 1.

90   Hume, *Of the Standard of Taste*, p. 81.

91   Ibid., pp. 49–51, 57. For a succinct and elegant discussion of Hume's attitudes on taste,
     morals and utility, as put forth in *An Enquiry Concerning the Principles of Morals* and in
     Dialogues Concerning Natural Religion, see Wind, *Hume*, p. 6.

92   Hume, *Of the Standard of Taste*, pp. 51–2.

93   Wainwright, *Romantic Interior*, pp. 109–46.

94   Ibid., pp. 139–40.

95   Though such discussion is beyond the purview of this book, Beckford's notorious oriental

romance *Vathek* is surely in the category of literary connoisseurial expressions that animate the oriental other and make them a part of the connoisseurial self in highly controversial ways. See Beckford, *Vathek*, ed. Roger Lonsdale, (Oxford, 1983).

96   Wainwright, *Romantic Interior*, p. 113.

97   Robert Anthony Bromley, *A Philosophical and Critical History of the Fine Arts, Painting, Sculpture and Architecture …* (3 vols, London, 1793), vol. 1, p. 407.

98   Ibid., vol. 2, p. 47.

99   Hume, *Of the Standard of Taste*, p. 57.

100   Peake, *Memoirs*, vol. 1, p. 100; see also vol. 1, pp. 90–92. On Rome and reactions to it in the eighteenth century, see Wrigley, "Crossing Boundaries and Exceeding Limits: Destabilization, Tourism, and the Sublime," in Chloe Chard and Helen Langdon (eds), *Transports*, and for Vesuvius and Naples see Hamblyn, "Private Cabinets."

101   Peake, *Memoirs*, vol. 1, pp. 9, 30.

102   Ibid., vol. 1, pp. 26–7.

103   Brewer, *Pleasures*, pp. 264–8.

104   George Colman Jr., *Broad Grins and Eccentricities for Edinburgh* (repr. New York, 1977), p. 31.

105   Ibid., pp. 30–31.

106   George Colman the elder, Letter to Elizabeth Inchbald (3 March 1786, Victoria and Albert Museum, F 48.G.3/12).

107   He draws her into this paternalist realm, where he owns her and her work benevolently, also in his letter of 29 November 1785 to her (Victoria and Albert Museum, A F 48.G.3/11).

108   Sussman, *Consuming Anxieties*, pp. 50, 60–61.

109   Black, *British Abroad*, pp. 40–41.

110   Wrigley, "Crossing Boundaries."

111   Carol Barash discusses the similar mortiferousness of creole and Jamaican female sexuality to English people in "The Character of Difference," pp. 407–24.

112   Colman, *Inkle and Yarico*, p. 7.

113   His attitudes also suggest that he is an Enlightenment empiricist and progressivist (Trumpener, *Bardic Nationalism*, pp. 29–30).

114   References to "interest" occur on pp. 12, 23, 43, 48, and 55. In Act III, pp. 49 and 51, Inkle also refers to his "labor" (in making Yarico marketable) in enabling his interest (see in this regard the discussion above on use value and exchange value created by labor). "Interest," a central term in the late eighteenth-century discourse upon commerce and capital, also appeared in Colman's other colonially derived play, *John Bull* (in Elizabeth Inchbald's *British Theater* [London, 1805], vol. 21). In it, the worldly and savvy Tom Shuffleton tells the less up-to-date Sir Simon Rochdale, a country aristocrat, "Don't talk about your heart, Baronet; – feeling's quite out of fashion … We make a joke of the heart now-a-days; but when a man mentions his interest, we know he's in earnest" (Colman, *John Bull*, p. 25).

115   Irigaray, "Women on the Market," p. 181.

116   Steele, *Spectator* 11, 1711, in Felsenstein, *English Trader*; Hulme, *Colonial Encounters*, p. 235.

117   Colman, *Inkle and Yarico*, pp. 14–15.

118   Ibid., p. 47.

119   Sutcliffe, *Plays*, p. 103.

120   Hulme, *Colonial Encounters*, pp. 228–48.

121   Ibid., pp. 249–59.

[122] Maxine Berg and Helen Clifford, "Commerce and the Commodity: Graphic Display and Selling New Consumer Goods in Eighteenth-century England," in Michael North and David Ormrod (eds), *Art Markets in Europe, 1400–1800* (Brookfield, 1998), p. 197.

[123] Anonymous reviewer in *Literary Journal*, vol. 1 (London, nd.), pp. 381–2, quoted in Bagster-Collins, *George Colman*, p. 157.

[124] As I hope I have sufficiently foreshadowed in the Introductory chapter of this book, this chiasmic construction of "materiality" and "culture" is intended to underscore the paradox of the concept of "material culture." The conflict between collecting and connoisseurship is, in large degree, the conflict produced by the synchronic duality of materiality and culturalism.

[125] Wainwright, *Romantic Interior*, p. 14.

[126] Brewer, *Pleasures*, pp. 220–21.

[127] Ibid., pp. 229–31.

[128] Ibid., pp. 244–6.

[129] See Tasch's introduction to *Plays*, vol. 1, pp. xv–xvi, li.

[130] I am influenced in this formulation by James Thompson's analysis referred to above.

[131] Two of the best accounts of gender and abolitionism are Clare Midgley's *Women Against Slavery: the British Campaigns, 1780–1870* (London, 1992) and Moira Ferguson's *Subject to Others: British Women Writers and Colonial Slavery, 1670–1834* (New York, 1992).

[132] "Remarks," *Inkle and Yarico*, n. p.

[133] Sussman, *Consuming Anxieties*, pp. 5–6. See also her chapter entitled "Women and the Politics of Sugar, 1792," in *Consuming Anxieties*, pp. 110–29.

[134] Catherine Moore, "Robinson and Xury and Inkle and Yarico," *English Language Notes*, 19/1 (1981): 27; see also Martin Wechselblatt, "Gender and Race in Yarico's Epistle to Inkle: Voicing the Feminine/Slave," *Studies in Eighteenth-century Culture*, 19 (1989): 198.

[135] Aeneas' Dido is an important precursor of Yarico in two ways: as a dark-skinned woman who is involved with a European man in an exploitative romance, and as a figure of the public reality of Europe's commodification, enjoyment and abandonment of non-European regions. Joseph Roach (*Cities of the Dead*) and Peter Merchant ("Robert Paltock and the Refashioning of 'Inkle and Yarico,'" *Eighteenth-century Fiction*, 9/1 [1996]: 42–3) have commented on this genealogy. Peter Hulme (*Colonial Encounters*) provides an extensive discussion of Dido as part of the political unconscious of *Inkle and Yarico*, especially in the common tropes of hospitality and return.

[136] However, Lawrence Marsden Price's exhaustive analysis of these mid-century epistles provides no support for Wechselblatt's conclusions (Price, *Yarico and Inkle Album* [Berkeley, 1937]). Price sees the heroic epistle form as embodying the lament of the oppressed, not of the guilty.

[137] Wechselblatt, "Gender and Race," p. 214.

[138] Young, *Colonial Desire*, pp. 29–54.

[139] Wechselblatt, "Gender and Race," p. 214.

[140] Hulme, *Colonial Encounters*.

[141] See Folarin Shyllon, *Black People in Britain 1555–1833* (New York, 1977), and Vincent Carretta, "Phillis Wheatley, the Mansfield Decision of 1772, and the Choice of Identity," in Klaus H. Schmidt and Fritz Fleischmann (eds), *Early America Re-explored: New Readings in Colonial, Early National, and Antebellum Culture* (New York, 2000), p. 203.

[142] Wood, *Poetry of Slavery*, p. 87; see also "The Morning Dream," in ibid., pp. 90–91.

[143] Moor, "Robinson and Xury," p. 27; Tasch, *Plays*, vol. 1, p. xvii.

144 Irigaray, "Women on the Market," p. 175; original emphasis.
145 Sutcliffe, *Plays*, p. 73.
146 Roach, *Cities of the Dead*, pp. 2–4. See further discussion of surrogation in Chapter 3.
147 Young, *Colonial Desire*, p. 158.
148 Colman, *Inkle and Yarico*, p. 49.
149 Ibid., p. 51.
150 Irigaray, "Women on the Market," p. 172.
151 For a useful summary of Colman's popularity and its decline in nineteenth-century critical opinion, see the introduction in Sutcliff, *Plays*, pp. 1, 3–5, 7–20.
152 Brewer, *Pleasures*, pp. 256–87.
153 Frances Burney, *Camilla, or, A Picture of Youth*, eds Edward A. Bloom and Lillian D. Bloom (Oxford; New York, 1999).
154 "The Traffic in Women: Notes on the 'Political Economy' of Sex," in Julie Rivkin and Michael Ryan (eds), *Literary Theory: an Anthology* (Malden, MA, 1998), pp. 533–60.
155 Thompson writes: "*Camilla*, then, is the story of the regulation of the female emotional economy, a making safe of the home … and the chief regulator is, of course, the husband" (*Models of Value: Eighteenth-century Political Economy and the Novel* [Durham, 1996], p. 167).
156 Claudia Johnson, *Equivocal Beings: Politics, Gender and Sentimentality in the 1790s: Wollstonecraft, Radcliffe, Burney and Austen* (Chicago, 1995).
157 Irigaray, "Women on the Market," p. 190.

Chapter 3

James Cobb and Colonial Cacophony: Doing the Enlightenment in Different Voices

"National history" must be transcended, and colonial history treated within a global context.[1]

Salman Rushdie's *The Moor's Last Sigh*[2] is a trenchant postcolonial *mise-en-scene* of the reformer's implication in the very oppression that she seeks to eradicate. In this intergenerational saga set in India around the time of independence from the British Raj, a family of the indigenous elite – the Zogoibys – become transcultural agents of social reform in ways that continue the hegemonic paternalism of colonial societies. In Rushdie's rich panoply of images for national struggle and self-representation, elephants signify legitimate national authority – traditional, indigenous, and ancient – not unlike the British historiography of Mughal legitimacy, later appropriated by the British themselves to justify their own rule.[3] Thus, Lambajan Chandiwalla, the one-legged gatekeeper of the Zogoiby family home *Elephanta* in Bombay, tells Rushdie's protagonist – the son of the Zogoibys – that Elephanta island near Bombay contains reminders of an earlier, grander era, when philosophical elephants ruled their subjects, the monkeys, benevolently. In the novel's pre-independence Indian national imaginary, therefore, elephants were divine emblems of a national past and identity. It is a historical irony that the elephant god later becomes the rallying emblem of Hindu fundamentalist forces in independent India, an abuse of originary myths that has continued under Hindu nationalist regimes. Festive locals in the novel celebrating the power of the elephant deity dance along the thoroughfare well below the elegant *Elephanta*, as indeed they do today in contemporary Mumbai.[4]

In the diegetic India, though, the mansion *Elephanta's* location well above the masses reflects the extant inequity of indigenous elite and masses in late colonial India. The reformer in this book – the protagonist's mother Aurora Zogoiby, herself of hybrid ancestry – is distanced from India's teeming, hybrid masses by her wealth, status, and possibly hybridity. But it is she who has named her mansion Elephanta, and fraternizes with the rabble everyone else considers dangerous. Rushdie takes great pains to emphasize how she ostensibly identifies with the colonized masses.

Elephants, reminders of a golden Indian past, and of hydra-headed imperialism and nationalism in this allegorical tale, are thus contested metaphors to be appropriated by a linked chain of post-enlightenment reformers from British colonialists to nativist elite hybrid Aurora Zogoiby. She, Aurora Zogoiby, teaches Lambajan Chandiwalla's pet parrot to repeat "*peesay saafed haathi*," a distortion of "pieces of eight! my hearties!" the cry of lusty British seafaring. "*Peesay saafed haathi*" translates roughly as "mashed white elephants." Now, the "saafed haathi" or "white elephants" of the parrot's unconsciously resistant nationalist articulation could very well be the "white" English who appropriated the "elephant," indigenous, nationalist symbol of political legitimacy, for their own ends. The British, as subaltern studies historian Ranajit Guha has pointed out, did in fact evoke the Mughals as their true political precursors in a mythical "golden age" India. Thus they claimed their status as saviors of a hopelessly degenerate colonial India. Thus far, Aurora's appropriation of and identification with the elephant suggest mimicking resistance to the British appropriation of Indian "essence": "*peesay saafed haathi*" could mean "mash the white colonialist." However, her gatekeeper recounts an unwieldy act of erasure by Aurora that hints at a "mashing" of the masses by Aurora herself.

Thus, in passionate revolt against the Indian National Congress' capitulation to England and its betrayal of striking Indian labor, Aurora herself "mashes" Lambajan Chandiwalla's leg under her elephantine American buick. She tries to atone for this by setting him up as gatekeeper of her own home, a deeply ambiguous act through which her son later understands his mother's implication in the colonial project and the imperialist allegory of the elephant. Aurora wrests the emblematic elephant from the British, the "*saafed haathi*," but despite her best intentions, she appropriates the megalithic elephant only to become one; indeed, she is and always has been one. As Lambajan Chandiwalla says, the elephant bit off his leg.

From this counter-allegorical allegory in Rushdie's *Moor's Last Sigh* I turn to the work of James Cobb (1756–1818), an office-holder of the East India company, whose late eighteenth-century plays about crosscultural encounters anticipate Rushdie's examples of the imagination of coloniality[5] at work on transnational fictions of reform. Aurora's meddling in creating the postcolonial "nation," as I will show, is not unlike the colony's 'reform' by globe-trotting heroines in Cobb's plays. As I will show throughout this chapter, however, when women are involved in crosscultural "reform," they are often blamed disproportionately for its excesses or its blind spots, and in this regard they often share the fate of the subaltern whom they are employed to subdue. Thus, whether they are "virtuous" and pure or dabblers in local clutter, their situation vis-a-vis the colonized as well as the colonizer is precarious, and the heavy hand of patriarchy is ever ready to "mash" *their* deviation from policy and propriety, as Aurora is mashed later in Rushdie's novel. Through the lens of postcolonial storytelling we see that Cobb's tales of colonial reformers anticipate the continuing torment of the enlightenment's bequest to postcolonial nationality: its colonization of those it seeks to liberate. For all who meddle in "reform" and "progress" must exchange the quiet eddies of their lives and homes for the maelstrom of bodies, things and cultures, which makes "reason" return as a nightmare version of cacophonous siren songs from the edges of the known world.

Whereas some later colonial writers saw colonial identity as stable, unitary, and unquestionable, even in the late eighteenth century, despite the normative narratives of the enlightenment, British identity abroad was itself broken up into acceptable and unacceptable types. This itself, however, was in the embittered aftermath of a vigorous and almost routine heterogeneity of British identity in India, as William Dalrymple has amply demonstrated in *White Mughals*. In his book, Dalrymple documents not only the sexually adventurous and ambiguous behaviors of many eighteenth-century Englishman in India, but also documents the indigenous and metropolitan reactions to those "adventurous" behaviors.[6] In the later eighteenth century, a British colonial identity came under more strict regulation and dramatists like Cobb participated in the official dismantling of heterogeneity. Cobb's plays usually depict two scenarios for British national identity, both foreshadowed in Dalrymple's work. The first scenario involves heterogeneous exploration, maritime commerce and military aggression. The second, later scenario is that of homogenous romance and marriage, a familial comedy of manners involving disguises, crossed identities, and happy rediscoveries and reunions (including the rebuttal of cynical age and the vindication of youth). The development of these evolving themes will be explored here primarily in Cobb's *The Humourist; or, Who's Who* (1785), *The Strangers at Home; A Comic Opera in Three Acts* (1786), and *Love in the East; or, Adventures of Twelve Hours* (1788), this being a by no means comprehensive list of Cobb's plays.[7]

As to the first scenario of exploration and aggression, Cobb's age was one of rapid global changes triggered by commerce and global warfare. When Cobb celebrates "Anglo-Saxon liberty" against this volatile global backdrop, he shows a particular face of the enlightenment dream: that of a global cacophony of language and performance. The cacophony of global others – endlessly subjugated and resurrected in various relations of difference or identity with the self produced anxiety. Another term for resurrection is "surrogation," formulated in Joseph Roach's *Cities of the Dead*;[8] a surrogate, Roach explains, is that which helps a culture to come to terms with its memory of connection or debt to an "other" context, historic and spatial.[9] A surrogate enables a culture to refigure its aggression and annihilation of an other as an act of appropriation and recontextualization, even as a form of orchestrated pantomime like blackface. In such surrogation, aspects of the unfavorable conduct of that annihilated other are, however, allowed to remain as traces, justifying annihilation as a reaction to the threat. The mimicry in surrogation thus encompasses an identity in difference: always already an assimilable oscillation of semblance and dissimulation.

In any case, colonial surrogations or resurrections required remembering oneself through connections with strange cultures and peoples. Linda Colley writes, for instance, that "throughout the seventeenth century and in the early 1700s, England's (and subsequently Britain's) most widely known and controversial contacts were with the so-called Barbary powers, Morocco, Algiers, Tripoli, and Tunisia, the last three all regencies or military provinces of the Ottoman empire … over the course of the seventeenth and eighteenth centuries, there were probably 20,000 or more British captives of Barbary."[10] The anxiety of resurrection and the effort of surrogation lead to Cobb's divided plots wherein an engagement with the other is inevitably corrected by repressing that other, using gender politics as a convenient nationalist ideological tool for repressing true difference.[11]

The presence of women engenders the second scenario of Cobb's plays – the marriage and romantic liberation plot – while the role of racial others in the first scenario is to dramatize British male identity founded on homosociality and global aggression. In reality, each plot incorporates some tincture of the other, demonstrating that the era's private, conjugal mores were actually inseparable from its public discourse.[12] Choreographically, for instance, both plots are liberally sprinkled with music, spectacle, and performances. *Love in the East*, for instance, opened on 25 February 1788, at Drury Lane, with a variety of new scenery, including a view of Calcutta from an on-the-spot painting by Hodges, and dress and decorations to match.[13] This bears out two critical insights. First, the heightened scale of theater shows that late eighteenth-century theater architecture mandated a more spectacular dramatic style.[14] Second, the incorporation of colonial margins as scenery in this spectacle metonymizes the nation represented as both home and mart, home and the world.

In the bigger, showier, and "English" theater, British greatness prized for guarding the gate of the bourgeois home and companionate marriage was, as ever, created by accelerated cultural exchanges and debts. Heterotopic and hybrid cultural images and performance linked together representations of private, public and global. The two insights together indicate the spectacularity of British identity at the intersection of the expansionist public and the retreating private. Remembering themselves as a nation refulgent in past and present glory, the British also implicitly understood their intimate history through their relations with colonial subjects and neighbors.

However, though imitation is the highest form of flattery, wielding the eraser is yet a greater power: "the relentless search for the purity of origins is a voyage not of discovery but of erasure."[15] Cobb's female characters enact such erasures while engaging in playful cross-dressing performances. An example of these voyages of discovery through erasure – resurrection through surrogation, one might say – is that of Eliza in search of her British lover in the play *Love in the East* (1788).[16] Eliza's disguise as Alexander McProteus, a stock device in colonial plays – which in this instance harks back to the "testing" motifs of Rosalind in Shakespeare's *As You Like It*, as well as to the legendary female soldier Hannah Snell – serves to establish a festive European empire of love, not a "despotic" oriental one:

> Eliz. None can pay more sincere homage to Cupid, than we laughing lovers. You sighing folks make him an eastern despot, and fall prostrate before him; with us, he is an European prince – we bow and simper at his levee: you degrade him to the mere tyrant of slaves; we exalt him to a glorious situation – the monarch of happy subjects.[17]

Thus, slavery, that non-western curse and racialized global enterprise, is both evoked and circumvented by a female cross-dresser.[18] Her masquerade marks victory over two kinds of "slaves" – men and non-western others – and celebrates women's sentimental and amorous empire, an empire defined civilizationally, however, and not racially.

Love in the East begins with Englishmen in India declaring their intention to go transnational or, as some might say, "native":

> We be three, who *doom'd* to *roam*,
>   Have *dared* the dang'rous seas;
> That land becomes our dearest *home*,
>   Which gives us *wealth* and *ease*.
> No other climes will we explore,
>   Nor *search* the world around:
> Our choice is *fix'd* on India's shore;
>   Our *home* shall be this ground.[19] (*Love in the East*, I.i.5–6; emphasis mine)

If we follow carefully the sequence of italicized words above, we see the graft of "home" and "roam," the warp and woof of "daring" and "ease," and the playful strain of searching for utopia and finding it in dystopia. Being in India also becomes synonymous with possessing it, just as being lovers, fathers or husbands of women becomes synonymous with having power over them as commodities.[20] The same may be said about owning slaves. But it is the refining and sentimentalizing agency of British women that saves this master, the European man, from nativization and degrading transnationalization into "slave" cultures.[21] Western women visiting "slave" nations (as in *Love in the East*) adopt masculine disguise to redeem their men from embroilment with a slavish culture.

Still, though female cross-dressing in *Love in the East* saves Europe from refiguration *as* enslaved nations politically and socially,[22] Europe must acknowledge slavery in the process of disavowal itself. Both disguises and disavowals show hidden racialist anxiety about displacement and what Homi Bhabha has called "recognition" of alterity's real presence. The initial enthusiasm expressed by Cobb's characters for cultural and civilizational similarities gives way to much greater anxiety about racial and sexual contamination, and a revised civilizational impulse apparently spearheaded by women is deployed in fiction to contain the resurgent racial anxieties. Whereas in the mid-century fiction analyzed by Roxann Wheeler, men are the agents of civilizational discourse,[23] Cobb's women assume such apparent agency due to related shifts in the sentimental ideology of gendered spheres that have been well documented by James Thompson and others and discussed at length in Chapter 2. Even these brave acts, though, repress but cannot erase slavery as indelible memory in the western psyche.[24]

The disguises entail expedient self-transformation – thereby actual partial self-loss. For instance, Mrs Mushroom says to Eliza disguised as Alexander McProteus: "that is very disinterested to remember your friends while you *forget yourself* …."[25] She is referring in particular to the changes in Eliza's accent, which the latter has assumed to go with her disguise as McProteus. Indeed, the characters in Cobb's plays often need to lose both physical selves and linguistic control to have themselves and their desires, a phenomenon also capturing the essence of transcontinental exploration, colonization, trade, and of course slavery. Discourses and practices of liberty and manhood, like those of femininity and the empire of love, are evidently affected by the discourse and practices of slavery, a more serious loss of identity. In *Love in the East*, this protean European self has to be ratified, moreover, by slaves and subjects. Thus Rosario, the stereotypical ethnically unspecific "native"[26] muses about Warnford, his good English master: "He be good massa – give me money for my poor father – never say to me rogue – rascal – but always speakee kind, and call my own name."[27]

Identities vacillating between slave and master, woman and man, can also be found in one of Cobb's more famous plays, *The Strangers at Home*. This play, both mainpiece and afterpiece, dramatizes the return to Europe of a band of freed Barbary-coast white slaves. It first appeared on Drury Lane in December 1785. In the 1785–86 season it was performed at least 16 times; in the same season the afterpiece *Omai* – chronicling Captain Cook and Polynesian local color – was staged 49 times.[28] However, it was performed only once in 1800, the year preceding which Sheridan's *Pizarro* was performed 67 times. I offer these contemporary performance records to suggest that *The Strangers at Home* shows evidence of riding a small wave of popularity during an era enthusiastic about exploration and resistance to the barbarian, and suffering a decline when *Pizarro*'s whig rhetoric resisted expansionist and colonialist moods in an England inhospitable to transnationalizing identity politics.[29]

At its very opening, we find some white men liberated from Barbary slavery who have returned to Florence, seeking their past lovers.[30] The secondary theme in the play, again, is that of women's amorous government, a common enlightenment motif. One of the returned ex-slaves is Montano, who remains in love with Laura, a Florentine gentlewoman. Laura's old guardian Aldobrand tries to prevent Laura and Montano's reunion, but is eventually thwarted and fooled after several sets of disguises and tricks leading to the lovers' reunion. The liberated European men's desire to enslave their women romantically turns at the play's end to the women's empire over these men.[31] The languages of love and of warfare are also mutually interpellated.[32] The supposed importance of women's governance is archly indicated in the play by Laura's cross-dressed maid Rosa (played by that acclaimed cross-dresser, Mrs Jordan) passing for the husband of Laura. Thus, Rosa says to Laura: "Am not I the best of husbands? … Ah! you will never know my value, till you have got your beloved Signor Montano; and then you'll soon find the difference between us!"[33]

This female empire complements the homosocial, public male context of the play. In the character of Firelock, the English soldier released from white slavery, we find that military masculinity is characterized by conviviality: singing, dancing and, needless to say, drinking (I.i.13). This carnivalesque conviviality, which apparently cuts through national and cultural boundaries, characterizes male culture in the play, while female identity remains nationally and domestically demarcated. In other words, conviviality is corrected as well as complemented by the female empire of conjugality. Perhaps these complex and interdependent relations of identity are best summed up in the words of Firelock:

I hardly dare call myself an Englishman while I wear the badges of slavery. Our noble captain, Ibrahim, has kindly presented me with the very cloaths in which I was taken by the Algerines: so, within an hour, you shall see me in that character which commands respect in every part of the world – a British soldier! – and then I shall want nothing but a mistress to make me compleatly happy … Love, I take it, is an universal language, much the same in most countries … Besides, if even a mistress should be coy, I have yet my bottle to comfort me.[34]

The freedoms to be English, men, lovers and bon vivants join in the above declaration of identity. Gender and national identities interpellate each other into a transnational Britishness that might incorporate even some elements of Islamic social identity.

Yet virtuous female domestic gender arrangements are threatened by men of 'other' colors and costumes. At a critical moment in the play, Montano appears to Laura as Ibrahim the Turk, and her response to him as the Turk is highly ambivalent. That the white man should approach his estranged female lover as a subject of a despotic culture is in itself evidence of persistent fascination with the polymorphousness and ambivalence of race and national identity throughout the eighteenth century. It encourages a more open view of the reality of slavery and transnational gendered struggles. However, it also reminds us that white men who enslave their women in marriage – like Aldobrand, the old guardian – are slavers as much as Turks who enslave white men. These subject positions of slaver and slave continue to be slipperily ascribed throughout the play, while the language simultaneously pirouettes between the masks heightening these slippery identities. Cultural cross-dressing is, indeed, one of the major modes of transcultural male identification in the play.

At the point of irreversible danger, that of actual inter-racial sex, however, distinct racial identities are reinforced by consumerist national identities. "Hunger is a bitter enemy to gallantry!" exclaims the Florentine Laurence, also freed from Barbary coast slavery,[35] when he is asked by his wife Alice whether he did not attempt to ingratiate himself with any of his Muslim master's wives or courtesans. European men's appetite for exotic women is acknowledged, but even for working-class men the bitter tonic of reverse enslavement is to have one's appetite for exotic women taken away and replaced by a keener tie to one's economic and cultural rights as an individual of an oppressed race belonging to a "superior" civilization. In Laurence's case, the identity of white men as slavers is repressed, while women's status as commodities defining the racial antagonism of men is foregrounded.

As Beth Fowkes Tobin has shown, cultural cross-dressing and other mimicries and hybridities do not always have the effect of subverting hegemony; sometimes they have the paradoxical effect of re-inscribing that hegemony.[36] The position of the cross-dresser determines some of these outcomes. Cross-dressing abroad has an array of meanings different from cross-dressing upon return. One of those meanings upon return, in Cobb's work, is the use of demonized alien cultures for domestic purposes.

European women like Laura were the vehicles of cultural and biological reproduction of Europe, the keepers of children as well as of ancestral memories. But besides being surrogates through which Europe remembered itself, they were sacrificial effigies[37] too, and like slaves, symbolized consumerist excess, always nodes of anxiety in a culture.[38] In Cobb's plays, therefore, their role of "savior" is the bright side of the symbolic violence of containing their energies in the fashion described in Burney's *Camilla*'s case (see Chapter 1). They redeemed European culture from the moral guilt of excess, saved themselves and their men from contamination by lesser humans, and attributed to those lesser humans a merely instrumental "nature." But violence was done to their own images as well.

While serving as the limits to homosocial consumerism, women themselves are one of the commodities in circulation among men. Mary Wollstonecraft's famous enlightenment feminist passage linking patriarchal double standard and western exoticism illuminates this perception of women's commodification in Cobb's day:

> Females have been … stripped of the virtues that should clothe humanity … [and] decked with artificial graces that enable them to exercise a short-lived tyranny. Love, in their bosoms, taking place of every nobler passion, their sole ambition is to be fair, to raise emotion instead of inspiring respect; and this ignoble desire, like the servility in absolute monarchies, destroys all strength of character. Liberty is the mother of virtue, and if women be, by their very constitution, slaves, and not allowed to breathe the sharp invigorating air of freedom, they must ever languish like exotics, and be reckoned beautiful flaws in nature.[39]

However much Eliza in Cobb's *Love in the East* may align herself with a masculinized "liberty" and energetic Anglo-Saxon reform of "slavish" colonial societies, Wollstonecraft here shows the impossibility of European women's attaining that sort of free selfhood as long as they are treated like slaves and commodities by their own men. Even their reign, contrary to Eliza's declaration in *Love in the East*, must then be the reign of slaves turned despots.

Human "nature" is used to put cultures and women in their appropriate places within enlightenment hierarchies, to transform so-called cacophony into harmony. But danger remains. As with the slippery threshold of European versus non-European identity vis-à-vis slavery, in the discourse on women, racial slave and master reverse ranks when it comes to commanding their women: "the Infidels have ways of keeping their wives to themselves, which we have not yet attain'd," says Laurence.[40] While a matter of debate since the famous Aaron Hill-Lady Montagu controversy, comparisons of the relative power and freedom of oriental versus European women contribute to the deeper ambivalence about European versus non-European nature. The nexus of anxieties surrounding gender, slavery, marriage, and national identity is evoked endlessly in the play. In the very next interchanges, Alice, Laurence, and Viola (the last being another young gentlewoman loved by the noble Octavio but persecuted by the villain Aldobrand) in turn revive the notion of love as slavery for women, for men, and again for women with physical beauty or commodifiable qualities, criteria applying to marriageable European women as well as to female slaves.[41] Viola refers to her impending marriage with Aldobrand as "this living death," a term commonly used to refer to slavery. In Act II, the concluding catch revives this theme:

'How great is the pleasure, how sweet the delight,'
When Love's silken bands willing captives unite!
Well pleas'd in their bondage, his vot'ries remain,
And, proud of subjection, exult in his chain:
   Oh, Love! how blissful's thy meed!
   The pray'r of thy vot'ries is – ne'er to be freed.

The prevalence of disguise among "strangers at home" – European ex-slaves – indicates that they cannot forget their experience of subordination, literally their emasculation, in an alien culture that they were used to revile and dominate. This drives their polymorphousness or disguise, not merely their desire to test their women's "love" for them. But slaves in *Strangers at Home* also haunt the disguised encounters in another sense, for Turk or slave, the disguised men hint at pervasive fears of sexual and economic contamination, another threat of identity-loss that interpellates gender relations as gender interpellates racial or national confraternity and conviviality.[42] I am considering the obvious anxieties surrounding Montano disguised as Ibrahim, but also the scene in Act II where Aldobrand fears that Regnalto, Viola's returned brother disguised as a "mute" – one without another kind of social identity – may be her "slave" and she his "mistress" in a lascivious sense.[43] The task of reclaiming masculinity and national superiority also must recall the hypothetical case of slavery, for it is the memory of that "living death" that haunts these men needing resurrection from the violent memory of "Many Thousands Gone." Colley has written of the ceremonies to greet redeemed "Barbary coast" slaves in the mid-eighteenth century that "in the redemption processions held in December 1721 and again in November 1734 [in London], the former captives were instructed to wear their 'Moorish' or 'slavish habits,' the clothes they still had from their time in North Africa."[44] This cross-fertilization of performance by memories of immobilization significantly indicates the "surrogation" of European captives for the triumphalist and spectacular performances of the redeeming nation-state. The ceaseless anxious male play on women's and slaves' unstable and interchangeable commodity identities evokes "an effigy in the process of symbolic substitution … of gender difference for racial difference, and of one commodity for another."[45]

Oddly, feudal patriarchy also stands in this play for the brutalized domestic surrogate, as the villainous guardian Aldobrand. Aldobrand is evidently worsted in the play so that the demise of feudal absolutism can complete the triumph of bourgeois paternalism. This romantic exposure of the older male guardian's avarice and moral turpitude,[46] hints first at political and moral reform of feudal patriarchy personified by Aldobrand in this play, or by the turncoat overlord Useph in *The Siege of Belgrade*.[47] However, this reform-mindedness might also illustrate that paternalist nationalism draws exaggerated attention to domestic reform in order to deflect attention from its "exploits" abroad. Indeed, when Montano intervenes in Aldobrand's seduction of his beloved Laura, he forces Aldobrand, then disguised as a friar, to exchange his Turk's habit with him, to "Turn Mahometan!" as Aldobrand says.[48] Aldobrand rather succinctly expresses his erasure within the glorification of a new national culture refined by women as displaced transmission and effigy-making:

> Ah! 'tis all over with me! Here am I, in my rival's house, with another man's cloaths
> on my back; having lost my character, my wife, my mistress, and almost lost myself!
> I am an actual numeration-table of losses; they rise upon me by tens, hundreds, and
> thousands.[49]

In the very language of change alley and the counting house, the "mahometanized" Aldobrand describes his loss of privileged European masculinity, a transnational tripping up. He is stripped and alienated; the sacrificial expenditure[50] of his male, European and material substance allows the refiguration of European bourgeois identity. Vested with the roving symbol of non-western savagery and despotism, he is at the same time made expendable at home. He is necessarily erased in order to make Mahometanism and the Barbary threat risible. Critically, it is losing his female possessions that completes his defeat. In the old guardian's expenditure or in his rein-"vest"-ment as the real Turk in Europe, then, we see a reiteration of all the motifs of spectacular sacrifice associated with transnationally defined gender and commodity fetishisms.

Such fetishisms keep appearing in Cobb's work, reintroducing the distinction between connoisseurship and collecting encountered in chapter two. In *The Humourist*, first acted on 27 April 1785 at the Drury Lane as an afterpiece, a hinterland of commodified cultures, peoples and things – similar to that which produces the "strangers at home" – informs the sense of European bourgeois and aristocratic male identity.[51] In this play, the eccentric collector Sir Anthony Halfwit mistakes his daughter's prospective suitor Beaumont, a young gentleman just returned from the Grand Tour, as a rival collector, and abetted by his mischievous friend Frolick, proceeds frantically to protect his most valuable acquisition, an Egyptian mummy, from Beaumont's imagined clutches.[52] The treatment of collectors in Cobb's work is thus distinctly similar to that found in Colman's play: collectors are stupid and indiscriminate hoarders who bear no comparison to true judges of worth, that is, connoisseurs. Beaumont, introduced to Sir Anthony as Mr. Medallion, is a connoisseur in that wide-ranging sexual and cultural sense of the term, and has eyes for no one but Sir Anthony's daughter Diana.

By chance, Diana's exits and entries are usually in an identical line of view with the place of the mummy's concealment, adding fuel to the baronet's suspicion. In this farce, as in Inchbald's *Lovers no Conjurors*,[53] a collector father, especially one absorbed by the "antiquity" of "other" cultures,[54] has lost touch with reality, and in his magisterial collectorhood, devalues his living womenfolk for his "mummies." Flesh and blood women and servants are renamed after figures of antiquity,[55] and Diana and her aunt Mrs. Matadore are mistakenly called "the mummy" by several characters.[56]

The task of evoking the exotic and the antique falls on the mummy. Disguise appears as another motif of polymorphousness, as we saw before in *The Strangers at Home*. The male characters, Sir Anthony and Frolick, "appear" in each other's characters, thanks to Frolick's practical joking, but while all identities are in question and fluid, the displacement of real women by Egyptian mummies underscores the former's devaluation. The older woman, Mrs. Matadore, is ridiculed for being nearly as old as the mummy,[57] this commodity of circumatlantic collection – a veritable usurpation of England's domestic pivot, its women, by the "living dead," conferring prestige and social eminence, "collected" from the circumatlantic flow of commodities.[58] Diana's value is also confounded with that of the mummy by Sir Anthony, especially in the scene where Beaumont speaks of her while Sir Anthony speaks of the mummy, after she has left the room through the door near which the mummy is concealed:

> Sir A. (Aside) Curse that fellow I don't like his looking so earnestly at my mummy (Beaumont's eyes are directed towards the door where Diana went out and where the Mummy stands.)
> … …
> B. Sir there is a lovely female thief in your house who has stolen my affection.
> Sir A. An impudent dog – he means my mummy.
> … …
> Sir A. But the Lady is rather too Old for so young a Man as you Mr. Medallion.
> Beaumont. Too Old Sir!
> Sir Anthony. Aye Sir – why I have had her my self these forty years.
> B. Forty years Sir – impossible.
> Sir A. I bought her forty years ago I'll assure you.
> Beaumont. Bought her – I thought she had been your own Sir.
> Sir A. Well Sir and so she is as I have paid for her – she cost me more money than you would give for her I believe.[59]

Later Sir Anthony cautions his daughter thus: "don't trust yourself with him [Beaumont]. – He may take it in his head to run away with you instead of the Mummy."[60]

Though the two men, one possessing both women and circumatlantic treasure, speak at cross-purposes to the audience's delight, it becomes gradually clear that underlying the circular discussion of the costs of women and mummies lurks another unnamed but ubiquitous reality of the west's commodity relations with another "monstrous double": the slave. The farce can be read as a covert concession of the nation's history of participation in trade in the socially dead. In this sense, in Roach's terms, the slave or mummy are "effigies" for Diana, the marriageable daughter and emblem of surrogation. Sir Anthony appears not to value his daughter nearly as much as he does his mummy.[61] Women who found themselves the marginalia of family and empire compared themselves with slaves and lent support to abolitionism.[62] But the suppressed, half-forgotten memory of the "living dead," the slaves of America and the Indies, lay under many other cultural practices, enthusiasms, and self-consolidating gestures of eighteenth-century England. In *The Humourist*, Cobb, with his own links with intercontinental exchanges and flows of commodities,[63] makes comic capital out of the reality of flows of slaves and exotic commodities, exchanges of women, and consolidations of the self in England.

Even though the term "miscegenation" was coined only in 1864 in America,[64] in 1772 and 1774 the West Indian planter Edward Long wrote about the simultaneous attraction and repulsion felt by the west towards its non-European other, demonstrating thereby the inner conflict of enlightenment racial theory.[65] This theory was marked by its inability to either deny or accept hybridity or transculturality as a viable category.[66] As Young details in his book's central argument, the central axis of this conflicted self-construction – whether one resembles many others or many others resemble one – is the figure of interracial mingling or sexuality. Long wrote:

> In the course of a few generations more, the English blood will become so contaminated with this mixture [of dreaded racial otherness], and from the chances, the ups and downs of life, this alloy may spread so extensively, as even to reach the middle, and then the higher orders of people, till the whole nation resembles the Portuguese and the Morisco in complexion of skin and baseness of mind. This is a venomous and dangerous ulcer, that threatens to disperse its malignancy far and wide, until every family catches infection from it.[67]

Undoubtedly, Cobb's plots reflect the dialectical tension between difference and universality found by Young in racial theories like Long's, and like in those theories, his resolutions are determined upon the axes of sexual and commodity relations.

In the institution of the Grand Tour, classical culture and the antique past were super-imposed on women, whom Chloe Chard has termed "surrogate antiquities."[68] These women were usually Europeans, however, and like the notorious Emma Hamilton, renarrativized European antiquity from within European culture.[69] Mrs. Matadore and Diana are thus fulfilling a classic role for the female within collector culture. But something additional happened when racial difference was added to this configuration of taste for the spatially and temporally remote. Especially in their ability to evoke the thrill of a mysteriously viewed past, which then became "normalized" and "naturalized" as both female, quotidian, private, and exotic, enlightenment Grand Tourists as well as Cobb's collector perform one of the enlightenment's central dramas: the museum-ization of the globe.

Denise Albanese remarks upon post-Renaissance Europe's relations with antiquity: starting with an attitude emphasizing the continuity of past and present and the patrilineal supremacy of the past, the Renaissance moved, however, to a controlling and instrumentalizing relationship with history. The discovery of exotic lands, femininity and commodities played a large part in this demystification or domestication of the "other" of space, whose time was considered commensurate with the early stages of the west, hence with the "past." History thus lost its pride of place when it became the present tense of lesser peoples.[70] The treasure of history itself became commodified. This shifting relationship with history, its magicality and authority devalued as news and commodity as it began to be seen as the present of lesser beings, is seen in the Grand Tourists' and Collectors' attempts to re-enchant as well as colonize antiquity and its female symbols, as in Sir Anthony's attempt to read the mummy as well as his daughter and sister as his everyday possessions. In

The Humourist, the living women involved are English and at home. The collector's desire for the strange and the magical focuses on the commodified circumatlantic female dead – the mummy – which evokes the past and the other but also parades their threatening otherness.

For instance, in George Colman's *A Turk and No Turk* (1785), an Englishman disguised as a Turk rambles collecting exotic mistresses, though returning to England to find a moneyed English wife. His servant Presto describes him thus:

> a ... blockhead ... looking over all the world for a wife – and hasn't picked up one with a few guineas in all the four quarters he has scamper'd thro'. No wonder, for whenever he sets out for a spouse, he is stop'd in the way by a mistress. In Egypt he mumbled all the female mummies. In Spain, mahogany brunetts – and in Italy he fed upon *Olives* – and then in Constantinople – oh Lord – we had a seraglio. Master was stark mad – and the women – oh *they* were stark – well – now we are in England – and in London too – unmarried as we left the country – the best of it is, he is arrived from abroad (*according to one of his last whims*) in a Turkish habit (*for he is never confin'd to customs*) – so the foolish people in the hotel here take him for a foreigner.[71]

The mummy here signifies live female exotica, as the other females of this libidinous Englishman's collection also denote strangeness and otherness.

An antagonistic relationship thus develops with history, which then becomes something to dominate as well as suspect, like women. But this cheapening of history as evidence of the tangibility of other cultures also requires a redemptive movement, or else a sense of history as one's own legacy vanishes threateningly. Thus, history needs to be re-invested as national treasure. The threat too is eventually to be controlled by the family's women, who reproduce the civilization that collects dead histories. Then, like women and like other races, history is idealized as the redeeming discourse of western heritage rather than the mark of commodifiable difference. In this idealized phase, it is frequently resurrected ideally, as are women, as a savior for present corruption; that is, as a civilizational force.[72]

Thus, constructions of alien versus domestic femininity reflect and shape male exchanges; while the enslaved, foreign commodities are sometimes remembered and symbolically cherished by male confraternities, the conjugal romance plot eventually subjugates the masculine conviviality plot, and the focus shifts to liberty for Englishmen and women to marry despite paternal tyranny. This plot depicts the bourgeois refinement of oppression, not its end. Cobb's *The Humourist* serves as a useful reminder of women's central role in mediating and accommodating awareness of transnational exchanges in the intercultural zone so that they became "normal" and normative to the average Englishman or woman. When the Englishman's relationship with the "other" is antiquarian and circumatlantic, domestic women change from being effigies and mummies to being practical homemakers. It is no coincidence that at the play's end, women like Diana are put in charge of preserving circumatlantic commodities' commodity status in a rather gruesome image:

> Sir A. Come let us into the next room [sic] I long to give the young Couple my blessing in a bumper – may their Sons be all Members of the Royal Society and may their daughters revive the art of embalming and understand pickling Mummies as well as any Egyptian since the Creation.[73]

The ending controls, but just barely, the volatility induced in English identity in incorporating women and slaves as commodities and doubles. In the end, neither home, marriage, and womenfolk, nor commerce, commodity and venture capitalism, slavery, and homosociality can be understood in isolation from one another. In their recent book, Barbara Ehrenreich and Arlie Russell Hochschild have unearthed how male interests are reaffirmed in the global trafficking of foreign women through the collusive "domestic" supervisory agency of western women.[74] Cobb's Diana is an eighteenth-century forebear of the western woman today whose better home and garden are made possible by the forlorn foreign maid or nanny, the trafficked commodification of care.

The projection of undesirable traits onto "others" morally condemns them. This is also a type of self-definition which is useful in maintaining class and racial distinctions and political authority over native or subject peoples. But such projection also makes any primordial pure identity suspect or partial, because it whispers that undesirable traits in the other are reflections of the same in the apparent wholeness of European identity. The opposite of such self-definition is a radical destabilization of distinct categories of racial purity. Thus, representations wherein "others" are realized as undeniably human occur continuously, in the form of ruptures and changes in the narratives of European identity that are early precursors of transnational discourse. Robert Young, who demonstrates the importance of racial hybridity in British cultural self-definition in the eighteenth and nineteenth centuries, writes: "the races and their intermixture circulate around an ambivalent axis of desire and aversion: a structure of attraction, where people and cultures intermix and merge, transforming themselves as a result, and a structure of repulsion, where the different elements remain distinct and are set against each other dialogically."[75]

In Cobb's plays, radical and "impure heterogeneity," polyphony, and playful experiments with the self appear to be the wayward nature of the boyish man; the woman, the fixed foot of the anchor, returns him to his sense of boundaries, most often through romantic and conjugal love. Women are thus seen as the limits of transnationality, at a time when actually unprecedented numbers of women were in global circulation.[76] Men are involved in a carnivalesque world, while women usually reinforce the staying powers of romance with the girl next door. Male social energy, expressed in war as well as camaraderie and riot, is tamed by the contrary pull of the romance narrative, articulated by the racially and ethically pure female. The fiction of femininity helps recuperate the loss of self and historical memory sustained through the "structure of attraction" with other cultures, replacing it with the "structure of repulsion."

It is precisely the hesitant, divided quality of Cobb's triumphalist plots and declarations that make him really worth study in his context. The first reason for a serious look at Cobb's apparently pulp-fiction-like work is its dividedness and mercuriality that seem to allow, indeed solicit, a questioning of it as a work with defining certitudes. This dividedness is made possible partly by his constant de-centering of the static and stable nation state and national identity. It is also enabled by his repeated demonstrations that encounter with difference changes the discourse upon self and other, difference being defined both by gender and by race. Second, his work is important for his depiction of nations as cultural "flows" rather than as rigidly mapped territories: it suggests a keen awareness of the "global flows" of culture, men, women, armies, national myths, artifacts, money, languages, ideologies, and performances. Cobb describes nationality as commodity- and exchange-based in his many "enlightened" representations of sexual and racial encounters, though such flows must also be regularly dammed to keep the nation pure from the taint of unregulated commerce with otherness. Not only is gender discourse – liberatory for women and salvific for men – to be found in the midst of male huzzahs and hoorays, but the interweaving of the two with slavery suggests, once more, Cobb's divided response to the serious pressures of a decentering, de-essentializing engagement with the other.

Cobb's subjects' encounters with the other are riddled with excitement as well as ambivalence, frequent slippages in self-possession, and the potential hybridization of enlightenment rationality and universality. Cobb's ambivalences emerge even in his "romance" plots, wherein national boundaries and traditional paterfamilias are repeatedly debunked, acquisition and commerce are repeatedly defetishized, and liberty is repeatedly reconceptualized, but with a surrogate effect. Difference congeals into an identity that insufficiently conceals its own hybridity. Unlike the historical actuality of preponderant and prevalent hybridity and exogamy experienced, even embraced, by many eighteenth-century Englishmen, Cobb's plays pull such hybridities back into a regulated and regulating conjugal framework wherein gender operates – as it did in *Inkle and Yarico* but with utterly inverse subjects – as the modality within which race must be lived. Within his hymeneal and "romance" plots, revaluations of "Englishness" are portrayed as salutary reform of patriarchal tyranny. Cobb's cacophonous chronotopes,[77] on the other hand, are transnational scenes of male convivial encounter with the other which imperil western subjectivity.

As to real expertise as an orientalist, Cobb is a fledgling at best. Despite his career with the East India Company, as a storyteller he appears to lack all of the sophistication, and most of the scholarly acumen, of truly serious orientalist scholars such as Sir William Jones. But he effectively metamorphoses the margins of the world into sites of British transformation and transvaluation. This relocation and redefinition of identity has been discussed in the context of the "national tale" by Ina Ferris, who has described the national tale as an autoethnography, performative enunciation and strong representation, or as an encounter of the material body with the material "other," which reinforces the colonial location's power "to move the metropolitan subject/reader into [an estranging and] potentially transformative relation of proximity."[78] But as Gary Kelly has argued, this potentially transformative relationship triggered a later fearful reaction to such dizzying polyglossia, which enforced a resumption of "standards" of literacy and expression. The "standard," a truly civilizational enlightenment concept, was "an assertion of the power of the standard language and its owners. For this reason ... literature using language to represent the 'nation' as diversity-in-unity became especially powerful."[79] Even before the simultaneous post-revolutionary triumph of the "mother-tongue" and "standard English" administered by several women writers whom Kelly mentions, women were serving as instruments in standardizing the nation and its narration much earlier, as we have seen in the discussion of plays by Cobb.

Cobb also both creates and undoes transnational "types," both favorable and unfavorable, who signal the absurdity of exclusive "national" superiority.[80] Again, women reaffirm the boundaries between national self and transnational other. Women save both home and the political realm, and influence and soften the hegemonic discourse of masculinity. Masculinity is defined in Cobb's work not only as military might and a fighting spirit, but through the father's line, which women perpetuate. The converse of imagining oneself through distant others is re-interpreting home. In his attempt to recreate English origins as partly imitating and partly challenging other traditions, Cobb even naturalizes the long-dead Moliere to enlist support for comedy, a genre that Cobb claims the revolutionary French have forgotten, as they have forgotten their own true national poet.[81] Thalie and Josie converse:

> Thalie. Jupiter alas, wearied ... Has Commanded Me Along with Momus ... to descend on this Terrestrial Globe, and Carry him back to the Abode Of Thunder, some new work which can Enliven.
> Josie. You will find it a Difficult task, The Scene is greatly Impoverish'd.[82]

In contrast, Cobb's "free" Englishmen alternately carouse with or fight enemies abroad, thus defining maleness by equal portions of military camp and homosocial comedy. Once more, we see a familiar process at work: the play identifies French comic tradition, then appropriates that tradition to form part of a strengthening and centralizing of English national tradition.

Cobb's work thus demonstrates a tension between free and easy flows of culture and male identity moderated by the so-called feminine domestic instinct. As to literary precedents for this style, accommodating more than one voice or "strain" of argument or rhetoric is nothing new in itself in the eighteenth century; critics have noted this attempt to contain and sometimes liberate multiple voices in the eighteenth-century discursive form of the dialogue,[83] while the novel is, of course, the most prominent example of a form that struggles to contain and order as well as liberate psychological, social, and evidentiary narratives.[84] The third Earl of Shaftesbury had suggested as early as 1709 that a dramatically divided self could lead to self-knowledge, conferring upon the most rational, coherent part the status of leader, assigning to other parts of the self the role of followers, who would learn from the leader.[85] Shaftesbury suggested, moreover, that one of the ways that an unrestrained dialogue could be obtained was by absenting the author from the narrative, by replacing overt authorial didacticism with mimesis. This could be a program for conducting literary truth-telling from epic to dialogic to novelistic to dramatic modes, literally, wherein magisterial authors progressively fade, and characters in action work out their own destinies.[86] Needless to say, these mimetic, "strong representations" are also scenes of transformation, as are dialogues, novels, or the carnivalesque aspects of Cobb's plays: Cobb's dramaturgy there shows the reliance on mimesis, and the division of the fictional self. The transformative nature of strong representations appears, perhaps, in this near-total free-for-all of character and circumstance in Cobb's carnivalesque and transnational plots.

Many of these plays exhibit the aesthetic problem of formal containment and substantive unity. Different writers throughout the century had found different solutions for this problem. As mentioned above, Shaftesbury had characterized dialogue as an attempt to unite the several personages and characters in one action or story. Addison, in his *Spectator* essays on the Pleasures of the Imagination had grappled with the various components of volume, expanse and limit of prospect, color, the senses, artifice versus nature, variety in unity, etc., that made his aesthetic a complex mental and sensual activity.[87] Hogarth had determined variety to be the principle of beauty, and had found the embodiment of that aesthetic principle in the curved line or serpent as well as the beautiful woman.[88] Cobb's plays show similar efforts to contain in a fictional compass the strains and tongues of variety, an effort wherein the author's presence is muffled by the dramatic form. If the dramatic dialogue was a quintessentially enlightenment form of rational polemics, always troubled by many voices, Cobb's vision of a polyphonic or even cacophonous form exceeded as well as extended the enlightenment to the west's shores, peripheries and borders – perhaps made it a "polylogic" interval. In this way, reading Cobb's plays inform us of the role of the other – Shaftesbury's dialogic opponents, or racial and cultural others – in modifying the legacy of the enlightenment.

Cobb's project of presenting plurality and polyphony is manifested also in the formal aspect of his writing and is characteristic of some other contemporaries. I wish to draw attention to the repeatedly participial nature of many of the line-endings of Cobb's choruses and songs. These musical numbers have a parodic, vaudevillian refrain, reinforcing a quality of quotidian flux and agitation. Some randomly chosen samples from Cobb's plays will serve as examples. At the conclusion of *The Haunted Tower*, set in Norman England, when a marriage impends between a French noblewoman just arrived and Edward the son of the usurping English baron, the unwilling bridegroom Edward sings to delineate the themes of marriage as well as staged military arts:

> Air–Edward. While swords and shields are clashing,
>   Archers aiming, cudgels thrashing,
>   The ale to none denying,
> Flaggons far and wide supplying,
> With tilters fencing, wrestlers boasting.
> Bonfires blazing, oxen roasting;
> And all the vassals flock around,

What pleasures now abound!
Now all in preparation,
For the nuptial celebration.[89]

This eulogy serves to delineate the momentary fusion of social classes even while it asserts the coronation of hierarchy. In *The Siege of Belgrade*, in a eulogistic hymeneal finale, European women threatened by Muslim conquerors and then released from that threat by nationalist resistance sing:

Lilla and Ghita.	Bright the laurel of victory gracing,
	The manly brow merit marks it to wear.
Chorus.	Doubly dear is that laurel while placing,
	By the loved hand of the favourite Fair.
	Toils forgetting, pleasure courting,
	Beauty beaming, smiles transporting.
	Bright the laurel of victory gracing, &c[90]

These musical numbers are hymeneal finales or expressions of amorous crises just as often as they are comments on power struggles. They express social reality as mediated by personal and political stresses, while also testifying to hierarchical ways of organizing reality. They express quotidian flows and vibrant scenarios as they endorse the status quo and spheres of power. Compare this with the writing of another of Cobb's contemporaries, Mary Robinson in, say, "January 1795."[91] In suggesting hurry, class indistinction, and quotidian action including "incongruities,"[92] Robinson too repeatedly uses participial endings that impart a sense of hurry, flux and contingency to each line and make them literally flow into and depend on one another for overall meaning. For instance:

Pavement slipp'ry, people sneezing,
Lords in ermine, beggars freezing;
Titled gluttons dainties carving,
Genius in a garret starving.

Lofty mansions, warm and spacious;
Courtiers cringing and voracious;
Misers scarce the wretched heeding;
Gallant soldiers fighting, bleeding[93]

Or:

Tents, marquees, and baggage-wagons;
Suttling-houses, beer in flaggons;
Drums and trumpets, singing, firing;
Girls seducing, beaux admiring;
Country lasses gay and smiling,

City lads their hearts beguiling;

… …

Lordly gen'rals, fiercely staring,
Weary soldiers, sighing, swearing![94]

What a different world from Cobb's, and yet how similar. The above poems show Robinson's awareness of complementary social and individual turmoil and hierarchies,[95] and her sense of a society in flux. Judith Pascoe has noted how her whirlwind social life and her insistence upon mobility, and upon a panoptical vantage point on a constantly mobile society, led her to maintain a carriage that consumed a good portion of her income.[96] She has noted also Robinson's interest in the urban scene as a busy social milieu involving much action, movement, and exchange.[97] The rhetorical and visual similarities in Cobb's and Robinson's work, therefore, are not incidental. Though Robinson seeks to highlight and showcase the active involvement of women in the late eighteenth-century public life and marketplace while Cobb seeks to repress it,[98] they are aesthetically aligned in their vision of the times. This vision entails aestheticizing crisis and flow: the assault of social, political, and cultural modernity upon tradition may be said to have reached one finale in the Revolutionary era. Both Robinson and Cobb attempt to convey a sense of its bustling activity by similar syntactical strategies. Cobb's work incorporates flows and attempts to contain contradictions or incongruities inevitable in his time.

The tumult and cacophony in his plays may be a reflection of the fact recognized by Shaftesbury, Addison, and others, that representing global, social, and individual turmoil necessarily involved engaging with clutter. Even more critical is the fact that engagements with absolute difference entailed a potential hermeneutic free-for-all and a transfiguration of tradition. At least potentially, accepting plural voices would mean acknowledging in the abstract the transformative possibilities of scattered global phenomena and cultures. Hence, perhaps, the madness, the enthusiasm and extravagance of some of Cobb's works, though significantly limited by a normative patriarchal gender discourse.

The apollonian side of this polymorphism of gender and race was the enlightenment project to throw light on the true "nature" or essence of things and people. If philosophes such as Diderot and Voltaire had believed that such a "nature" could be recuperated by enlightened despotism guided by the philosophes, anti-philosophes such as Rousseau had contended that human nature – often blamed by materialists such as Hobbes for all that was wrong with the world – suffered precisely from the philosophes' opportunistic reconciliation of public virtue with "sociable" self-interest. The philosophes' society and sociability were rejected by Rousseau in favor of an enlightened republicanism wherein human beings would, to some degree, recover their lost nature – or essence – at least that found in the golden age between barbaric savagery and effete, corrupt civilization.[99]

Enlightenment thinkers' pursuit of origins and "nature" continued in their application of enlightenment principles to the peripheries. This is evinced in the engineering of the Anglo-Indian Permanent Settlement (1793) in eighteenth-century

Bengal by Sir Philip Francis, Warren Hastings' contemporary and implacable adversary.[100] Like his physiocratic forebears, Francis outlined for Bengal a reform plan which would root out accreted corruption, attendant upon "misgovernment." More radical than the mainstream philosophes who stroked secular power while challenging theological authority, less radical than Rousseau who attacked both and advocated return to a putative "pristine" political and psychological structure, Francis' theories yet displayed the reformist paradox that sought to return the object populations of reform to their supposed "permanent" precolonial essence. Corruption, Francis argued, was inevitable if a high "civilization" such as Britain, with its elaborate jurisprudence and alien venal system, intruded upon a flourishing eastern order. Francis declared that the East India Company, in its judicial and revenue operations, should seek to revive the practices of the Mughals, India's indigenous enlightened despots, and to maintain for itself as much of a behind-the-scenes profile as possible.[101] The Mughals, according to Francis and many others, had ruled by fiat, but benevolently, and Bengal had been rich and stable under them.

At the same time, Francis reconciled enlightened autocracy with the European idea of a right to private property, as had Voltaire and Holbach in France. Hence, while endorsing a political regime that remained faithful to a supposedly authentic native past, Francis, like other philosophes, sought to define native culture as universally as possible, and attempted to re-plant European enlightenment in Indian soil.[102] While Francis believed that Britain should not colonize Bengal, he also believed that it should administer Bengal with a firm hand, allowing physiocratic and some free trade principles to work for its agricultural, commercial, and manufacturing "improvement." Reform sought both to liberate the "native" and to prescribe the terms of the liberation by "uncovering" British and whig ideals of property and subjecthood in the indigenous cultural and social arrangements. The similarities with Colman's social manifesto cannot but begin to be obvious here. We have also seen the postcolonial rendering of this story in Rushdie's Aurora Zogoiby.

These enlightenment projects which confronted difference, thus, by chanting both the praises of the indigenous system and of the enlightenment's universalist ideals, provide the ideological analogs for plays like Cobb's. His drama, set in India and other exotic places, shows European characters who similarly oscillate between accepting and reforming the native. Their opening of local selves to the globe means that eventually they impose their local norms on the globe. On the one hand, men in Cobb's plays seem to encounter difference in a male public world primarily in the form of male consumption, recreation, and amorousness: drinking, carousing, lovemaking, and fighting. His male characters' frequent assumptions of the disguise of another, as in *The Strangers at Home* or in *The Humourist*, suggest hints of a radical instability of essence, acknowledging a "universality" that exists only through change and radical alterity. But the potential threat of such blurring of "essence" always generates its own reaction.[103] Even within the male public sphere, transnational carnivalesque male "culture" is gradually replaced by the absorption of private sphere ideology into the public sphere in the garb of "family values."

Chloe Chard's analysis of the Grand Tour also speaks potently to this issue: "Travelers of all periods express a wish that the foreign should proclaim itself as dramatically different from the familiar. At the same time, they also register a hope that the topography will not in the end prove entirely resistant to intellectual and imaginative appropriation ... the two qualities demanded of the foreign [are] ... mystery, on the one hand, and relative accessibility, on the other."[104] Universality is deferred but not abandoned. Moreover, she also finds this dialectic of the universal and the same embodied in women who both mystify and familiarize antiquity for the male citizen of the republic of taste. Women in Cobb also trigger delicious self-loss as well as firm self-possession.

European women clearly served as effigies useful in both commemorating and erasing difference lodged in the crannies of the national unconscious as repressed memory. Elsewhere, Partha Mitter has pointed to the same enlightenment propensity to gather the unknown and the strange into the folds of consciousness through the aesthetic motif of "schemata."[105] Mitter anticipates Roach's critique of enlightenment European genealogies of performance as being based on aesthetic surrogation and displacement of the other. The earliest European travelers displaced non-western substance by transforming it into a stereotype of something closer to home.[106] Difference has always haunted the imagination of the self. Michel de Certeau describes how sixteenth-century western ethnography of the Brazilian Tupinamba converted the latter's speech, space, and body into writing, history, and culture in the west.[107] De Certeau shows – as do Mitter and Roach – that western identity is initially predicated on the experience or enjoyment of difference, but that difference is then funneled into making western representation, space, and time – the three props of western identity.

Cobb's work too embraces difference avidly, until its specificity vanishes. To use another metaphor, Cobb's writing "translates" the other into self, echoing and re-presenting the other's ravishing but also threatening speech and sounds.[108] Globalizing and pluralizing impulses are tempered by the regularizing impulses of colonialism and conquest, however anxious. His excited, tumultuous dramatic rhetoric – with characters and plots perpetually in tumult, falling in turns into song, drunken riot and melodramatic battle with equal alacrity – suggests his attentiveness to the ultimate unmanageability of human nature, and its cacophonous self-expression. But the opposing universalist imperative emerges also to deploy this male public culture of song, drink and militant fraternity in the service of heterosexual romance nurturing a stratified society, wherein the "human" is categorized and hierarchized. Female agency seems to deepen this instinct for structure quiescent in male homosociality. Indeed, as Felicity Nussbaum has shown, enlightenment writers anxiously scrutinized the state of female culture as an index of the general superiority of cultures. The potentially raucous, supposedly equalizing, cacophony of male public culture is tamed and striated by the harmonious polyphony of the empire of decent women and men.[109] The carnivalesque fraternal impulse is thereby channeled into social repression.

Evidently, my suggestion has been that colonial patriarchy used the construction of women and gendered spheres as an ideological tool to fend off racial threats to its identity, however much women seem themselves to have been implicated in "enlightenment" reform. I now return to Rushdie in closing, especially to his characterization of women and power. The work of empire was done by men, but women provided its symbolic arsenal. Even if in comparison with mid-century fiction women's reform is triumphant in Cobb's plays,[110] the erasure of female reformers' true autonomy is implicit in the punitive controls ever imminent on transgressive women. That seems true of imperial as well as Rushdie's postcolonial representations of female agency. Would the story of Aurora Zogoiby have been different had she told it herself? Would the women in Cobb's plays act any differently if they did not dance at the capricious commands of colonial patriarchy? These are important questions to ask of colonial and postcolonial representations of genders, races and nations. Women's deployment in containing the nightmares generated by enlightened Reason and nationalistic Passion is a story nearly as fascinating as that of their embodiment as cultural monstrosities. In the end, Rushdie's Aurora, who is herself smashed by her fall from her Olympian height to street level, embodies the contradictory fate of the elite who is also woman and native, identities that shift contextually. By fraternizing too closely with the subalterns, and generating irresolvable anxieties by this transgression, Aurora's fate resembles that of many European women of colonial narratives who are contaminated in the process of colonial reform and must be purged as effigies. Their virtuous antithesis is idealized in Cobb, but such virtue is always instrumental, not chosen. The centrality as well as instrumentality of women in both Cobb and Rushdie keep us aware that the need to keep a strict eye on the politics of gender discourses – colonial or contemporary – continues.

Notes

1   Gwendolyn Midlo Hall, *Africans in Colonial Louisiana: The Development of Afro-Creole Culture in the Eighteenth Century* (Baton Rouge, 1992), p. xii. Especial thanks go to Kenneth Warren and Mita Choudhury for their early reading and helpful criticism of this essay.
2   Salman Rushdie, *The Moor's Last Sigh* (New York, 1995).
3   See Ranajit Guha, *A Rule of Property for Bengal: An Essay on the Idea of Permanent Settlement* (Durham; London, 1996), pp. 22–4.
4   Mumbai is today's name for Bombay, reflecting a neonational attempt to shake off colonial renaming by returning to an "original," precolonial name for the city. Certainly, the metropolitan infection remains.
5   I deliberately use the term "coloniality" rather than "colonialism" as one that connotes attitudes, conscious and unconscious, while the latter connotes actions and practice.
6   Dalrymple, *White Mughals*, pp. 38–43.
7   Full citations are as follows: *The Humourist; or, Who's Who*, Farce in 2 acts, 1785, British Library Add. Ms. 25912; *The Strangers at Home; A Comic Opera in Three Acts* (London, 1786); *Love in the East; or, Adventures of Twelve Hours* (London, 1788).
8   Roach, *Cities of the Dead*, pp. 2–4.
9   The related term "mimic" is also well known, of course, as Homi Bhabha's formulation

of what happens to language and identity in imbrications of colonialist and subaltern cultures (*Location of Culture* [New York, 1994], p. 88). The main distinction between mimicry and surrogation seems to be the former's connotation of subjectivity and the latter's associations with greater objectification. To these two theoretical models one might add Georges Bataille's concepts of pure and impure social heterogeneity in his *Visions of Excess: Selected Writings, 1927–1939* (Minneapolis, 1985), vol. 14, pp. 139–44. Bataille's "pure" heterogeneous society is one very close to a homogenous and controlled one, in that it "orders" the chaotic, tumultuous impulses of a diverse society in the interests of its privileged groups. An "impure" heterogeneity represents a society where the hierarchy of the privileged and the masses is not as clearly established. In this regard, see also Gretchen Gerzina's *Black London: Life Before Emancipation* (Newark, 1995), esp. p. 5.

10 Colley, *Captives*, pp. 43–4.

11 In terms of contemporary cultural analogs for the dual plots and the tension between race and gender observable in Cobb, I have found helpful Andrea Most's analysis of the American musical in "'We Know We Belong to the Land': The Theatricality of Assimilation in Rodgers and Hammerstein's *Oklahoma!*," *PMLA*, 113/1 (1998): 77–89. She claims that American musicals in the 1940s and 1950s showed national identity being negotiated through the tension between dual plots of individuality and musical collectivity. A musical like *Oklahoma!* typically depicted the plot of individualistic identity as running counter to the musical carnival that establishes community and national identity. In Cobb's work, however, the oppositions are reversed: coherent national identity is threatened by carnivalesque performance dominated by men, and fostered by the restricted plot of individual romance dominated by women.

12 See Jurgen Habermas' *The Structural Transformation of the Public Sphere: An Inquiry into a Category of Bourgeois Society*, trans. Thomas Burger and Frederick Lawrence (Cambridge, 1989), pp. 43–51. Habermas pioneered the argument that the mores and conditions of the privately defined self influenced bourgeois public life in the eighteenth and nineteenth centuries. The work of cultural historians like Catherine Hall and Leonore Davidoff lends extensive support to Habermas' formulation of the private springs of public spheres in *Family Fortunes: Men and Women of the English Middle Class 1780–1850* (Chicago, 1987). Among literary critics, Nancy Armstrong is one of the best known to have argued that the first modern individual was a woman, in her reading of literary forms like the novel (*Desire and Domestic Fiction: A Political History of the Novel* [New York, 1987]).

13 See Charles Beecher Hogan (ed.), *The London Stage* (Carbondale, 1968), pt 5, vol. 2, p. 2.

14 John Loftis remarks that in J.P. Kemble's Drury Lane, three-dimensional and realistic stage props had replaced the painted flats of Dryden's Drury (*Sheridan and the Drama of Georgian England*, [Cambridge, MA, 1977], p. 138). Cobb started staging plays before Kemble became manager of Drury, but the innovations in stage and scene setting had preceded Kemble. Mobile spectacle such as Cobb's – complete with music, dress, decorations, and machinery – would be particularly effective on the three-dimensional stage of the later eighteenth century. See also Robert Hume, "The Multifarious Forms of Eighteenth-century Comedy," in *The Stage and the Page: London's "Whole Show" in the Eighteenth-century Theater*, ed. George W. Stone (Berkeley, 1981), pp. 3–32, and the introduction to *The London Stage*, pt 5, vol. 1, pp. xix–ccxviii.

15 Roach, *Cities of the Dead*, pp. 5–6.

16 While disguises, mistaken identities and concealments are common in comedies, farces,

and "Spanish" plots in Georgian drama (Loftis, *Sheridan*, p. 65), in Cobb's plays it is the addition of colonial motifs to the motif of disguises that emphasizes how the conventions of drama are imbricated with the apparatuses of empire.

[17] *Love in the East; or, Adventures of Twelve Hours: A Comic Opera in Three Acts* (London, 1788), p. 8.

[18] Colley, indeed, writes that "only a minority of Britons seem to have acknowledged any parallel between their own risk of being captured at sea by North African corsairs, and the much greater threat that British slaving ventures increasingly posed to men and women in West Africa" (*Captives*, p. 46). See also ibid., pp. 47–8, 54–6.

[19] Cobb, *Love in the East*, pp. 5–6.

[20] Women are explicitly referred to as commodities in *Love in the East*, p. 72.

[21] Male tyranny and insurrection are found repeatedly in Cobb. They appear in *Lausus and Lydia* and *Mezentius*, two classically inspired unperformed plays by Cobb (both undated but late eighteenth century). In *Lausus and Lydia*, while at first the son Lausus is constructed as a courageous warrior in his father's battles, the subservient filial relationship is interrupted by conflict over a woman, whom both father and son desire. But the revolution is contained by the woman herself who becomes the mediator between father and son, and who re-humanizes the tyrannical father; masculine paternalism as well as patrilineage is interpellated by this obsession with possessing a woman. In *Mezentius*, certain passages strongly demonstrate the contested woman's instrumentality to reproduce and mediate the filial relationship of father and son, while never allowing their potential for conflict to be forgotten (pp. 15r–16r). In the end, kingly fathers relinquish their ungoverned and impolitic desires and claims.

[22] See Nussbaum's discussion of the importance of female development for assessing the superiority of civilizations during the enlightenment (*Torrid Zones: Maternity, Sexuality and Empire in Eighteenth-century English Narratives* [Baltimore, 1995], p. 11).

[23] Wheeler, "Complexion of Desire," p. 328.

[24] Bhabha, *Location of Culture*, p. 73.

[25] Cobb, *Love in the East*, p. 12.

[26] It is unclear if he is West Indian, East Indian, African, or other.

[27] *Love in the East*, p. 15. Rosario is ethnically unspecific precisely perhaps because the feminized reform ideology of the play requires attention away from racial issues, and on to civilizational issues. Robert Young argues that the pluralistic, relativistic, and hybridizing theories of culture and ethnicity that prove so *liberating* for us today share certain formal similarities with eighteenth- and nineteenth-century *reactionary* racial theories which, the more they accepted the concreteness of other cultures, also implicitly or explicitly equated evidence of cultural "difference" with evidence of racial polygenesis and hierarchies of race (see also Alexander O. Boulton, "The American Paradox: Jeffersonian Equality and Racial Science," *American Quarterly*, 47/3 (September 1995): 485). Initially meant to challenge the comforting Eurocentrism of enlightenment universalism, these seemingly relativist and "multicultural" theories – Herder's and Matthew Arnold's, for instance – were used by conservative thinkers, paradoxically, to argue for western racial and cultural imperialism, once culture had been dissociated from civilization and had come to stand for racial essence after the 1770s. Roxann Wheeler persuasively traces the antecedents of such civilizational discourse – emphasizing Christian belief – in mid-century novels (Wheeler, "Complexion of Desire," esp. pp. 310–12, 328). The threat of hybridity first and miscegenation later intensified this urge to differentiate and devalue "other" cultures defined as other races or species (Young, *Colonial Desire*, pp. 29–54), and hence it became critical to re-impose a civilizational universality on them.

28 Hogan (ed.), *London Stage*, pt 5, vols 2–3.

29 Loftis, *Sheridan*, pp. 124–41.

30 Barbary slavery had been a menace for European navigators for a century at least. John Wolf shows that Cromwell was concerned with the ransoming of enslaved Englishmen (John Wolf, *The Barbary Coast: Algiers Under the Turks, 1500–1800* [New York, 1979], p. 159). See also Stephen Clissold, *The Barbary Slaves* (New Jersey, 1977), chapters 8 and 9. It is useful to dispel notions that Barbary slavery and transatlantic slavery were somehow numerically as well as psychologically comparable phenomena (Colley, *Captives*, p. 62). However, Colley also makes the related argument that Barbary slavery was, nevertheless, extremely "real" for Britons in the seventeenth and eighteenth centuries. Britons' own experience of enslavement also sometimes made others' slavery more "real" to them (ibid., p. 64). On the other hand, Britons' grudging concession of the "civilizations" of Islam may have also made a partial identification with those "slave" cultures more possible for them (ibid., pp. 104–13).

31 Cobb, *The Strangers at Home*, pp. 9–10, 22.

32 This is also evident in Cobb's *The Siege of Belgrade*, p. 11.

33 Cobb, *The Strangers at Home*, p. 27. Since Mrs Jordan's cross-dressing was thought by contemporary admirers to enhance the power and charm of femininity, demonstrated in an elaborate and enjoyable game of paradoxical make-believe between audience and actress, these lines from Rosa might easily reinforce the ascendant power of femininity in this play.

34 Ibid., pp. 13–14. Warnford expresses the same universalist hope in *Love in the East*, p. 20.

35 Cobb, *The Strangers at Home*, p. 33.

36 Beth Fowkes Tobin, *Picturing Imperial Power: Colonial Subjects in Eighteenth-century British Painting* (Durham, 1999), p. 90.

37 Roach writes: "The effigy is a contrivance that enables the processes regulating performance – kinesthetic imagination, vortices of behavior, and displaced transmission – to produce memory through surrogation" (*Cities of the Dead*, p. 36).

38 Ibid., p. 123. See also Beth Kowaleski-Wallace's *Consuming Subjects: Women, Shopping, and Business in the Eighteenth Century* (New York, 1997), and my *Reading the Splendid Body: Gender and Consumerism in Eighteenth-century British Writing on India* (Newark, 1998).

39 Mary Wollstonecraft, *A Vindication of the Rights of Woman*, ed. Mary Warnock (London, 1992), p. 41.

40 Cobb, *The Strangers at Home*, p. 33.

41 Ibid, p. 34.

42 Colley has discussed reputed Barbary sexual perversions such as sodomy in *Captives*, pp. 56–7, 128–29. See also *The Case of Many Hundreds of Poor English-Captives, in Algier, together with some remedies to prevent their Increase, Humbly Represented to Both Houses of Parliament*: "their frequent forcing of Men and Boys by their execrable *Sodomy*, also their inhumane abuses and force to the Bodies of Women and Girls, frequently attempting *Sodomy* on them also …" (1680, n.p.). Indeed, such equitable violence dismantles gender distinctions and hierarchies themselves, one might say.

43 Cobb, *The Strangers at Home*, p. 36.

44 Colley, *Captives*, p. 79.

45 Roach, *Cities of the Dead*, p. 217.

46   Cobb, *The Strangers at Home*, pp. 42–3, 49.
47   Cobb, *The Siege of Belgrade*, pp. 31, 34.
48   Cobb, *The Strangers at Home*, p. 53.
49   Ibid., p. 54.
50   In George Bataille's sense of profitable waste or economical excess, in Bataille, *Visions of Excess*, vol. 14, pp. 138–47. A redefinition of authority within bourgeois ideology causes Aldobrand's "type" to become superfluous.
51   Recent scholarship urges the need to read western material cultural history – including subject-forming phenomena such as the Grand Tour – with relation to the west's imbrication in other exchanges, travels, and flows of things and people. For instance, Kay Dian Kriz argues for situating "the Tour within a larger network of international travel and exchange that involved the circulation of bodies and luxury goods not only within Western Europe, but also within the European powers and their overseas colonies, and between Western Europe and other nation states … celebration of Western culture and scientific technology involves comparison with narratives of exotic peoples and natural curiosities 'discovered' outside of Europe" (Kriz, "Introduction: The Grand Tour," *Eighteenth-century Studies*, 31/1 [1997]: 88–9). It is in this sense that I use the term "hinterland of commodified cultures" here.
52   I am indebted to Mita Choudhury for reminding me that "collector" meant also the British revenue or tax collector in British India, a fact Cobb with his East India connections no doubt knew. "Collecting" as aesthetic and economic practice are then clearly interwoven in a colonial matrix that lends support to my argument in this essay.
53   *Lovers no Conjurors*, a farce in two acts, 1792, Huntington library manuscript LA 952.
54   Greek, Roman, and circumatlantic.
55   Gretchen Gerzina writes that it was common eighteenth-century English practice to give classical names to black slaves and servants (*Black London*, p. 16). Sir Anthony's status as father, collector, and male master of the household can thereby be seen as disturbingly aligned with the practices of slave owning.
56   Carol Barash also points out that Jamaican slave women were often given names from classical mythology, such as Psyche and Diana ("Character of Difference," p. 412).
57   This ridicule also points up the ageism of classic misogyny. James Thompson has written, for instance, that the eighteenth-century novel frequently "illustrates the multiplicity of subject positions assumed by the dependent female. Wife, mother, widow, and spinster are all devalued, while young women are suspiciously overvalued" (*Models of Value*, p. 176).
58   This is a farcical version of the later idealizing conflation of European women with antiquity, demonstrated by Chloe Chard: "During the late eighteenth and nineteenth centuries, travelers very frequently select as noteworthy objects of commentary those sights that elide antiquity with versions of femininity … living women … resemble ancient sculptures" ("Grand and Ghostly Tours," 102). Mrs. Matadore's displacement by the mummy in turn triggers the reactive staging of European women to reappropriate history and civilization as European (and universal), safe and venerable.
59   Cobb, *The Humourist*, pp. 17–20. There are haunting echoes of potential incest here, such incest being an actualization of potential abuse of women by their male possessors. This echoes also Cobb's *Love in the East*, where a benevolent but disguised father, Colonel Bentley, is for some time feared as his natural daughter Ormellina's potential suitor. Significantly, Ormellina's name evokes that of Robert Orme, an eighteenth-century

historian of India. Besides incest, in the scene above, collectors' desire is also pictured as a sexual and commercial relationship, that of paid possession, with the circumatlantic object, usually gendered.

60 Ibid., p. 23.

61 Similarly, in Inchbald's *Lovers no Conjurors*, Sir Samuel Prejudice is willing to let his prospective son-in-law "alter" – impregnate or possess – his daughter, but panics at the thought of change to one of his collections. Once more, this is a preference for the dead commodity over the living relation. When cultural surrogation produces anxiety or guilt rather than confidence and self-approbation, the culture produces an "effigy" to be an expendable "monstrous double" for the redemption of the surrogate. See also Chard ("Grand and Ghostly Tours," 102) on figures in whom "a remote past assumes a ghostly, semi-visible presence," which role is more literally fulfilled here by the mummy, and not by European women.

62 See Ferguson, *Subject to Others*, and Midgley, *Women Against Slavery*.

63 There is a "Memorandum of Correspondence relative to a Pearl ..." at the Oriental and India Office Collections, London (O/6/10. 317–20, 1817), wherein in an unknown hand are transcribed various details of correspondence between Cobb, Messrs de Vry, and a Governor-General Ruffles of Batavia, relating to a pearl whose sale value was expected to discharge the debt owed by Messrs De Vry to the East India Company. While the value of the pearl (£2,000) and the litigation surrounding recovery of the debt owed to the Company vie for space in the extracts recorded from these letters, the travels of the pearl from London to Batavia to Calcutta suggest something of the global flow of commodities, even minutiae, with which Cobb personally had to be involved.

64 Young, *Colonial Desire*, p. 144.

65 Ibid., pp. 150–51.

66 Ibid., pp. 36–43.

67 Long, *Candid Reflections upon the Judgment lately awarded by the Court of King's Bench ... On What is Commonly Called the Negro Cause, by a Planter* (London, 1772), pp. 48–9, cited in Young, *Colonial Desire*, p. 150.

68 Chard, "Grand and Ghostly Tours," p. 102.

69 Ibid, 102–3. See also Brewer, *Pleasures*, pp. 268–9, for examples of Emma Hamilton being specifically identified with exotic antiquity, even with a mummy.

70 Denise Albanese, *New Science, New World* (Durham, 1996), pp. 29–58.

71 Tasch, *Plays*, vol. 1, p. 3.

72 This unstable relationship between poetic and empiricist truths about the past – the devaluation of history from embodied romance to anonymous novel, and the reaction and return to romance – is also explored at length in Michael McKeon's *The Origins of the English Novel: 1600–1740* (Baltimore, 1987).

73 Cobb, *Humourist*, p. 66.

74 Barbara Ehrenreich and Arlie Russell Hochschild (eds), *Global Women: Nannies, Maids, and Sex Workers in the New Economy* (New York, 2003), pp. 8–13.

75 Young, *Colonial Desire*, p. 19.

76 Colley, *Captives*; Deidre Lynch, *The Economy of Character: Novels, Market Culture, and the Business of Inner Meaning* (Chicago, 1998).

77 Mikhail Bakhtin's coinage in *The Dialogic Imagination: Four Essays*, ed. Michael Holquist, trans. Michael Holquist and Caryl Emerson (Austin, 1981), quoted by James Clifford in *The Predicament of Culture: Twentieth-century Ethnography, Literature and Art* (Chicago, 1986), p. 236.

[78] Ina Ferris, "Narrating Cultural Encounter: Lady Morgan and the Irish National Tale," *Nineteenth-century Literature* (1996), pp. 288–9, 291–2, 295.

[79] Kelly, *Women, Writing and Revolution,* p. 186.

[80] While influenced naturally by contemporary political developments, Cobb's perhaps unconscious rejection of the theme of a "pure" national identity seems strikingly similar to that of the contemporary Charlotte Smith, who also contested the notion of a pure "Anglo-Saxon" identity and argued for a tolerance of things and persons French. My reference here is to Cobb's *The Haunted Tower* (Dublin, n.d.). The *Biographia Dramatica* gives this play as acted in 1789, and unprinted except in the pirated Dublin edition; see David Erskine Baker, Isaac Reed, and Stephen Jones, *Biographia Dramatica* (London, 1812), vol. 2, pp. 285–6. Here a "Norman" baron proves to be the true heir to an "English" castle. Similarly, in Charlotte Smith's poem *Beachy Head*, she suggests geological evidence of past English and French unity. For the point about Smith, see Matthew Bray, *Sensibility and Social Change: Charlotte Smith, Helen Maria Williams, and the Limits of Romanticism*, PhD thesis (University of Maryland, 1994), and "Removing the Anglo-Saxon Yoke: The Francocentric Vision of Charlotte Smith's Later Works," *The Wordsworth Circle*, 24/3 (1993): 155–8.

[81] In Cobb's unpublished farce, *The Age of Moliere*, which is a good instance of the late Enlightenment recovering its own "origins" from the past, and staging such recovery. In the farce, Momus and Thalie are sent from heaven by Jupiter to see if the spirit of Moliere is still alive among French people, a quest that reaches no true conclusion except that revolutionary fervor has seriously disrupted the knack for laughter (*The Age of Moliere*, a comedy in twenty-two scenes, 179?–, BL Add Ms. 24856). John Loftis discusses Moliere's influence, as a writer of comic but "chaste" plays, on eighteenth-century dramatists including Sheridan and Goldsmith. Cobb's re-incarnation of Moliere underscores Moliere's existing reputation as a model for "English" comedy, but excoriates the French for losing sight of their own national treasure.

[82] Cobb, *Age of Moliere*, vol. 3, p. 21.

[83] Michael B. Prince, *Philosophical Dialogue in British Enlightenment Theology, Aesthetics, and the Novel* (Cambridge, 1996), and of course Mikhail Bakhtin's work cited above.

[84] Mikhail Bakhtin in *The Dialogic Imagination*, calls this heteroglossia. The idea of the novel as evidentiary narrative is also derived in part from Alexander Welsh's *Strong Representations: Narrative and Circumstantial Evidence in England* (Baltimore, 1992).

[85] Anthony Ashley Cooper, Third Earl of Shaftesbury, *Characteristicks of Men, Manners and Opinions* (3 vols, London, 1711), vol. 3, pp. 195–6.

[86] Ibid., vol. 3, p. 191 ff. This privileging of mimesis over didactic authorial presentation parallels Welsh's thesis that in the novel as it developed over the course of the eighteenth century, circumstantial evidence and legal inference became more accepted modes of representation than more direct forms of absolute evidence or pleading (Welsh, *Strong Representations*, pp. 7, 16, 24, 28–9, 40–41).

[87] Joseph Addison, *Spectator*, no. 412, 1712, ed. Donald F. Bond (5 vols, Oxford, 1965), vol. 3, pp. 540–42.

[88] Ronald Paulson, *The Beautiful, the Novel and the Strange: Aesthetics and Heterodoxy* (Baltimore, 1996), pp. 32, 47.

[89] Cobb, *Haunted Tower*, p. 30.

[90] Cobb, *The Siege of Belgrade*, p. 38.

[91] I am indebted for this comparison to Stuart Curran's discussion of "quotidian," particularist

realism in Robinson's work in "Romantic Poetry: The I Altered," in Anne K. Mellor (ed.), *Romanticism and Feminism* (Bloomington, 1988), pp. 190–92. "Perdita" Mary Robinson (1758–1800), sometime mistress of the Prince of Wales, wrote at the height of the French Revolutionary crisis. Her first novel sold out on the day of publication, and her 1791 *Poems* was a success before publication (Judith Pascoe, "The Spectacular Flaneuse: Mary Robinson and the City of London," *The Wordsworth Circle*, 23/3 [Summer 1992]: 166).

92   Curran, "Romantic Poetry," p. 191.
93   "January 1795," cited ibid., p. 190.
94   "Windfield Plain; or, a Description of a Camp in the Year 1800," cited ibid., p. 191.
95   Robinson is credited with imparting a strong sense of her personal drama to her poetic work; as Pascoe has argued, her personal forte is her ability to show women in the male world of markets and politics, as she brings herself into that world as a poet and not merely a royal ex-mistress, as a spectator and not merely a spectacle ("Spectacular Flaneuse," pp. 168–70).
96   Ibid., p. 167.
97   Ibid., pp. 168–70.
98   Ibid., pp. 167–9. But see ibid., p. 170, where Robinson at the apogee of her disembodied spectatorship of the city is compared to Romantic writers at their most imperialistic height.
99   Hulliung, *Autocritique of Enlightenment*, pp. 26–33.
100   Guha, *A Rule o Property*.
101   Guha notes Voltaire's analogous commendation of an enlightened absolutism for China in his *L'Orphan de Chine* (*Rule of Property*).
102   This universalism has also been called "uniformitarianism" by A.O. Lovejoy; for this and related ideas see G. Rousseau and Roy Porter (eds), *Exoticism in the Enlightenment* (Manchester, 1990), p. 2.
103   Acknowledging difference can cause its depreciation. This reactive self-definition of the west has also been studied by Robert Young. In Cobb, we see a similar recognition of the "reality" of other cultures and their disavowal under pressure to construct "pure" heterogeneities of race, aesthetics, class, and gender in the west, known alternatively as "civilization."
104   Chard, "Grand and Ghostly Tours," p. 101.
105   Mitter, *Much Maligned Monsters: A History of European Reactions to Indian Art* (Chicago, 1977), p. 5.
106   Ibid., pp. 3–5.
107   See Michel de Certeau, "Ethno-Graphy: Speech, or the Space of the Other: Jean de Lery," in Tom Conley (trans.), *The Writing of History* (New York, 1988), pp. 209–43.
108   Michel de Certeau discusses the analogous dynamic of speech versus writing, performance versus ethnological science, and body versus scripture in Jean de Lery's encounter with the Tupis of Brazil ("Ethno-Graphy," pp. 218–37).
109   I am indebted to Nussbaum's discussion in *Torrid Zones*, pp. 14, 17–18 for the idea of the "empire of women."
110   Wheeler, "Complexion of Desire," p. 314.

Chapter 4

Sheridan's Follies: Auctioning Ancestors in *The School for Scandal*

In an age when connoisseurship and collecting were commonplaces of public speech and thought, it is no surprise that Sheridan's *The School for Scandal*, played 261 times between 1776 and 1800,[1] appears to be a collection of fables about collecting and connoisseurship.[2] When one looks, merely, at the string of grotesques who appear in Sheridan's plays,[3] or when one considers the ways in which scandal delineates character in *The School for Scandal*, one is obliged to acknowledge the prevalence of matters of taste and connoisseurship in *The School for Scandal*.[4] In Act II of the *School*, Sir Benjamin speaks of the Widow Ochre as though she were a bad collector's bargain, or junk: "it is not that she paints so ill – but when she has finish'd her Face she joins it so badly to her Neck that she looks like a mended Statue in which the Connoisseur sees at once that the Head's modern tho' the Trunk's antique."[5] In one other scene of the play, at least, one sees the prevalent tropes of collection, connoisseurship and real or junk value. This is the famous picture auction scene, wherein the dissipated but good Charles Surface, a proverbial improvident younger brother, decides to auction off family portraits, including those of his East Indian nabob uncle Sir Oliver, to pay off his duns and creditors. The actual Sir Oliver, posing as a customer, recognizes Charles' true moral worth when Charles is unable despite his circumstances to part with Sir Oliver's "ill-looking" portrait simply because the portrait and the East India connection apparently has a "symbolic" value for Charles.

Before this can happen, however, the value of collectibles is thrashed out persistently in terms of commercial versus symbolic value. As this chapter will show further on, is not easy to assign to moral genealogies to commercial activities merely on the basis of who is selling what where: nationalism and geopiety are often unreliable when it comes to colonially influenced commerce. The moral status of British metropolitan and colonial agents is often ambiguously interdependent or interchangeable. Controversial transnational criteria and chronotopes often underlie provenances and evaluations of things and people in such scenes as the auction scene. Prior to the actual auction, Charles and Sir Oliver (the latter disguised as Mr. Premium) have the following conversation:

> Sir Oliver. … You have no land, I suppose?
>> Charles. Not a mole-hill, nor a twig, but what's in beau-pots out of the window!
>> Sir Oliver. Nor any stock, I presume?
>> Charles. Nothing but live stock – and that's only a few pointers and ponies. But pray,

Mr. Premium, are you acquainted at all with any of my connections?
    Sir Oliver. Why, to say truth, I am.
    Charles. Then you must know that I have a dev'lish rich uncle in the East Indies, Sir Oliver Surface, from whom I have the greatest expectations.
    Sir Oliver. That you have a wealthy uncle I have heard, but how your expectations will turn out is more, I believe, than you can tell.[6]

Charles' material Britishness is assessed first on the basis of fixed, immoveable property – land, livestock, or use value (inalienable, non-transferable property) – and the lack thereof then forces a discussion on venture capital and venture capitalist colonialists such as Sir Oliver, that is, on fungibility, exchangeability, alienability of value characterizing mercantile society. Sir Oliver has indeed remitted or transfused colonial wealth into the British body. The question remains whether such wealth remains fungible and commercial, or inalienable and intrinsic worth; at this point, this is more than anyone can tell.

As will be seen, however, the strange and rich cargo of colonial transfusions alter forever British taste and values that come to the assessment of metropolitan collections and moral genealogies in the auction scene. When in the guise of an impoverished supplicant Sir Oliver inquires of Joseph Surface, Charles' elder brother and the scoundrel prince of social hypocrisy, whether their uncle has "transmitted you bullion – rupees, pagodas?" Joseph replies, "Oh, dear sir, nothing of the kind! No, no. A few presents now and then – china, shawls, congou tea, avadavats, and India crackers. Little more, believe me." In disbelief, Sir Oliver then discloses in an aside that he has already disbursed £12,000 to his British family.[7] The colonial transfusion enables and triggers the auction scene's exchange mechanisms, in fact, because while Charles' mind wanders to the profits of colonial ventures, Sir Oliver repeatedly seeks to test Charles' moral worth against an inventory of family collections such as trophies, books, and, of course, most famously, pictures.[8] A system of invisible exchanges between moral and fiscal value – symbolic and commercial capital – is set up by the advent of Sir Oliver upon the British scene.

Of his invaluable, inalienable family collections Charles offers Sir Oliver a bargain. At this Sir Oliver evokes tropes of dismemberment, disemboweling, etc., strong indicators of the demise of the body: "What the plague, have you no bowels for your own kindred? Odd's life, do you take me for Shylock in the play that you would raise money of me on your own flesh and blood?" Sir Oliver strives to represent auctioning off one's metropolitan genealogy as almost a murderous crime, as a base act of destroying the foundations of the metropolitan self. Still harping on exchange value and not intrinsic worth, Charles asks in surprise, "What need you care if you have your money's worth?"[9] Later he reinforces his misrecognition of the value of preserving moral genealogies when he exclaims: "When a man wants money, where the plague should he get assistance if he can't make free with his own relations?"[10]

However, Charles' auctioning of family portraits almost seems at one point suicidal, an act of self-cannibalism, because he recklessly applies genealogical emblems to the destruction of genealogy: "What parchment have we here? *Richard, heir to*

Thomas. Oh, our genealogy in full. Here, Careless, you shall have no common bit of mahogany – here's the family tree for you, you rogue. This shall be your hammer, and now you may knock down my ancestors with their own pedigree."[11] Not only is this a parricidal[12] scene, but the auction as an attack is driven deeper and deeper into the genealogical body when Careless declares that the parchment will "serve not only as a hammer but a catalogue into the bargain."[13] And yet, the displaced other self is everywhere in the very performance of the self-cannibalizing auction. Not only does the auction and devaluation of the family halt upon encountering Charles' sentimental and symbolic attachment to the colonial Sir Oliver's portrait – an object whose worth is harder to settle than that of the other ancestors' portraits[14] – but references to mahogany,[15] and the burning of ancestors[16] evoke the tropics, specifically the East Indies, from whence Sir Oliver is returned.

Mahogany is, after all, a tropical tree, yet Charles exhorts its fungibility with the British family tree of the Surfaces. The othering of the self accompanied by genealogical devaluation is also highlighted when Charles' response to Careless' "Oh, burn your ancestors!" is "No, he [Sir Oliver as Premium] may do that afterwards if he pleases."[17] This quite possibly, if not beyond a doubt, alludes to the Indian sacred ritual and funerary practice of cremation. The scene – rich in colonial and connoisseurial allusions – points up the irony of the transnational homo economicus returning as reformer of metropolitan commercial, connoisseurial and genealogical irresponsibility, and judge of metropolitan cultural and moral connoisseurship. Charles says at the auction's end: "I find one's ancestors are more valuable relations than I took 'em for!"[18] This makes a telling statement upon how intricately commercial transactions are interwoven with symbolic, genealogical and moral transactions and identity.

Thus, Sir Oliver's presence at the auction scene necessitates rereading the British auction in the light of colonially influenced connoisseurial discourse that overturns claims to metropolitan superiority over the colonial by transnationalizing moral authority. Yet, even postcolonial readings of Sheridan's plays have rarely noticed this colonially inflected connoisseurial discourse and aesthetic that suffuses this scene of his comedy. Mita Choudhury has alerted us to the colonial market for plays like *The School for Scandal*.[19] David Garrick sent both play texts and theater people to India upon request by East India Company officials. Though it would have been very interesting to know just how the auction scene in *The School for Scandal* would have played to knowing audiences in this terrain,[20] such an analysis is, however, beyond the purview of this chapter, which will concern itself with questions of taste and value being negotiated at home, in England, with the peripheries as matrix and focus.

The auction scene serves as an illustration of anthropological rereading of the commodity fetish scenario. As Nicholas Thomas has written, "artifacts can have peculiarly personal value arising from some association with an individual's biography, that … passes largely unrecognized in both collective scales of value and in the systemic dynamics of transaction."[21] Sir Oliver's portrait was about to pass into such obscurity, the auction transaction supremely indifferent to its sentimental value for both seller and buyer. However, it is a remarkable fact that its intrinsic value emerges at the moment of its value being imminently denied in the moment of circulation. The sociality of exchange is, therefore, what gives the portrait its value, while said value is said to inhere in its non-exchangeable, inalienable personal status. The portrait, like Sir Oliver, is not what it seems to be. It is a treasure masquerading as commodity that sends conflicting signals about its worth and manages to be rescued from its own intrinsic indeterminacy as a valuable object, not being after all a very good portrait, but still good enough to be unsold: "evaluations of particular artifacts will often conflict; a situation of exchange, or one in which one party attempts to impose exchange upon another, is thus inevitably a politicized field entailing compromise, subordination, acquiescence, refusals, and so on. In cross-cultural exchange on colonial peripheries, in particular, the discrepancies between estimations of value are one of the crucial sources of conflict."[22] The valuation and exchange processes in the auction scene thus might belong to colonial, not metropolitan contexts, or to a metropolitan context with a colonial cast, or vice versa, or might reduce the antipodality of colony and metropole.[23]

Auctions and auctioneers haunt the play's mise-en-scene as well as its production history. Cecil Price has noted the absence of any early manuscript of the auction scene. [24] He speculates that the idea for it may not have come to Sheridan until late 1775. The extreme lateness of the appearance of the play itself – 8 May 1777 – has also rightly led Price to speculate on possible contextual links. Price touches upon Sheridan's acquaintance with an auctioneer, Robert Langford, while speculating upon the origin of the Jew Moses in the play (see Figure 4.1). He suggests that the character of Moses is based upon an actual Jacob Nathan Moses who was a creditor of Sheridan's fellow proprietors of Drury Lane, the debt-ridden, Charles Surface-like, Willoughby Lacy.[25] I suggest, based upon the cultural evidence provided by auctions and auctioneering in Sheridan's day, as well on Sheridan's known tussles with an auctioneer named Robert Langford, that not only is the auction scene – the focus of this chapter – a significant scene and indeed dramaturgical tour de force of the play, but auctions and auctioneers imbricate and dominate the play's performance history in yet another way.

First and incidentally, according to Choudhury, the play was produced in Kolkata (then Calcutta), India in 1782, in a theater called the New Playhouse or Calcutta Theatre established in 1775 by George Williamson, an auctioneer.[26] Second, and crucially, Robert Langford, who attempted to purchase Willoughby Lacy's moiety of the Drury Lane Theatre and thereby divert sole control of the theater from Sheridan and his partners, was prevented from so doing in 1776, a few months before *The School for Scandal* opened. The transactions for purchasing Garrick's share of the theater and the threatened loss of control of the theater upon Willoughby Lacy's attempt to sell his share to Edward Thompson and Robert Langford are demonstrated in Sheridan's letters of 31 December 1775 and 31 January 1776 to Thomas Linley, and of 15–16 October 1776 to David Garrick. [27] The fate, performance history, and mise-en-scene of *The School for Scandal* thus seem to have been tied to auctions and auctioneers,

Figure 4.1   Robert Baddeley as Moses in *The School for Scandal*, painted
by Zoffany. National Museums Liverpool (Lady Lever Art
Gallery). Produced by permission.

and this should guide readers in understanding the symbolic function of the auction scene within Sheridan's play.[28]

Langford was one of the principal villains in Sheridan's struggles with Willoughby Lacy, the remaining second shareholder after Garrick's share of Drury Lane was sold to Sheridan and his partners – Thomas Linley and James Ford – in 1776.[29] Langford appears to have also gained a villainous because usurious hold over Lacy, who was in his debt during and after the Drury Lane transactions, forcing Lacy to purchase a $500 annuity for life for Langford in 1778.[30] *The London Chronicle* of 15–17 July 1777 went so far as to report that Sheridan and his partners, the holders of Garrick's former share of the theater, were about to sell their moiety to "Mr. Langford, Mr. Bateman, and attorney of Maiden-Lane, and Mr. Duberly, the army taylor."[31] Sheridan wrote with relish to Garrick about the foiled scheme to split Lacy's share between two theatrically inexperienced men of business. Sheridan himself had threatened to quit the theater's management if Langford bought in. The actors, especially those who would later play prominent parts in *The School for Scandal* – Mrs. Abington, Mr. William Smith, and Thomas King – were principal leaders of the actors' rebellion against the proposed sale. Thomas Moore writes in his *Memoirs* of the theatrical fracas occasioned by Sheridan's intransigence regarding this transaction, and the umbrage expressed by at least one newspaper, *The Selector*, at the seemingly haughty attitude of a mere theater manager who thought himself principally injured.[32]

Faced with the collapse of their enterprise, Langford, Thompson, and Lacy abandoned their scheme to have the former two buy out Lacy's share of Drury Lane.[33] The theater was once more Sheridan's in 1778,[34] but the lasting resonance of this event was redoubled and renewed in the mise-en-scene of auction in a play that opened on 8 May 1776. That play was *The School for Scandal*.

An auction, as Charles Smith has written, is quintessentially a crucible of value uncertainties that are resolved by a communal consensus.[35] Value in an auction should ideally reflect not so much the actual price or commercial worth of an object, but what legitimate members of a community can agree upon to be its worth.[36] In the case of one-of-a-kind auctions, moreover, it is in the process of such valuation and its attendant community-building that the object morphs from a commodity of exchange to treasure or a valued collectible.[37] Thus Smith writes, "auctions, through competitive bidding, seek to establish standards of worth through price … Price determines value."[38] This last factor in essence drives in the confused and confusing interdependence of value and price, of moral and economic genealogies, of treasure versus commodity status, of objects in an auction.

The English auction is, moreover, as Cynthia Wall has written, a narrative of dismantling and remantling, greatly dependent on the personality and charisma of the auctioneer.[39] Before 1770 and 1777, the firm of Abraham Langford and son Robert Langford held at least 74 major auctions.[40] Between 1778 and 1785, they held approximately 18, a significantly reduced number. Of the Langford auctions, several were the sale of possessions of antiquarians and other collectors of curiae both British and foreign.[41] What caused the number of auctions by this firm to drop off so sharply? In connoisseurial circles the name of Langford may have gained an additional notoriety from its connections with Sheridan, Drury Lane, and *The School for Scandal*, with its famous auction scene. The connection between Langford's thwarted attempt to buy shares of Drury Lane, the auction scene in *The School of or Scandal*, and the post-1776 disappearance of the prominent firm of Langford and Sons from the auctioneering firmament has gone largely unremarked. So has been the concatenation of revaluations of material culture and its purveyors in the commercial, cultural, and dramatic context in eighteenth-century England.

Choudhury writes that "the relationship between Sir Oliver and Charles Surface reflects and codifies with a degree of accuracy the kind of reciprocity that marked the relationship between the East India Company and David Garrick: characterized by mutual respect that veils an irrepressible pecuniary interest."[42] If in Calcutta, Sir Oliver and Charles appeared in such coded valences of enlightened pecuniary self-interest, what other measures, discourses and systems of value could the play's picture auction scene invoke to a metropolitan culture of auction-goers? Choudhury's comments, again, are instructive:

> Sheridan's *School for Scandal* appeared at a time, almost two hundred years after the death of Elizabeth, when the expression of British expansionist motives was characterized less by the rhetoric of trade and commerce and increasingly by the rhetoric of government and control. The thematic, metaphoric, and symbolic elements of Sheridan's play, when juxtaposed against the trajectory of the then London-Calcutta connection, transform it into a unique cultural product in which commercial and aesthetic impulses are indistinguishable.[43]

While agreeing completely with Choudhury about seeing the play's cultural capital, its habitus, as foregrounded as well as founded on a commercial matrix, I nevertheless would point to such elision of commercial and aesthetic impulses as occurring primarily in the context of auctions and auctioneering, a whole other chiaroscuric metropolitan context of pecuniary transactions whose particular object was to assign value to objects and associations of disputed, uncertain, or dubious value.

Horace Walpole – an avid auction-goer and connoisseur – wrote gloatingly, bitterly, and voluminously of the shady and shadowy business of auctioneering and auction-going in his correspondence. Thus, he writes in 1762 that his domestic collections will not suffer "as long as there are auctions and I have money or *hoards*."[44] Yet in 1758 he had written to a fellow connoisseur, Sir Horace Mann: "our glaring extravagance is the constant high price given ... pictures do not monopolize extravagance; I have seen a little ugly shell called a ventletrap sold for 27 guineas."[45] In 1767, while exulting upon acquiring a "little Caligula" whose "muscles play as I turn it round," he still complains that "at the sale of Monsieur Julien's cabinet ... everything sold as extravagantly as if the auction had been here [in England]."[46] And as late as 1790, he again crows to, of all persons, Hannah More: "I employ mine [money] better at *auctions and in buying pictures and baubles, and hoarding curiosities*, that in truth I cannot keep long, but that will last *forever* in my catalogue and make me immortal!"[47]

Auctions also provided, most crucially, a matrix for genealogical reflections and assessments by this prolific correspondent and connoisseur. Acutely conscious of the fiscal fluidity underpinning connoisseurial ambitions, Walpole reconciles such uncertainty with the certainty of status accrued through connoisseurial ownership, however temporary. Thus, though connnoisseurial objects are hereby seen to be alienable and exchangeable, again, following Nicholas Thomas' insight, the focus of analysis should not be the "pure" status of the commodity, but on the status networks conferred by sociability of possession and of exchange. Indeed, even Walpole's mournful reflections on the mutability of human life and fortunes are circuitously derived via a reference to the genealogy and status of the Walpoles in England: "what signifies what baubles we pursue? Philosophers make systems, and we simpletons collections, and we are as wise they – wiser perhaps, for we know that in a few years our rarities will be dispersed at an auction; and they flatter themselves that their reveries will be immortal, which has happened to no system yet. A curiosity may rise in value; a system is exploded. Such reflections are applicable to politics, and make me look on them as equally nugatory … was not Sir Robert Walpole an abominable minister?"[48]

It is also instructive to attempt to gauge the broader currency of the auction trope in Sheridan's culture. Sheridan found successors in the drama who would continue his preoccupation with valuations and moral and cultural genealogies as exemplified by auctions and auction-goers like Walpole. Hannah Cowley, a significant female playwright of the 1780s, not only depicted an auction in *The Belle's Stratagem* (performed on 22 February 1780, a few years after *The School for Scandal*), but also cited Sheridan in Act III, Scene ii of her play, in the words of the character Mr Hardy planning to borrow the actor John Quick's costume for the Jew Isaac Mendoza in Sheridan's *Duenna* (1779).[49] *The Belle's Stratagem* is also notable for its echoes of Sheridan's play, not merely in the wittily grotesque auction scene as in *The School for Scandal*, but in its maintenance of double romantic plots, one comic and one sentimental, as in Sheridan's earlier play *The Rivals* (1775). It was a very popular play. Linda R. Payne writes: "Acted 118 times in London by 1800, ranking fourth of all full-length plays written between 1776 and 1800, it continued to be frequently produced in both England and America through the nineteenth century."[50]

Achieving about half of *The School for Scandal*'s production run, the play is arguably a significant successor to the auction metaphor for society articulated by *The School for Scandal*. Though not as much critical attention has focused on its less articulate and elaborate auction scene as on that of *The School for Scandal*, a brief analysis of that scene and its place in Cowley's play is instructive in understanding public attitudes to auctions and connoisseurship. In Act I, Scene iii Doricourt, the rakish hero who will later be united to a pure English beauty, says of her:

> English beauty! 'Tis insipidity; it wants the zest, it wants poignancy, Frank! Why, I have
> known a Frenchwoman, indebted to nature for no one thing but a pair of decent eyes,
> reckon in her suite as many counts, marquises, and petits maitres as would satisfy three

dozen of our first-rate toasts. I have known an Italian marquizina make ten conquests in stopping from her carriage and carry her slaves from one city to another, whose real *intrinsic* beauty would have yielded to half the little grisettes that pace your Mall on a Sunday.[51]

To this his rather more "English" friend Frank Saville responds: "So Miss Hardy (Doricourt's intended) with only beauty, modesty, and merit [intrinsic, non-commodified qualities], is doomed to the arms of a husband who will despise her."[52]

It is particularly only women, though, who have been revaluated by Doricourt's grand tour lessons in connoisseurial discernment; in his friendships with men he prefers and remains "truly English,"[53] a fact that carries us back to the previous chapter's examination of the gendering of early modern gendered transnationality. The discourses of transnationalized revaluation and gender ideologies interpellate each other throughout the play; corrupted, continentalized, and false connoisseurship is to be redirected here to its true object, female English beauty. The connoisseur himself is to be refined.

In real life women were often seen to be misguided collectors and buyers rather than connoisseurs, and connoisseurship itself was sometimes ridiculed as effeminate. In the poem *The Connoisseur*[54] it is proclaimed:

> And what the Girls were deem'd in Ages past,
> Are our Top Beaux, and modern Men of Taste.
> But now so lessen'd is the Progeny,
> That the next Race will only Women be;
> And tir'd Nature, having lost its Force,
> Stop Propagation, and so end its Course.[55]

The gendering of a principle of natural selection would change in the course of the century to a more selective gendering discourse where a form of heroic masculine connoisseurship would generate and engender the proper public man, cultivated and discerning, like Sheridan's acquaintance the Duke of Portland. Yet such engendering is reliant on the maintenance of distinct gendered spheres and behaviors. Charles Surface is a hybrid of such a heroic public man – struggling to maintain principles of Taste and morality – and a more effeminate and feeling failed connoisseur, not unlike Sheridan himself as we shall see later. In another part of Cowley's playworld, however, a revaluation of auctions, tastes, and auction-goers proceeds to a moralized (trans)nationalization of Taste. Now, true Taste becomes not only ambiguously gendered, but the heroic public connoisseur also becomes nationally ambiguous or transnational.

As the play's very next scene reveals, in an apartment in Miss Hardy's father's house, Mrs. Racket and Flutter discuss a recent auction they have witnessed. I quote at length:

Flutter. A propos des bottes, there was the divinest Plague of Athens sold yesterday at Langford's! The dead figures so natural you would have sworn they had been alive! Lord Primrose bid five hundred. 'Six,' said Lady Carmine. 'A thousand,' said Ingot the Nabob. Down went the hammer. 'A rouleau for your bargain,' said Sir Jeremy Jingle. And what answer do you think Ingot made him?

Mrs Racket. Why, took the offer.

Flutter. 'Sir, I would oblige you, but I buy this picture to place in the nursery: the children have already got Whittington and his Cat, 'tis just this size, and they'll make good companions.'

Mrs Racket. Ha, ha, ha! Well, I protest that's just the way now. The nabobs and their wives outbid one at every sale, the creatures have no more taste -

Villers. There again! You forget this story is told by Flutter, who always remembers everything but the circumstances and the persons he talks about: 'twas Ingot who offered a rouleau for the bargain, and Sir Jeremy Jingle who made the reply.

Flutter. Egad, I believe you are right. Well, the story is as good one way as t'other, you know.[56]

Sheridan having set the stage, Cowley helps herself to another jab at the auction firm of Langford holding an auction where dubious objects are being sold for dubious reasons to unqualified buyers: a connoisseurial nightmare that worsens as one realizes that Flutter's report itself is unreliable and unsound. If the audience had initially prepared oneself to laugh at the nabobs and colonial *nouveaux riches* (knowing that Cowley's husband himself had left her with three children in London to go seek his fortunes in India[57] would make such condemnation of nabobs particularly saucy), the rational and sober Villers quickly settles Flutter's gossipy overflow by reversing the attribution of bad taste in the account from the nabob to the English collector. Here too, as we saw in Chapter 2 in the discussion of Cook's sailors in Polynesia, it is the English who do not know how to discern and value things. Neither nabob nor Lord is discriminating, obviously: a painting where the dead look alive is a suspicious article of taste. Ingot's aesthetic principle based on similarity of dimensions is an execrable one; Sir Jeremy Jingle's acquisitive hunger to compete with those such as Ingot is presumably in worse taste. And yet worse would be the state of connoisseurship if an English nobleman bought a bad picture for an outrageous amount – the very situation that Horace Walpole frequently exclaimed at – and then agreed to sell it to an oriental despot for profit motives alone.

And yet, the exchange is striking precisely because it confirms the reality that connoisseurship could and did problematize clear national boundaries and destabilize masculine nationalities: in some cases it could create identities that mimicked one another to reinscribe difference. A nabob's bad taste could be confusingly similar to an English peer's bad taste, and indeed connoisseurial principles were themselves in disarray. This exchange on the inversions of transnationalism is not far wide of the ambiguous transnationality of British identity revealed in an exchange between Rowley and Sir Peter Teazle, characters in the sentimental main plot, in *The School for Scandal*. Sir Peter discloses to the audience and to Rowley that the brothers Surface are both indebted to Sir Oliver for their current status in British society: "Sir Oliver's eastern liberality gave them an early independence."[58] Sir Peter's unequivocal weaving of oriental value into the fabric of British fortunes precedes an evaluation of British worth that is, in this instance, completely off: "Of course, no person could have more opportunities of judging of their hearts, and I was never mistaken in my life. Joseph is indeed a model for the young men of the age. He is a Man of Sentiment, and acts up to the sentiments he professes; but for the other, take my word for't, if he had any grain of virtue by descent, he has dissipated it with the rest of his inheritance. Ah, my old friend Sir Oliver will be deeply mortified when he finds how part of his bounty had been misapplied."[59]

This utter misjudgment sets the course for a revaluation of the true relationship of colony and metropolis, value and worth, and transnational and national in the picture auction scene, where though the potential for further misjudgment is as rife as in Cowley's scene above,[60] true values are indeed settled according to the tenets of heroic virtue and taste. The difficulty of appropriating and territorializing connoisseurial discernment as British was not a new one, however; at least as early as 1735, the Connoisseur exclaims:

> But think not all our Follies are at Home,
> From *France* a Cargo of Fresh Mimicks come,
> …
> Our Ancestors with plain sheer Wit were well content,
> But we must have some Flight, some strange Event;
> Our Modern *Connoisseur's* Applause to win,
> Let Tragic Actors roar, and Comic grin;
> Then they'll be sure to please at small Expence,
> For all have *Ears*, and *Eyes*, tho' *Few* have Sense.[61]

The rhetorical hypernationalism of connoisseurship is materialized in some auction catalogues. Two British worthies amply represented in James West's collection of prints[62] – Shakespeare and Addison – are the two favorites also in *The Connoisseur*.[63] The poem proceeds upon a gendered and national basis for distinguishing between true and false connoisseurs. Effeminacy was supposedly characterized by sensuality rather than rationality, and false connoisseurship relates most to "foreign" sensual corruption. In this regard, it is also instructive to quote an inscription the author of *The English Connoisseur* Thomas Martyn noted on a Venus de Medicis in William Shenstone's grounds at Leasowes:

> To Venus, Venus here retir'd,
> My sober vows I pay;
> Not on her Paphian plains admir'd
> The bold, the pert, the gay.
>
> Not her, whose amorous leer prevail'd
> To bribe the Phrygian boy;

Not her who, clad in armour sail'd,
To save disastr'ous Troy.

Fresh rising from the foamy tide,
She every bosom warms;
While half withdrawn she seems to hide,
And half reveals her charms.

Learn hence, ye boastful sons of taste,
Who plan the rural shade;
Learn hence to shun the vicious waste
Of pomp at large display'd.

Let sweet concealment's magic art
Your mazy bounds invest;
And while the sight unveils a part,
Let fancy paint the rest.

Let coy reserve with cost unite
To grace your wood or field;
No ray obtrusive pall the sight,
In ought you paint, or build.

And far be driv'n the sumptuous glare
Of gold from British groves;
And far the meretricious air
Of China's vain alcoves.

'Tis bashful beauty ever twines
The most coercive chain;
'Tis she, that sov'reign rule declines,
Who best deserves to reign.[64]

This hypernationalist exhortation to British "sons of taste" to eschew foreign vices and sensualities accommodates the contradictory and simultaneous impulses toward commercial and symbolic capital by seeking the aid of the idealized feminine – Venus – as a locus combining both worth and value. Transnationalization and privatization of connoisseurship were often firmly interwoven: the grand tourists and the great traveling scientists who were often as cosmopolitan as English were usually the owners of foreign treasures. Despite his protestations, in its pornographic coyness Martyn's poem cannot but recall Isaac Teale's "Sable Venus" (1765), where the slave woman in Middle Passage is sexualized, consumed, and deified, all within the norms of classical taste and connoisseurship (see Chapter 2). Though not as crudely and violently exploitative of women and other cultures as Teale's verse, and though indeed explicitly eschewing such motives, Martyn's observations on Shenstone's garden are also a ringing reminder of the anxiety of finding a Venus de Medici in an English landscape, and of reconciling the paradox of simultaneous transnationalization and privatization.

The auction ideally had to privatize transnationality, as the foreign object changed its genealogy along with change in private ownership.[65] Sheridan's picture auction scene would have resonated especially for contemporary audiences because in it they saw the actual threat of alienation of that which should be ideally inalienable: family heirlooms and genealogical artifacts. Transnationalization or alienation had overtaken and disabled privatization and genealogical principles. This threat is so palpable because an auction so often proclaimed the reverse kind of movement – to imbricate nation and property, to absorb the foreign into the body, or at least to maintain a circulation of treasure within the body politic – while in actuality effecting its opposite.

Charles Smith lucidly details the object-cathexes, personifications and reifications of commodities involved in auctions. Smith writes that auction participants' motives can be threefold: desire for personal aggrandizement, professional publicity OR anonymity, and market control.[66] With regard to the first motive, though, too frequent recourse to auctions as a means for self-aggrandizement can become a losing venture.[67] On the other hand, while an auctioned item can make a person famous, objects can also take on their buyers' or owners' attributes: "participant-related uncertainties … are generated, or at least made possible, by the auction itself … Provenance and ownership of items – past, present, and future – are often equally important defining characteristics as price."[68] Moreover, auctions also entailed a significant change in social identity: the earliest reported auctions are of wives, as reported by Herodotus.[69] Slave auctions operated on the principle of publicly establishing a social identity for people changed into things, and especially for establishing their legitimate owners; despite public outrage against slavery, these were two reasons for auctioning slaves publicly.[70] Women and reviled minorities being prime auctionables tells the story of how these two groups also served as agents and objects of moral values and social genealogies. Hence, precisely because of the symbolic attributes of commercial transactions, auction-goers had to tread carefully in the treacherous quagmires of values and genealogies of people and things that auctions generated, and those who could not ended up in Sheridan and Cowley as objects of ridicule or pity. A family auction where the family portraits are being auctioned off dramatically threatens the principle of genealogy; it is a parricide and a self-murder. The auction scene may even have echoed recent anxieties surrounding slave ownership; the Somerset case had set in motion a strong distinction between property in foreign goods which could be alienated and those which could not.

Notably, in *The Belle's Stratagem*, Villers' revelation of the interchangeable tastes of the nabob and the British peer parallels the porosity of the line between the public and the private, the transnational and the national, the commercial and the cultured where connoisseurship is concerned. The transnationality and the privatization of connoisseurship were undeniable, challenging and complementary yet interpellatory.[71] The transnationalism of connoisseurship was indeed always evident in the reticulated discourses of preference for Italian, Flemish, Dutch, or English styles, a controversy that Joshua Reynolds may have settled for a while by his distinct preference for and domestication of Italian masters.[72] Connoisseurship in Sheridan's culture was a complex phenomenon because it was a precarious and porous realm of social experience, where the potentials for moral heroism and what Bourdieu has called "Distinction"[73] on the one hand, and for turpitude, degeneracy, and folly on the other hand, are equal contenders and determinants of Britishness. The multitudinous texts of his era that represent auctions and collections bear up this observation. Feminization was foreign, and yet connoisseurship was intimate and privatized. The paradoxical crossweaving of connoisseurship's transnational and private characteristics became matter for conscious comment by British connoisseurs as the age of empire and commerce spurred the public connoisseurial fervor, and public accountability was demanded of private ownership of collectibles (see Chapter 2). Connoisseurship had to adjust to bear the responsibility for refining National public taste.

In his preface to *The English Connoisseur* Martyn wrote of the need for connoisseurial guidance through the private collections of the wealthy, while gesturing at the confusing European varieties of aesthetic possibilities that British connoisseurs of art needed to navigate:

> without such catalogues it must be confessed little use can be made, by the yet uninformed observer of these valuable collections, besides that general one of pleasing the eye and the imagination, by viewing a *variety of delightful objects* ... It should be observed in commendation of the taste which our illustrious countrymen in general have shewed, that they have preferred the greatness of design and composition in which the Italian masters are so well known to excel, before the gaudy Flemish colouring ... At this time he could scarcely help felicitating his own countrymen, upon their not having produced artists of sufficient eminence, to give them a pretence of burying a taste for real merit and greatness under national prejudice.[74]

Martyn also wrote that the private and hoard-like nature of some collections was a bar to the nascent national improvement of connoisseurship: "The polite arts are rising in Britain, and call for the fostering hand of the rich and powerful: one certain way of advancing them, is to give all possible opportunities to those who make them their study, to contemplate the works of the best masters, that they may not form a bad taste and a poor manner upon such productions as chance throws in their way... It should be mentioned to the honour of the French nation, that their collections are come at, even by foreigners, with great facility."[75]

The crosscultural and ambiguously transnational language and affect of connoisseurship seeped into the also ambiguous sphere of intimacy – relationships and marriage – and penetrated daily idiom. Thus while Doricourt finds Letitia an insufficient connoisseurial object, as we have seen already, Letitia finds him much improved:

> Letitia. ... The blooming boy who left his image in my young heart is, at four and twenty, improved in every grace that fixed him there. It is the same face that my memory and my dreams constantly painted to me, but its graces are finished and every beauty heightened. How mortifying to feel myself at the same moment his slave and an object of perfect indifference to him![76]

Mrs Racket, though a jaded and non-exemplary female character, sets Letitia right in her expectations of being found desirable by an equally desirable connoisseur type: "Can you expect a man who has courted and been courted by half the fine women in Europe to feel like a girl from a boarding school?"[77] Her view lends force to the connoisseurial character of the marriage contract between a rake and a country girl: English beauty and character are found insufficient by refined connoisseurs who transform social settings into auction settings in their search for treasure. Of course, as the reader sees, English aesthetic and English values triumph at the end of Cowley's play – this is an English play, after all – and supposed connoisseurial sophistication is chastened and improved into homegrown and domestic excellence, pruning in the process the associations of connoisseurship with vice and excess and foreignness.

Letitia and Doricourt are not the only characters framed within connoisseurial discourse in the progress of their relationship; Lady Frances, the wife of the jealous and devoted Sir George Touchwood, is in the same situation. Doricourt who is almost obliged as the connoisseurial rake to seek out pretty women says disingenuously to Sir George: "'Tis hard one can't have a jewel in one's cabinet but the whole Town must be gratified with its luster. (Aside.) He shan't preach me out of seeing his wife, though."[78] Of this jewel Mrs. Racket later speaks in similar terms: "Her father kept her locked up with his caterpillars and shells and loved her beyond anything – but a blue butterfly and a petrified frog!"[79] Her father, thus, was not so much a connoisseur – a lover of truly refined objects – but an unglamorously idiosyncratic and quixotic indiscriminate collector. Marriage had catapulted Lady Frances into connoisseurial status as well as from country to town. Mrs. Ogle, another lady of no particular quality but great pretensions, says of Lady Frances' genealogy: "Well, 'twas a cheap way of breeding her: you know he [her father] was very poor, though a lord, and very high-spirited, though a virtuoso. In Town, her pantheons, operas, and robes de cour, would have swallowed up his seaweeds, moths, and monsters in six weeks."[80] In an auction environment that women both inhabited and personified, all other things and people are also morphed into a collector's nightmare. As *The Belle's Stratagem* progresses, it becomes clear that this is the play's true particular predicament and representation of crisis.

In words reminiscent of some auctioneers' prefatory rationale (as we shall see below in the preface to the Duchess of Portland's auction catalog by Skinner), Sir George touches upon precisely this taxonomic and valuative chaos characterizing and exemplifying auctions:

> Sir George (to Mrs Racket). And what is the society of which you boast? A mere chaos in which all distinction of rank is lost in a ridiculous affectation of ease and every different order of beings huddled together as they were before the creation. In the same *select party*, you will often find the wife of a bishop and a sharper, of an earl and a fiddler. In short, 'tis one universal masquerade, all disguised in the same habits and manners … Now I defy to tell from his appearance whether Flutter is a privy counselor or a mercer, lawyer, or a grocer's prentice.[81]

This is reminiscent of Horace Walpole's consternation or amusement – or both – that "Gideon the Jew and Blakiston the independent Grocer have been the chief purchasers of pictures sold already [at Houghton]."[82]

The indeterminacy of value – of things and people – that connoisseurs find an opportunity, collectors find a delight, Sir George finds a headache. In the actual auction scene in this play (II.ii) there are many more references to untrained viewers and buyers and cheating auctioneers and their agents. Perhaps the auctioneer Silvertongue is an especially ineffectual auctioneer, because clearly social boundaries are uppermost in the minds of the viewers, and Silvertongue has been unable to draw these to the background, as his approach to a lady is marked by her as that of a "familiar monster."[83] However, Wall gives an account of how liminal and precarious even the famous auctioneer James Christie's public image was.[84] Abraham Langford, the father of Robert, was also caricatured as Smirk, and his predecessor Christopher Cock as Prig, in Samuel Foote's play *The Minor*.[85] The lady herself mistakes a David and Bathsheba as a Diana and Actaeon, which shows her upbringing as deficient in both Christian and connoisseurial virtue.[86] The auctioneer Silvertongue's puff Mask rattles off his acquaintance with the names of the most coveted Italian and Flemish painters of the art market, namely Parmegiano, Salvator Rosa, Gabriel Metsu, Gerard Terborch, Jan Vermeer, Wouvermans, Teniers, Claude Lorrain, Ruysdael, Tintoretto, Vandyke, and Correggio.[87] And this is also where Courtall, a rich rake and a continental traveler, targets the unidentified Lady Frances as the object of his scandalous connoisseurial regard. Misidentifications, inexpertise, braggadoccio, and conceit abound therefore in the charged context of valuations and revaluations that is the society of auction as well as the auction of society.[88]

John Picker writes, "As Sheridan makes clear throughout the play, scandal works to fragment personalities, to reduce multifaceted individuals into monochromatic cartoons."[89] Scholars who have drawn attention to the play's inimitable, unremitting and tense interplay between representation and re-presentation – rhetoric and voice – have paved the way for a consideration of how such a textual tension between rhetoric and voice or foundations and surface evoke the related contemporary tensions between value and price.[90] Indeed, the tensions between representation and re-presentation are more than broadly hinted at by Charles Surface's repeated fulminations in the scene about the "bad art" in his family, that being the pictures he wishes to dispose of: "all stiff and awkward as the originals, and like nothing in human nature beside!"[91] As Jack Durant has suggested, the scene turns upon an issue of taste: "What really enables Charles to sell the family portraits is that they are hackneyed or inferior as art …."[92] Indeed, Sheridan's reference in this scene to the Modern Raphael Sir Joshua Reynolds identifies "the scene with contemporary instructional efforts in behalf of the pictorial arts by bringing it into accord with prominent commentary on the subject by Reynolds and … Richardson."[93]

Reynolds saw "'likeness' as the product of a merely mechanical skill, and … as the lowest form of imitation, the one in which 'the slowest intellect is always sure to succeed best.'"[94] Jonathan Richardson made similar commentary on portraits producing "likeness" to originals.[95] He used the difference between mere resemblance and representation to connote the essence of connoisseurship: "*he that stops at These as at what Constitutes the Goodness of a Poem is a Bad Critic, He is an Ill* Connoisseur *who has the same Consideration for these Inferiour Excellencies in a Picture.*"[96] And indeed "bad art" is a prevailing concern for all in a play whose famous "scandal session" is played out entirely in the language of connoisseurships, antiquities, and forgeries.[97]

While preserving the individuality and uniqueness of the original, therefore, the object of connoisseurship, the object of truly good taste, enables one to see its "higher" qualities, its ethereality, its ineffability, its aestheticization precisely; Charles, in demanding of art that it be poeticized, romanticizing of the original, to be good, is demanding no more, it would appear, than what the high portrait theory of his day commanded. However, this is not all that is going on in this scene; the scene also commands a recognition that aesthetic value is generated not by mere re-presentation, but by representation, which involves the act of cleansing the tainted original and redeeming it from commodity into treasure and a connoisseurial object. This is what Reynolds means by "universal rectitude and harmony" in representation.[98] The seventh of Reynolds' *Discourses* was presented at the Royal Academy on 10 December 1776, a few months before the opening of *The School for Scandal.*[99]

The emphasis upon representation as opposed to re-presentation was also echoed in the ensemble style of acting popularized by the greatest eighteenth-century actor/ manager, Sheridan's ally, and one-time business partner, David Garrick. As Mark Auburn writes: "His [Garrick's] emphasis upon ensemble acting countered a tradition of *formal* and *individualistic* presentation which had marked London acting for several decades: actors portrayed the universal rather than particular truths of their characters; they represented the passions which they found in their roles; they acted exemplars rather than people."[100] Auburn's delineation of another important aspect of "ensemble acting" – team performance of actors to create a seamless illusion[101] – is also partly applicable to my argument about auctions and connoisseurship creating a seamless illusion of culture and genealogy.

Indeed, Sheridan could also have been reacting in this scene to negative reviews of *The Rivals*, such as the *Morning Chronicle*'s 18 January 1775 complaint that "characters such as Malaprop were not 'copied from nature,' and her language was a 'defect' in the playwright's skill."[102] Such criticism must have seemed misplaced to Sheridan, and perhaps the diatribe in *The School* against the principal of reproducing bad "originals" as bad "art" evinces his response to earlier reviews of his work and his representation of "real" characters. As was the case with *The Rivals*, the audience did not at once find Sheridan's characters in *The School for Scandal* "believable," and the fault, he must have felt, was in their corrupt aesthetics rather than in his dramaturgical incompetence.

To fully make this last point I should mention that ensemble acting's rejection of the "formal" and the "individualistic" and its endorsement of the "universal" echoes, one can see, Charles' vituperation in the auction scene against family portraits "all stiff and awkward as the originals, and like nothing in human nature [here to be understood as universal, not particular human nature] beside." It is the re-presentation or faithful copy of the real, defective original, the forebear fresh from the trenches of a discredited past, the jaundiced "real" relative, though metropolitan, who is unacceptable to Charles. It is the refined gold of Sir Oliver's character – though transnational and processed and reprocessing colonial experience – that the connoisseurial Charles treasures.

In order to examine closely the process of Charles' reformation from an auctioneer to a connoisseur, one must inevitably examine actual auctions in Sheridan's time. What flows of value and worth did an actual eighteenth-century auction entail? If the slave trade, for instance, was a pathogen-conduit, as well as the largest global migration of people in human history,[103] what might have been the colonial kaleidoscope part of the total experience of a mirage of objects and values represented in an auction? All flows of things and people, including auctioned items from the Caribbean, the Indies, and Africa carried upon themselves traces of the contaminations of those shores, as did sailors and "colonials" like Sir Oliver.[104] However, the true picture is more complicated than that: the colonial may indeed be effecting metropolitan reform.

Indeed, in the first act and scene of *The School for Scandal*, Crabtree and Joseph Surface discuss the odds of metropolitan morality from the colonial perspective:

> Sir Benjamin Crabtree. ... O lud, Mr [sic] Surface, pray is it true that your uncle Sir Oliver is coming home?
>
> Joseph. Not that I know of, indeed, sir.
>
> Crabtree. He has been in the East Indies a long time. You can scarcely remember him, I believe? Sad comfort, whenever he returns, to hear how your brother has gone on.
>
> Joseph. Charles has been imprudent, sir, to be sure; but I hope no busy people have already prejudiced Sir Oliver against him. He may reform.[105]

Charles' reform, however, as we have seen, is situated in and generated by his uncle's transformative liminality. The colonial British provide the crucial context and transnational impetus for the reform of the metropolitan British. Until Sir Oliver's return and the cathartic picture auction scene, Charles' lifestyle and taste had been mere debt-riddled pomp:

> Sir Benjamin Crabtree. Yet no man lives in greater splendour (than Charles). They tell me when he entertains his friends he will sit down to dinner with a dozen of his own securities, have a score of tradesmen waiting in the antechamber, and an officer behind every guest's chair.[106]

Through every gesture of elegance and taste the bared fangs of commercial exigency peep through. In Charles' revaluation of worth and value in the picture auction scene lies the key to his reform and recovery from consumerism to connoisseurship, leading to reinvestment in symbolic capital reinforced by affective investment in that assortment of significations called Sir Oliver.

What did a person like the colonial Sir Oliver, a liminal entity until rehabilitated into English national identity, transport back to England: dubious curiosities or connoisseurial treasures? And what would such transnationals have stood for, with their colonial associations trailing behind them: as dubious "jaundiced" curiosities, or as refined national treasure?[107] Or perhaps confusingly, threateningly, as both? I will present some data from catalogs of a few major auctions held in the 1770s, one of them actually held by Langford and sons, to answer the preceding question.

The Duchess of Portland's auction was conducted by Thomas Skinner in 1786, beginning on 24 April and continuing for 37 days thereafter. The Duchess was one of the greatest female collectors of her time, perhaps of any time, and also came from a long line of distinguished collectors.[108] Figure 4.2 reproduces the title page of the auction catalogue preserved at the Beinecke Library.

The Portland Museum was auctioned in several lots categorized as natural curiosities or as cultural artifacts and antiquities. The Museum was strongest in natural biological curiosities, itemized as "Shells, Corals, Petrifactions, Crabs, etc." The second most numerous category belonged to mineral curiosities itemized as "Ores, Minerals, Crystals, Spars, etc." The auctioneer prefaced the catalogue with the following rationale for its categorization:

> To give some Idea of its great Extent, it may be remarked, that the celebrated Linnaeus, who had studied the Subject [Natural Science], and methodized the Materials of it, has not described One Fourth Part of the Objects contained in the Museum now offered to the Public. It was indeed in the Intention of the enlightened Possessor to have had *every unknown* Species described and published to the World; but it pleased God to cut short the Design, not only by the Death of the ingenious Naturalist employed by her for that Purpose [note: Dr Solander]; but in a short Time afterwards, to the great and irreparable Loss of Science, by her *own* also. Had her Life been continued a few Years longer, it is possible that every Subject in this Catalogue would have been properly described and characterised; but in the present Mazes of Science, all that could be done by the Compiler was only to give in *general* the classical or popular Names to such Articles as were known to have any, and to leave the great Bulk of Non-descripts to the Examination and Determination of the Curious. Some Persons, perhaps, may object to the Promiscuous Assemblage of the various Subjects here exhibited, and be ready to wish they had been allotted in Order and Method, according to *Genus* and *Species*; and it must be confessed, that such a Proceeding would have proved extremely satisfactory to every true Lover of Science. Such would have been highly pleased to have seen each Article named, and stand in its proper Place. But however desirable such an Attainment might have been to a few *Cognoscenti*, it is very certain that the Majority of the World are not *Methodists*. They love Variety more than Order … In a methodical Arrangement, it must of Necessity have frequently happened, either that a Multitude of the *same Species* must be sold together in *One Lot* (which very few would chuse to purchase) or each Individual of that Species, must be disposed of *singly*, or in *Pairs*; which would have multiplied the number of Lots to such a Degree as would extend the Sale to as many *Weeks*, as it consists at present of *Days*.[109]

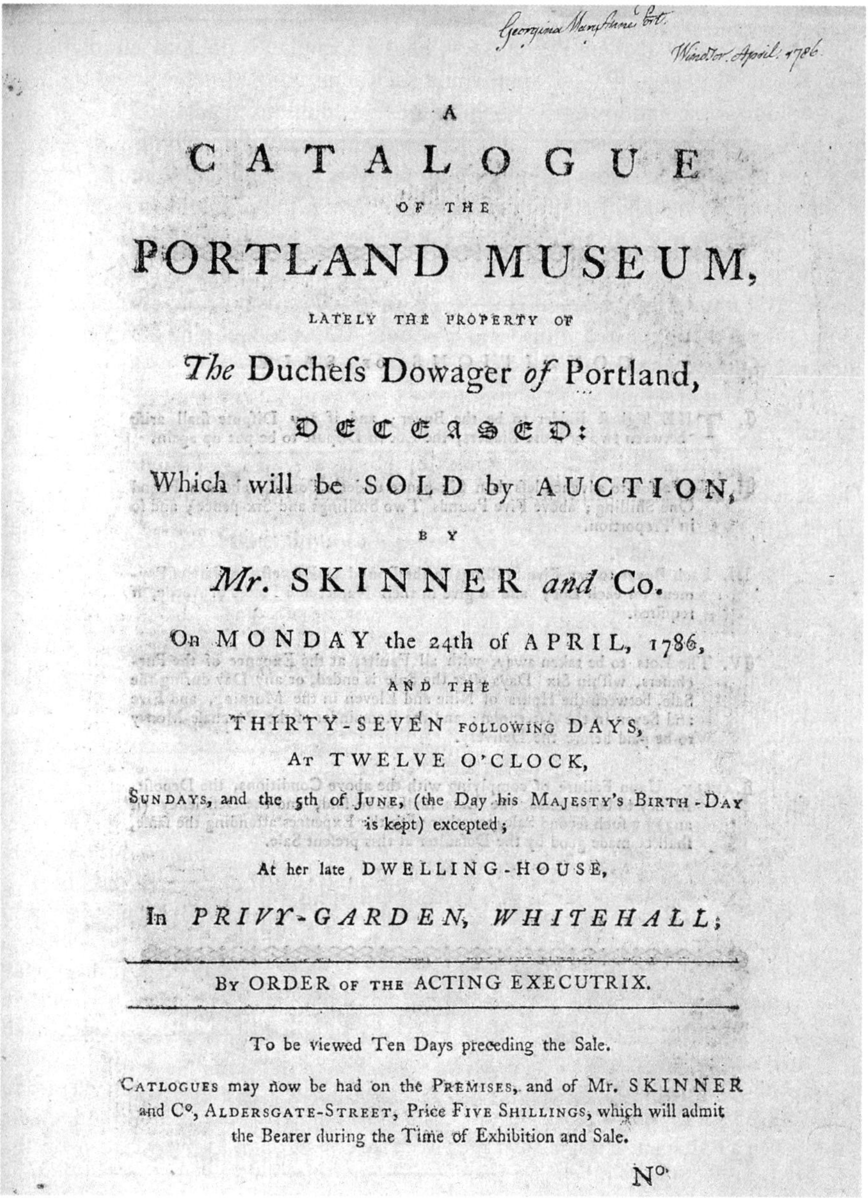

Georgiana Marq Shaner Port.

Windsor April. 1786.

A

CATALOGUE

OF THE

PORTLAND MUSEUM,

LATELY THE PROPERTY OF

The Duchefs Dowager *of* Portland,

𝔇 𝔢 𝔠 𝔢 𝔞 𝔰 𝔢 𝔡:

Which will be SOLD by AUCTION,

B Y

Mr. SKINNER *and* Co.

On MONDAY the 24th of APRIL, 1786,

AND THE

THIRTY-SEVEN FOLLOWING DAYS,

At TWELVE O'CLOCK,

Sundays, and the 5th of June, (the Day his Majesty's Birth-Day
is kept) excepted;

At her late DWELLING-HOUSE,

In *PRIVY-GARDEN, WHITEHALL;*

By ORDER of the ACTING EXECUTRIX.

To be viewed Ten Days preceding the Sale.

Catalogues may now be had on the Premises, and of Mr. SKINNER
and Cᵒ, Aldersgate-Street, Price Five Shillings, which will admit
the Bearer during the Time of Exhibition and Sale.

Nᵒ.

Figure 4.2   **Title page of *A catalogue of the Portland Museum: lately the
property of the Duchess Dowager of Portland, deceased: which
will be sold by auction, by Mr. Skinner and Co. on Monday
the 24th of April, 1786.* Beinecke Rare Book and Manuscript
Library, Yale University.**

In his defense of a commercial logic for categorizing, allotting and selling the Portland Museum's vast collection of natural curiosities, the auctioneer keeps in focus one crucial method and motif of an auction's madness: the importance of allowing the value of objects to be determined by a legitimate communal consensus.

This principle may be contrasted and compared with Richard Gough's lament on the disrespect for James West's collection of prints and portraits as a privileged text purveying a coherent narrative whose parts can be sundered only at the expense of the formal integrity of the script; he writes of the avarice of print collectors and their buyers who literally tore up West's magnificent collection.[110] This collection was auctioned by the firm of Langford beginning on 19 January 1773 and contained a truly astounding variety of portraits, etchings and engravings by various European masters and English artists.[111] Gough's lament evokes in disavowal Skinner's principle of privileging the collective valences and evaluations of collections at auctions as opposed to the abstruse inner logic of a particular collection.[112] In Skinner's case, if "the Majority of the World are not *Methodists* [and if] … They love Variety more than Order," Skinner would and did oblige them by allotting objects according to a commercial collector's cultural logic of belonging or genealogy in objects, and not a scientist's strict lineage of the natural world. This in itself exemplifies use in an auction setting of the principle of the refinement of the "natural" into a connoisseurial schema of cultural recognitions and revaluations. Given such a "cooking" of the "natural" order of things, then, it is also instructive to recognize the genealogies of the items auctioned by Skinner, and to find and locate their geopolitical origins on a larger grid of values being set within the auction.

In brief, the objects closest to their original, that is to Nature, came from non-western and peripheral or exotic terrains, while the objects most recognizably "cultural" – that is, refined from their original source or material into civilizational symbols – tended to be from western and classical locations or collections. The 2,104 "shells, corals petrifactions, crabs, etc." at the Portland auction derived largely from the West and East Indies, the Cape of Good Hope, from Guinea, Coromandel, Martinique, Barbados, China, Jamaica, Ceylon, Madagascar, Africa, and Tranquebar. One single item, in this category (no. 1719) offers a remarkable instance of the cooking of nature into a cultural icon, this object being a walnut tree cabinet with 20 drawers, each drawer adorned by corals, butterfly wings, and shells from the island of Minorca to represent the arms of the late Duke of Cumberland – "*a most elaborate performance, by a private Soldier*" – and representing military portraits and triumphal scenes.[113] Twenty-seven other "Curious Shells" came from Guinea, Coromandel, and the East Indies. Seventeen "Dried Plants, Seeds, Fungi, etc." came from Africa, the Cape of Good Hope, and Jamaica. "Artificial Curiosities and worship" items numbering 41 came from China, Otaheite, Sandwich Islands, New Zealand, Cayenne, India, Angola, New Caledonia, Lapland, Quebec, North America, South America, Malaysia, Madagascar, etc. Exotic insects numbering 225 came from Africa, Cayenne, Jamaica, Brazil, Madeira, and Guinea. The 456 "Ores, Minerals, Crystals, Spars, etc." were from Eastern and Western Europe including England, Ireland and Scotland, with a few from

South America, China, Sumatra, Turkey, etc. Ninety-seven "Fine Old China" items were from Japan, 57 "Rare Old Gold and Silver" items were mostly from Japan, 15 "Very Curious Snuff Boxes" were from China and Japan. Fifteen "Curious Crystals" were from the Arundel Collection. All antiquities were from Europe and the British Isles. All 117 prints, 200 drawings, and 39 books of prints were by French, English, German, Flemish, and Italian artists and masters.

Gough and Skinner's differences regarding how to evaluate collections at auctions may have been determined at least in part by the geopolitical genealogies of those collections. It may have been easier to respect esoteric scientific logic with a collection not chock-full of exoteric objects, as the Portland collection was. James West's massive collection of prints and portraits – sold by the Langfords from 19 January 1773 – contained only works by European and English masters. Another Langford auction of the collection of the Suffolk antiquary John Ives, held on 13 and 14 February 1777, contained only one lot of "raw" items in the antiquities category: "A scalping knife, a wampum, a bastinado instrument, an Indian bag, and a pipe."[114] In such cases, it may have been far easier to perceive cultural logic and coherence – defined by fairly consensual Eurocentric standards on cultural, moral and geopolitical genealogies – than it would be when many of the collectibles at an auction were startling, palpable reminders of cultural, moral, and geopolitical otherness, as in the Portland auction.

No great ingenuity is required to estimate the view of global material culture and the comparative value of global "collectibles" yielded at the Portland auction. We see, from a comparative examination of geopolitical geneses of categories of "auctionable" items, how Africa, the Indies, the Pacific islands, and the Caribbean produced "natural," biological curiosities at English auctions, while Europe – both modern and classical – produced gems and "art." The tropics offered "collectibles," while the west generated "connoisseurial objects." And in this differential matrix of synchronous absorption of foreign matter into the English body, not only objects' geopolitical provenance, but their teleological associations with the raw and the cultivated worlds respectively generated distinctive cultural ontologies and moral genealogies. The difficult task of the auction scene, as that of the return scenes of many other "colonial" eighteenth-century plays – beginning from Richard Steele's *The Conscious Lovers* (1723), through Frances Burney's *A Busy Day* (1801), and Colman junior's *John Bull* (1805) – was to purify tainted colonial "returns" into just(ly)-recognized and cherished treasures. Item 1719 of the Portland auction, the Walnut Tree cabinet with its shells, corals, and portraits represents the sort of mingling and hybridity of natural and cultural origins and resources that could enable an "awkward" original to be refined and transformed into a cherished collectible, though ironically enough its transformation was effected via a military context and associations. Naturally, such objects were few and far between, and could at once be picked out by the trained or the untrained eye.

Sir Oliver's portrait in the auction scene of *The School for Scandal* occupies something of the same liminal position in the hierarchy of material and moral genealogies represented by the Walnut Tree cabinet in the Portland auction. The portrait's antecedents are clearly lowly, humble, too close to nature and too much of a "curiosity" for a connoisseur's comfort; yet it contains "capabilities," as the period might have said, that anticipated its own transcendence from raw material into art. On the other hand, a failure of synchronous absorption of foreign matter into the English body occurs in Miss Ogle's case, which Sheridan's characters anatomize with relish in another scene of revaluation, the scandal scene of Act II that takes place at Lady Sneerwell's. Here transnational geopolitical provenance hybridizes and distorts female beauty, as in Cowley's *Belle's Stratagem* transnational provenances confused the cultural ontologies and moral genealogies of both painting and connoisseur. Thus:

> Crabtree. Oh, to be sure. She [Miss Ogle] has herself the oddest countenance that ever was seen. 'Tis a collection of features from all the different countries of the globe.
> Sir Benjamin. So she has indeed. An Irish front …
> Crabtree. Caledonian locks …
> Sir Benjamin. Dutch nose …
> Crabtree. Austrian lip …
> Sir Benjamin. Complexion of a Spaniard …
> Crabtree. And teeth a la Chinoise!
> Sir Benjamin. In short, her face resembles a *table d'hote* at Spa, where no two guests are of a nation –[115]

Like an old-fashioned cabinet of curiosities, Miss Ogle's face cannot pass the connoisseurial test because in her the differential absorption of foreign matter has not been aesthetically synchronized and domesticated. The foreignness of her parts remain discrete and unassimilated, and the transcendence and transvaluation of raw nature is not realized. She is therefore a failed work of art.

This principle of transvaluation – a connoisseurial principle if there ever was one – remained critical throughout Sheridan's life and career. In his *Letters*, a younger Sheridan wove in the thread of nature versus culture into his cogitations on the condition of women and his proposals for their improvement. In his impetuous and effusive letter "To the Queen," written ca. 1772, he compares nations closer to barbarity and savagery and those that are "civilized" as in some parts of Europe,[116] and comes to a not uncommon enlightenment conclusion that civilized nations respect and treasure their women.[117] Woven into the discourses of culture, nature, value, and political genealogies is the gender discourse that cannot fail to return us to the significance of genealogy itself in Sheridan's day. And in discussing the refinement of women's nature his recommendations for reading are predicated on the observation that "As for Novels there are some I would strongly recommend. But Romances infinitely more. The one is a representation of the Effects of the Passions as the[y] should be, tho extravagant. The other as they are. The Latter is false[ly] called Nature, it is a figure of depraved and corrupted Society. The other is the glow of Nature."[118]

To Thomas Grenville he wrote in 1772, again, that "For my own Part when I read for Entertainment, I had much rather view the Characters of Life as I would wish they *were* than as they *are*: therefore I hate Novels, and love Romances. The Praise of the best of the former, their being *natural*, as it is called, is to me their greatest Demerit … Why should men have a satisfaction in viewing only the mean and distorted figures of Nature? tho', truly speaking not of Nature, but of Vicious and corrupt Society. Whatever merit the Painter may have in his execution, an honest Mind is disgusted with the Design."[119] One cannot but be reminded of Sheridan's adoption of a connoisseurial principle as exemplified in the auction scene and in his advocacy of Reynoldsian portraiture four years later when we read this vindication of nature's "glow" which is to be found in a vastly reworked original improved by non-mechanical, anti-realist representationalism. In the auction scene, his pictorial and literary theories, his awareness of connoisseurial culture, and his close tie to his culture's irresolvable ambiguity and anxiety about nature and its transvaluation as civilization and culture, converge unmistakably in the judgment – of and by – Sir Oliver, the colonial uncle.

The most significant and anxious transvaluation in the picture auction scene of Sheridan's play, arguably, is that of the orient itself. That eastern territory, from which Sir Oliver returns, is already identified by 1776 as a soon-to-be-highly contested space (as in the trial and impeachment of Warren Hastings) whose occupation and possession were already becoming fraught with moral anxiety and guilt since 1773 and the passage of the Regulating Act. The east and the oriental had to be cleansed of its taintedness as hoard or commodity, and only then could it be enjoyable as treasure.[120] What may have seemed thus far like a digression upon highbrow aesthetics and performance in Sheridan's era actually helps contextualize the re-evaluation of the orient in the auction scene. Indeed, a metropolitan re-presentational aesthetic must turn into a transnational representational aesthetic in the picture auction scene – Sir Oliver who is in the portrait an "ill-looking little fellow over the settee," bears no "realistic" resemblance at all to himself, to the real colonial Sir Oliver.[121]

Charles' fondness for Sir Oliver – beyond the jokes at the outset about his presumed expectations – is somewhat inexplicable, or at least never explained; after all, Sir Oliver is the absent colonial uncle. We must read this preference in terms of the encoded genealogical reform logic and the realization of an aesthetic of anti-realist representation of the uncle and the orient. Things are not as they appear, and this realization is triggered only by Sir Oliver's picture and no other relation's. Charles learns to look beyond re-presentation and at representation as the basis for true value, not best price, when he sees in his colonial uncle's portrait the possibility for genealogical pride, and then he becomes a true connoisseur who looks beyond the surface. In this way, Charles the auctioneer becomes Charles the connoisseur. through colonial interjections.[122]

By the "judgment" of and by Sir Oliver, however, must be understood both Sir Oliver's trial as a contaminated colonial entity, and his own assessment of British metropolitan proclivities and identities, that is, the judgment by and of Sir Oliver. The liminal cultural ontology that Sir Oliver embodies – part British, part colonial – and the cultural hybridity that he inserts perforce into British metropolitan national identity must, beyond enabling the dubious transnationalisms of Hannah Cowley's auction scene, rise into an unassailable moral genealogy, however necessarily and deeply complicated (and indeed perennially infected) by commerce and colonialism. Indeed, as to the latter point, the insertion of connoisseurial discourse in an auction scene forces recognition of the paradoxical interleaving of symbolic and commercial capital in eighteenth-century British consciousness. It is then entirely appropriate that the aesthetic discourse of symbolic capital should be inserted in an auction scene in Sheridan's play – the location highlights the anxieties, interleavings, and urgencies of commerce and culture in his day.[123]

That a representative of that commerce, a nabob like Sir Oliver, has also returned as a judge of Britons at home, mirrors the instability of Britishness – after nearly a century of global wars and losses – also found in Cowley's play ten years later. Sir Oliver's return as a judge of the Surfaces must have resonated to an audience attuned to the ambiguities of national and transnational identity, to "transnation." In Act III, Scene iii of *The School for Scandal*, Sir Oliver says with poignant uncertainty, tracing his own family tree in "Charles Surface's house" (as the play directions indicate), "sure, this was my brother's house?"[124] The usurer Moses smoothly replies, "Yes, sir; Mr Charles bought it of Mr Joseph, with the furniture, pictures, etc., just as the old gentleman left it. Sir Peter [Teazle] thought it a great piece of extravagance in him."[125] This instantly activates the normative chain of transvaluations. Sir Oliver begins to see the auctioning in a another, better, light: "In my mind, the other's [Joseph's] economy in selling it to him was more reprehensible by half."[126] This exchange already indicates that far from the profligate descendant that Charles' auctioneering might make him seem in the next act, he is intrinsically more cognizant of the value of genealogy and lineage than his brother Joseph, something that poor judge of people, Sir Peter, misses completely. In this light, Charles's "auction" will come to seem more a call for colonial rescue than an actual abandonment of British genealogy and identity.

This scene, like Cowley's auction scene, is also meant to point the dubious superiority of a British "judge" or moral connoisseur like Sir Peter Teazle over a colonial "nabob," a more didactic version of the Ingot and Sir Jingle drama. An awareness of a threatening yet enticing colonial otherness and hybridity pressing against metropolitan British consciousness creates a critically unstable discourse of value. How can Sir Oliver then be presented as a colonial worthy of inclusion in the British gallery of virtues, cleansed of colonial contamination? Ethnic, gender, and moral stereotypes are deployed to contain the uncertainties and anxieties about value generated by both commerce and culture, and yet those stereotypical certainties are repeatedly undercut by what can only be called the uncertainty principle of transnation, whereby the geopolitics of identity is overshadowed by the potentially transnational nature of moral and cultural connoisseurship.

In the ongoing revaluation of the orient, another transnational moral counter that appears auctionable is filial piety, a cultural value and virtue. Filial piety is highlighted in Sheridan's auction scene, as it was also in his speeches at the trial of Warren Hastings, particularly in the famous 1788 Westminster Hall speech,[127] as a charged counter in both colonial and domestic negotiations. In both contexts, however, while valuing filial piety Sheridan also privileged its Whig British definition as universal and pure. With regard to defining this "British universal" and distinguishing it from contextual corruptions, the questions that reverberated through the days and months of the trial led by Sheridan and Burke were as follows: Were Warren Hastings' corruptions orientalized or British? Did Hastings' contamination truly originate in the colonies and was it something individual that denatured and deracinated him, erasing him from the picture of British moral genealogy? Was Hastings a colonial mimic man who had come up for revaluation in Britain (it is noteworthy that in the early colonial era, the anxiety of mimicry noted by Homi Bhabha was generated by Britons,[128] not natives)? The colonies as geographical terrains play a complex role in this revaluation of Hastings as a violator of transnational principles of filial piety. The Indian colonial space stood in much need of refinement in the 1770s and 1780s, since at least the Regulating Act of 1773, and some of this need had to do with the destruction of oriental cultural values and moral genealogies by Britons, not Indians.

The charges Edmund Burke brought against Warren Hastings on 26 April 1786 reeked of India's despoliation, not preservation. India as a treasure was being pillaged and ruined. Articles 4, 5 and 6 of Burke's charge related to the ruin of the royal family of Oudh, of Oudh itself, and of the provinces of Farruckabad.[129] It was claimed by Hastings' apologists that some at least of Hastings' actions could be justified by the low state of Indian morals and ethics; this was furiously dismissed by Sheridan who resorted to universalist concepts of ancestor veneration. Hastings' conduct, Sheridan urged, was Hastings' alone; it implicated neither true Britons nor true Indians. This is the whig universalizing representation mentioned already in Chapter 3; suffice it to reiterate here that such universalism generally saw the oriental as a mirror confirming Europe's rationality, and not as a radically alternative ethical or epistemological context. In his first Begum speech on 7 February 1787 (the speech that reportedly stunned stalwart orators such as Burke, Fox, and Pitt as well as lesser parliamentary luminaries), Sheridan distinguished between true and false Britons: "however degenerate an example of Englishman some of the British subjects had exhibited in India, the people of England collectively, speaking and acting by their representatives, felt, as men should feel on such an occasion, that they were anxious to do justice, by redressing injuries, and punishing offenders, however high their rank, however elevated their station."[130] Liberty was seen as a value deeply contrary to auction-like tearing up of native royal families and indigenous feudal loyalties for purposes of plunder. And it certainly was not a value held dear only by the British.

Thus if the Begums of Oudh incident demonstrated a black record of subversion of filial piety by the monstrous Hastings, such subversion could not be justified, Sheridan would argue, by the Indianization of Hastings' character and judgment. It would not be condoned by true Britons as truly oriental practice. He wondered at explanations that would insinuate "that there was something in Mahomedanism which rendered it impious in a son not to plunder his mother."[131] Sheridan clung to this refutation of orientalist "nativization" in the face of flaming rhetoric in its support;[132] even his nineteenth-century biographer testified to the power of this popular perception of the Orient as a cradle of corruption.[133] Sheridan refused to saddle the orient with any innate propensity to vice; in the context of the impeachment of Hastings, he ridiculed and refuted apologies for Hastings' conduct speciously grounded by others in the "orientalization" of Hastings' life and morals.[134] Not only did he condemn imputations of inevitability, but to some extent he ridiculed definitions of "oriental vice," laying the cause of such vice entirely at the door of British misgovernment.[135] Sheridan was essentially engaging in the act of translation of national principles and transformations of national identities, an engagement that might be termed transnation.

The ambiguities of transnational imagining may be vividly demonstrated by related speeches in the parliamentary debate on the Cheyt Singh affair. Pitt himself spoke thus:

> in the first place he found himself under a very disagreeable necessity of adapting in some degree his sentiments on the subject of government to the principles of Indian politics. Those principles were certainly not conformable to European ideas, but they were in a great measure the only ones on which an European could take upon himself to judge of the transactions and conduct of an East Indian Governor. They were the principles of arbitrary power and despotism. But though the constitution of our Eastern possessions was arbitrary and despotic, still it was the duty of every Administration in that country to conduct itself by the rules of justice and of liberty, as far as it was possible to reconcile them to the established Government. He did not care whether the laws of Tamerlane, or of any other Indian Emperor, has laid down such a doctrine – it was enforced by a higher authority, by the dictates of nature and of common sense. On this ground he could not acquit Mr. Hastings of the whole of the charge brought against him; for he felt in his conscience that he had pushed the exercise of the arbitrary discretion, which, from the nature of the Eastern Government, was intrusted to him, to a greater length than he was warranted to do by the necessity of that service ....[136]

Pitt's massive and idiosyncractic historical sweep – from Tamer Lane to Warren Hastings – and taking in the Mughal emperor Akbar earlier[137]– achieves the complex task of transnation that his arch-rival Sheridan also aims for. Harnessing a defense of European universalism to the complex tasks of culturally singular governance, Pitt dematerializes the eastern context by his recourse to abstract and bloodless concepts of liberty, justice, etc. By contrast, Sheridan deliberately adheres to gory accounts of Hastings' British iniquities, his transnation being founded in near equal proportions on universalist abstractions and materialized, palpable perceptions of British possessions abroad.[138] The dying Indians, victims of Hastings' and Colonel Hannay's despotism, were said to have "encouraged their blood to flow ... rise to the common God of humanity, and cry aloud for vengeance on their destroyers ... Why did they rise? – Because they were people in human shape; because patience under the detested tyranny of man is rebellion to the sovereignty of God ... And ... never in any clime, where rude man ever had any social feeling, or where corrupt refinement had subdued all feelings, – never was this one unextinguishable truth destroyed from the heart of man ...."[139]

Corruption and coercion tainted all of Hastings' action in India, as his impeachers viewed it. The auctioning of ancestors and its reflections on moral value and genealogy were Sheridan's particular obsession in the Begums of Oudh speeches of the Impeachment trial. The three principal triangulated and embattled characters in his dramatization of the rape of filial piety were liberty, British political justice, and British commerce or auctioneering. Sheridan connected, explicitly, moral genealogies to the condemnation of Hastings' politically tyrannous and commercially extortionate actions, the mainstay of his rhetorical flourishes.[140] Hastings' actions were to be examined as moral artifacts whose provenance and value were determined against a "British yet universal" national map or background of moral genealogies and symbolic values that ideally transcended commercial values and bookkeeping. Sheridan, while ridiculing defenses of Hastings based on the supposedly inevitable oriental taint, poignantly evoked violated filial piety as deeply contrary to both universal (read also transnational) morality and ethics. In *The School for Scandal*, Sir Oliver had remarked: "I think it a rare Joke to Sell one's Family by Auction ...."[141] Ten years later, that joke re-echoed when Sheridan castigated East India Company officers in the Begums of Oudh case. Sheridan said on 3 June 1788:

> The present nabob ... owed to her [the Bow Begum, his mother] not only his birth and succession to the crown, but also the preservation of his life; for one day, his savage father in a rage attempting to cut him down with his scymeter, the Begum rushed between her husband and her son, and saved the latter through the loss of some of her own blood ... A son so befriended and so preserved, Mr. Hastings had armed against such a mother: he invaded the rights of that prince, that he might compel him to violate the laws of *nature* by plundering his parent; and he made him a *slave*, that he might afterwards make him a *monster*.[142]

A moral connoisseurship therefore underpinned Sheridan's dissection of commercial transactions both in his play and in his study of colonial misgovernment. Liberty itself could not be defined as unshackled self-interest – whether on an individual or a national scale – but had to be grounded in what must be called principles of moral connoisseurship. In later years, Sheridan returned to his preoccupations during the Begum charges, and spoke of his own political career as that of a connoisseur of party:

> And now, reviewing my past political life, were the option possible that I should retread the path, I solemnly and deliberately declare that I would prefer to pursue the same course; to bear up under the same pressure; to abide by the same principles; and remain by his [Fox's] side an exile from power, distinction, and emolument, rather than be at this moment a splendid example of successful servility or prosperous apostacy, though clothed with power, honor, titles, gorged with sinecures, and *lord of hoards* obtained from the *plunder of the people*.[143]

In Sheridan's parliamentary speeches the impeachment recounts a disgraceful British colonial auctioning of filial piety and genealogical fidelity not unlike the scandalous auction in *The School for Scandal*. Sheridan fulminated against Hastings' "auctioneering" in India in the following speech of 7 February 1787:

Groundless, nugatory, and insulting were the affirmations of Mr. Hastings, that the seizure of treasures from the Begums, and the exposition of their pilfered goods to *public auction* (unparalleled acts of open injustice, oppression, and inhumanity!) were in any degree to be defended … Treasure, which was the source of all the cruelties, was the original pretence which Mr. Hastings had made to the Company for the proceedings … women were, on the death of their husbands, entitled by the Mahomedan law only to the property within the Zenana where they lived … the … treasure, namely, that which was within the Zenana, was confessedly her [the Begum's] own … After this … could there be an argument as to the right of the treasure of the Begums?[144]

Sheridan also worked into the first Begum speech of 7 February 1787 a strong condemnation of the company as "*auctioneering ambassadors* and *trading generals*; – and thus we saw a revolution brought about by *affidavits*; an army employed in *executing an arrest*; a town besieged on *a note of hand*; a prince dethroned for the *balance of an account*. Thus it was they exhibited a government, which united the mock majesty of a bloody sceptre, and the little *traffic of a merchant's counting-house*, wielding a truncheon with one hand, and *picking a pocket with the other.*"[145] Indeed, the connection between the cases of Charles and the nabob of Oudh is apparent in their dissimilarity: Charles' filial piety would not allow him to auction off his ancestor, while the cowardly nabob was distinguished by his notorious willingness to submit to the auctioneering English.[146]

The Begums – the genealogical artifacts about to be auctioned – not only possessed treasure that the English coveted; their positionality made them oriental treasures themselves: symbols of transcendent worth and refinement in India. Sheridan spoke thus:

the Turks … are a mean and degraded race in comparison with many of these great families, who, inheriting from their Persian ancestors, preserve a purer style of prejudice and a loftier superstition. Women there are not as in Turkey – they neither go to the mosque nor to the bath – it is not the thin veil alone that hides them – but in the inmost recesses of their Zenana they are kept from public view by those reverenced and protected walls … But, in this situation, they are not confined from a mean and selfish policy of man – not from a coarse and sensual jealousy – enshrined rather than immured, their habitation and retreat is a sanctuary, not a prison … that leads them to regard liberty as a degradation, and the gaze of even admiring eyes as inexplicable pollution to the purity of their fame and the sanctity of their honor. Such being the general opinion … whatever treasures were given or lodged in a Zenana of this description must, upon the evidence of the thing itself, be placed beyond the reach of resumption.[147]

Hastings' revaluation is clearly a part of the discourse and debate upon morality and sentiment in Britain. Hastings' misdemeanor in selling out the Begums of Oudh, and the nabob's crime in countenancing the same, resemble Charles' potential misdemeanor in selling his uncle's portrait. Sheridan's play parallels his parliamentary activities in the agenda of sifting through contested representations of British colonial identities so that they did not besmirch British national identity in the process of eager absorption of

Indian fortunes. Always, commerce as a marauder made its metaphoric mark. Sheridan mocked Henry Dundas in Parliament as early as 1784 for attempting to defend the wealth of the "real trader" saying "he made no doubt but the rich merchant would be respected, cherished, and revered; what treatment he should meet with if poor, it was not for him to foresee or to foretell."[148] He also commented on 21 June 1786 upon Hastings' presentation of an "extraordinary" large Indian diamond to the king,[149] an event that was also widely satirized in contemporary prints.

Sheridan did not go to India, but Sheridan's early friend Nathaniel Brassey Halhed, with whom he had collaborated when they were young, had asked Sheridan in 1771 to go with him.[150] Halhed returned a supporter of Warren Hastings, and the relationship of the two former friends would be cool at best.[151] We shall never know what would have happened had Sheridan chosen the somewhat typical course for unsupported younger sons in Britain – a colonial career – but as Fintan O'Toole writes, "In theory, the distance between Sheridan and India ought to have made his rhetoric artificial and ultimately bloodless. But in fact, he brought to the task in hand a range of both public and private obsessions that echo through his work both before and after the speech itself. His scornful dismissal of the 'strange rebellion which was afterwards conjured up, and of which the existence and notoriety were equally a secret' looks back to the fabrications of *The School for Scandal ....*"[152]

Conjoining the revaluations thus far seen of the oriental and of the orient – of Sir Oliver and India – it emerges that Sheridan had to perform a materially grounded spectacle of transnation in Parliament as well as in Drury Lane. He had to counter prevailing discourse such as the abstractions of Pitt but also the speciously nationalist specificities of Major Scott, Hastings' arch supporter, who claimed that Hastings had exacted an exorbitant levy from Cheyt Singh only because patriotism, aroused by the French threat in Coromandel and Madras, made it crucial that food and money be sent from Bengal for the preservation of the British possessions in India.[153] Himself a "transnational" Irishman in England, Sheridan knew well the desperate need to vivify seemingly distant and obscure maneuvers of British policy abroad, and he showed them larger than life in the theater and in politics.[154]

Mapping this condemnation of Hastings against the picture auction scene in *The School for Scandal* yields the conclusion that one's genealogy can but should not be "auctioned."[155] In this regard, it is noteworthy that Sheridan almost always referred to the Begums' confiscated property as their "treasure" and the "plunder," "hoard" etc. of the English.[156] The difference of vocabulary should itself alert us to the differential genealogies of moral and immoral acquisitions of the English and their redeemability within the body politic: "He [Hastings] there congratulates his masters on the seizure of those treasures which, by the law of Mahomet, he assures them were the property of Asoph ul Dowlah. Thus the perturbed spirit of the Mahometan law, according to Mr Hastings' idea, still hovered round those treasures, and envied them to every possessor, until it at length saw them safely lodged within the *sanctuary* of the British treasury!"[157] The relentless criticism of Hastings' actions ensures that the audience may not acquiesce in a representation of Hastings' colonial hoard as true English treasure.

In the context of the Begums charge against Hastings, filial relations had been traduced by Hastings into mere commodities – plunder – to enrich the British coffers. Sheridan stood up the staunch defender of filial piety as an inestimable treasure, a cherished possession whose value was not translatable into common currency either in India or in Britain, and thereby immortalized in politics a stance that he had already sentimentally held in theater, when Sir Oliver, the one Surface forebear who had "orientalized," became for Charles a touchstone of moral worth, a treasure, a cherished possession whose worthiness could not be bartered or commodified. Sheridan's representation of Sir Oliver Surface bears ingrained marks, therefore, of these "Indians" he personally and professionally knew – they were an intimate enemy. Hence, the greater urgency to salvage something of British honor, however commercially cathected, from the ruins of colonial corruption.

Charles honorably preserves his moral genealogy in ridding himself of all that shows bad taste in his ancestral possessions and keeping the exemplar – despite appearances – of moral and genealogical probity, his uncle. That his uncle is, however, a colonial, a precursor of the Hastings type, against whose appearance at least domestic moral and cultural odds were stacked, both problematizes the genealogy and provides an opportunity for social connoisseurship. The opportunity for social connoisseurship lies in displacing received notions of value based on an object's transparent attractions and the comforts of familiar re-presentation or self-mirroring, and introducing in their stead privileged and novel standards of taste that unsettle received criteria of value. Durant has defined the unsettling effect of operations of the grotesque in Sheridan's plays. The grotesque is that which "generates a sense of alienation, a sense of removal from the familiar and trusted. A second general effect is that it aggravates ambivalence. It both disarms anxiety and creates it."[158] Indeed, a connoisseurial object too can be a grotesque until its value is recognized – to unaccustomed or untrained eyes, a tasteful object might take getting used to. Connoisseurs must also rub off the blemishes and taints of objects mauled and mishandled in transit and even exchange of ownership to discover their true status and to enshrine them. And indeed this rubbing off can continuously generate ambivalence and anxiety because the true nature of the object being tested might disappoint, might raise new anxieties and ambivalences, or never be fully knowable.

Still, the nature of connoisseurial inquiry is to take the chance and at least to proclaim success. Sir Oliver must likewise be reabsorbed into the Surface genealogy as a treasure and not commodity. Such reabsorption is only likely if the perceiver's optic can expand beyond surface similarity to the rest of the unpalatable family to include the wider, general, universal virtues which he embodies despite appearances. The scene accommodates England's commercial enterprise by allowing for its rehabilitation mediated by connoisseurial discourse. The embedding of connoisseurial discourse within an auction scene forecloses misremembrance of culture's complicity with commerce. And the classical moral psychodrama of temporary misrecognition of returned relatives as well as of the deep springs of one's own character and feelings only heightens the pleasure of the comedic resolution whereby all errors are laid aside and truth is seen to reside where it was least suspected. That this theatrical coup occurred at about the same time as Sheridan's move from Covent Garden, the lower house of comedy, to Drury Lane, its refined epitome, puts an additional seal of certainty on the involvement of *The School for Scandal* with multiple refinements of its time. Within it, the picture-auction scene is emblematic of Sheridan's consummate artistry in capturing one of the most symptomatic cultural discourses of his time: the problem of connoisseurship.

The theater was always intimate with politics, and vice versa: Sheridan's 1788 Hastings Impeachment speech became the theatrical event of the season, people vying for a chance to attend as they would at a sensational play (see Figure 4.3).[159] The theater of politics was in full swing,[160] both attempting to set national standards and codes for moral and social values flat in the face of the economic logic that actually governed both. Hence it is not only useful but necessary to compare Sheridan's attitude to auctioneering in *The School for Scandal* with his parliamentary impeachment rhetoric ten years later. Indeed, around that time, the auction scene in *The School for Scandal* was re-imagined as the reduction of the Prince of Wales' establishment at Carlton House, a shearing in which Sheridan was much involved, and which gained national notoriety as an instance of filial conflict and a genealogical debate: did George III's son have the economic discipline and filial piety that his country and his father needed (see Figure 4.4)? Figure 4.4 reproduces a contemporary print in which the Prince of Wales, as Charles Surface, is seen declaring "Careless, Knock down the Farmer" (that is, George III or Farmer George). The comparison between stage and politics affirms the view that Sheridan deployed his culture's existing debates on symbolic versus commercial capital and value as anxious contexts for true Taste throughout his public and creative life.

Sheridan was himself, of course, a failed connoisseur. Perhaps the similarity between his own world of theatrical and political shifting sands, and that of the "Specious Orator" James Christie would have struck him.[161] Like Christie the auctioneer, he attained rhetorical powers of revaluating material and social life, social contexts, and moral genealogies in his parliamentary career; again, like an auctioneer, while engaged in such revaluation he himself occupied an uncomfortable and ambiguous liminal position between elites and aspirants.[162] As a failed connoisseur, not only could Sheridan not retain the worldly emoluments of place, power, and influence toward which he had set out as a young man in the heady 1770s, as biographers have commented; he was also unable to own and control his own wife's portrait, truly a connoisseurial object. Sir Joshua had painted the beautiful singer Elizabeth Linley, then Mrs. Sheridan, as St. Cecilia in 1775, and exhibited her at the Royal Academy as well. Sheridan had refused to let his wife sing for money, citing specifically his right of ownership which meant that rights over her unique and remarkable talent had become alienated from Elizabeth's father Thomas Linley to himself. Thomas Linley the father would and did choose to commodify his treasure,[163] but in a letter to him shortly after their marriage, in turning down claims upon her performance contracted *before* her marriage, Sheridan asserted his refusal to commodify her voice as she was now *his* property, and any contracts prior to this exchange were now null and void.[164]

Figure 4.3   *The Raree Show*. **London 1788, published by W. Moore and W. Dickie. British Museum Prints and Drawings 7273. Copyright The Trustees of the British Museum. Produced by permission.**

Figure 4.4   **A Scene in *The School for Scandal*. London 1786, published by S.W. Fores. British Museum Prints and Drawings 6968. Copyright The Trustees of the British Museum. Produced by permission.**

The ownership of his wife as his wife entitled Sheridan, as he clearly stated in this letter of 1773 to his father-in-law, to terminate Thomas Linley's claims to her talents, skills, her worth, in other words. A total transfer of those values had been made to Sheridan; in the process, Elizabeth Linley's singing voice had become translated and transvalued from a commodity to a treasure.

Once again, connoisseurship shoots through the language of property and exchange to transform the discourse of value from within. Defining the domestic and the feminine – his wife and her sister – as private treasures beyond the sphere of exchange and exhibition, Sheridan felt more "proper" in his ventures into publicity and propriety. As St Cecilia, the patron saint of music, Elizabeth Linley was refined into a treasure, into symbolic capital, by Sir Joshua Reynolds whose theory of portraiture – as we have seen – revolved upon the goal of transforming natural human material into examples of "universal rectitude and harmony."[165] This picture of his first wife Sheridan was not able to retain. In 1790 Sir Joshua offered to sell Sheridan this picture for 150 guineas – the sum, however, was then beyond Sheridan's powers.[166] Fintan O'Toole writes that Sheridan did, however, possess this picture in 1815, but had to sell it then to pay off his debts, in a moment reminiscent of the picture auction scene of *The School for Scandal*.[167]

In Sheridan's own life, the transformation of private life and relations by commercial and symbolic capital and their ambiguous interleavings remained as true and inseparable as they did in his immortal play which looked closely and unflinchingly at a society's desperate attempts to distinguish the good, eternal and universal from the self-interested, temporal and particular. Like the theater, the auction was also a performance space, with connoisseurs, auctioneers and bidders being at once audience and actors. The auction – the site for the public display and dismemberment of private collections[168] – became then a particularly effective motif and trope for a society that exchanged and bartered goods and people at home and abroad and yet hoped to gain and polish a reputation for refinement and virtue.[169]

Indeed, refining the theater itself was another one of Sheridan's more serious connoisseurial ventures. In the 1780s he put some effort into a proposal for a new Theater at the corner of Hyde Park which was to be a superior and more tasteful theatrical space than either Drury Lane or Covent Garden. It would cater to a more elite audience. In part, however, the motivation was again as much commercial as cultural; part of the goal here was to prevent the "dormant patent" of Covent Garden Theatre from falling into the clutches of theatrical competition. That Sheridan later abandoned the scheme of building a new theater and instead purchased Covent Garden's dormant patent to replace Drury Lane's missing patent in 1792[170] does not change the fact that Sheridan has proposed a third London theater using Covent garden's dormant patent to be jointly operated by the existing theaters as early as 1777.[171] Commercial and cultural ambitions competed for pre-eminence: his commercial aim in establishing such a third theater using Covent Garden's dormant patent was to forestall the possibility of serious external competition by new theatrical management. His cultural goal, as stated in the proposal, was to attract "a higher class of People,"[172] to accommodate ladies of fashion, to accommodate persons of rank, for "superior elegance and accommodation," and for "additional Lustre" of the theater.[173]

An undated copy of an application (apparently by Thomas Harris, the proprietor of Covent Garden) to the Lord Chamberlain, and dated by Ian Donaldson as ca. 1784–85, bears the imprint of Sheridan's scheme of 1777 and 1783–84[174] and states the following objectives:

> The earliness of the Hour to those who give attendance to Parliament and other Employments together with the usual later hour of dining customary to people of rank, the small number of Boxes of commodious access for ladies who are dress'd … in a manner precluded the Theatres from the countenance of people of rank except on the nights the performances are Honor'd by their Majestys presence in consequence so many other places of Entertainment as Masquerades etc. etc. are establish'd which include not only people of rank … but other Orders also [sic] from these and other considerations it is humbly submitted whether the present dormant patent might not be unexceptionably employ'd in a Third Theatre, on a smaller scale, to be built (without Pit or Galleries) and the admission at superior Price, the entertainments to commence at 7 or 8 o'clock, and to be conducted in a manner more correct and magnificent than can possibly be executed in any of the present Theatres … in a Theatre so circumstanc'd it

will be readily believed that numbers of ingenious Authors of rank in literature wou'd
turn their labours to the support of the British drama and also perhaps many young
performers who now dread the decision of our noisy and ill qualified Galleries ....[175]

Again, in 1789–90 Sheridan was applying to the Duke of Bedford, the landlord of
Drury Lane Theatre, for a rebuilding of the theater with the assistance of Henry
Holland as surveyor and builder.[176]

In each case of theatrical renovation and rebuilding, while Sheridan made proposals
aimed at commercial self-preservation, he took care to dress them in the language of
cultural enhancement and refinement of theater as a national institution. Indeed, the
dressing of immense personal fortunes in the garb of connoisseurial ambition and
action was typical of members of the company he kept throughout his career, including
such persons as the Duke of Portland and the Duke of Devonshire. Sheridan's not-too-
warm Whig associate, the Duke of Portland, had an annual income of about £17,000
after his mother the Duchess of Portland's death in 1785 (a clear and significant
jump from £9,000 per annum before her death), while the Marquis of Rockingham
and the Duke of Devonshire had incomes in the range of £40,000 per annum.[177] The
conflict and attempted conciliation of commercial and aesthetic values – of beauty,
use, and profit – so characteristic of connoisseurial lives is evident in the design and
improvement of Portland's seat Welbeck by Humphrey Repton, as finely demonstrated
by Wilkinson.[178] Like Sheridan, Portland was also "self-consciously an improver" who
attempted to finesse and maneuver the aesthetic and commercial value of his property
simultaneously,[179] this being the cause of much of his later impecuniousness. After his
mother's death in 1785, his London residence Burlington house, fitted with valuable
European art, "fulfilled every expectation of the residence of a Whig grandee ...."[180]
Notably, the family fortunes in this case too were transmuting from raw nature to high
cultural artifacts. Of Portland's connoisseurship of landscapes and pictures at Welbeck,
Repton spoke eloquently.[181] However, Portland was also quite content to disregard
human experience for commercial exigency.[182] Connoisseurial ideals notwithstanding,
connoisseurial practice could rarely totally transcend commercial realities.

Like these notable contemporaries,[183] Sheridan was in the habit of drawing and
overdrawing upon his resources to "improve" his treasure, Drury Lane, and of being
debt-ridden and constantly renegotiating the economic worth and ownership of
Drury Lane, his treasure, when needed. The same may be said of his plays; in 1775,
when his first play *The Rivals* drew public criticism as a linguistically muddled,
overwritten, miscast, and seemingly anti-Irish play, Sheridan connoisseurially – like
a young Hercules, the *Morning Post* wrote, referencing Reynolds' famous subject
picture in passing – rose to the challenge, and refined the play into one of the theatrical
sensations of the times, determined still to keep his wife out of public view as she
seemed to be making plans to return to singing for money.[184] And yet in the end it
was the immediate commercial exigency that caused the cultural vision or mission
to be abandoned, though that did not keep the commercial property – the theater
itself – from harm either.[185] In thus failing at his self-appointed goal of theatrical
connoisseurship shadowed by profit motives, Sheridan's own career as theater

manager bears the imprint of the same contradictions of value and price that his play undertakes to expose.

In later life, Sheridan's immersion in the political turbulence of his times shifted direct dramaturgical focus away from questions of connoisseurship and cultural practices, at least to the extent observable in *The School for Scandal*. In Sheridan's *Pizarro* (1798), for instance, broadly political obsessions – issues of political liberty, justice, and indigenous rights – seemed to dominate the playtext and the performance records. However, even here, Sheridan's connoisseurial and redesigning activities – at least vis-à-vis the stage – were still in evidence. *Pizarro*, as scholars have pointed out, was a tour-de-force of the spectacularization of English drama in the late eighteenth century.[186] Anna Larpent called it "a flash of language,"[187] unrelated to logic or judgment, an assessment consistent with Sheridan's own assessment of the political climate of the late nineties and of his own practice.[188] However, since the political subtext of connoisseurship has been the subject of discussion throughout this chapter, it will not be out of place to relink Sheridan's life and work after 1777 to the real story of how politics and commerce are the subliminal ground of culture and rhetoric which in essence is the history of connoisseurship in late eighteenth-century Britain. *Pizarro*, with its spectacular eloquence in unveiling the conflict between indigenous South American right and Spanish colonial might, still keeps us aware of the connections between political cost, commercial profit, and moral connoisseurship.[189]

Notes

1   *Hogan, The London Stage*, p. clxxi. Thomas Moore provides a list of receipts from *The School for Scandal* in 1777 and 1778 which show the play consistently grossing higher receipts than other plays throughout the two years (Thomas Moore, *Memoirs of the life of the Rt. Hon. Richard Brinsley Sheridan* [2 vols, New York, 1858, repr. 1968], vol. 1, pp. 160–61). Moore writes, "I have traced it by the same unequivocal marks of success through the years 1780 and 1781, and find the nights of its representation always rivaling those on which the King went to the theatre, in the magnitude of their receipts" (*Memoirs*, vol. 1, p. 161).

2   Thus, for instance, Sheridan was introduced to his most enduring though in the end most unreliable political and personal friend, Charles James Fox, by John Townsend, the nephew of the well-known connoisseur, Charles Townsend, himself the nephew of Sir William Hamilton (Richard B. Sheridan, *The Speeches of the Right Honourable Richard Brinsley Sheridan, Edited by a Constitutional Friend* [3 vols, London, 1842; reprt. New York, 1969], vol. 1, p. iv).

3   Jack Durant, "Sheridan's Grotesques," *The Theatre Annual*, 38 (1983), pp. 13–30.

4   Jack Durant has outlined the appearance of the grotesque as staged struggle between the principles of beauty and ugliness in the dialogue and characters of *The Rivals, St Patrick's Day*, *The Duenna*, and other Sheridan plays ("Sheridan's Grotesques," pp. 14–22).

5   Richard B. *Sheridan, School for Scandal*, ed. F.W. Bateson (London; New York, 1989), pp. 54–7.

6   Sheridan, *The School for Scandal*, p. 74.

7   Ibid., p. 112.

Slavery, Colonialism and Connoisseurship

8   Ibid., pp. 76–7.
9   Ibid., p. 78.
10 Ibid., p. 79.
11 Ibid., p. 80.
12 Sir Oliver exclaims at this point: "an *ex post facto* parricide!" (ibid., p. 80).
13 Ibid.
14 Sir Richard Raveline, and the great-aunt Deborah, are much more conventionally discussed and disposed of earlier (ibid., pp. 80–81). However, as to Sir Oliver, Charles explicitly remarks that he must retain the "little nabob." Samuel Foote's play *The Nabob* (1772) had already popularized the word; in that play, the nabob is a despicable and vicious character, contributing to an already evolving stereotype.
15 Sheridan, *School for Scandal*, p. 80.
16 Ibid., p. 78.
17 Ibid.
18 Ibid., p. 85.
19 Mita Choudhury, "Sheridan, Garrick, and a Colonial Gesture: *The School for Scandal* on the Calcutta Stage," *Theatre Journal*, 46 (1994): 304.
20 While looking at the play text and promptbook of the Calcutta production of *The School for Scandal*, Choudhury offers a performance encoding of sorts. She extends her argument to "audiences in London and Calcutta" (p. 305) who were urged by the play, she argues, to elide commerce and culture, literary text and social text, as well as Britain and colony, and "to participate in British expansionism with humor" (p. 305). She does not, however, make claims about the play's reception by indigenous Indians in Calcutta, as in the 1780s such an audience would presumably not have existed (pp. 304–5).
21 Thomas, *Entangled Objects*, p. 30.
22 Ibid., pp. 30–31.
23 This formulation is significantly indebted to ibid., p. 32.
24 Sheridan, *The School for Scandal* (1777), in Cecil Price (ed.), *The Dramatic Works of Richard Brinsley Sheridan* (Oxford, 1973), vol. 1, p. 295. I have alternately used this edition of Sheridan's play in order to avail of Price's invaluable editorial commentary.
25 Ibid., vol. 1, p. 302.
26 Choudhury, "Sheridan, Garrick," p. 304.
27 Price (ed.), *Letters of Richard Brinsley Sheridan* (Oxford, 1966), vol. 1, pp. 93–5, 99–101, 104–8.
28 Bruce Redford and Cecil Price have provided excellent backgrounds for and early drafts of *The School for Scandal*. Redford's compilations appear in *The Origins of the School for Scandal: "The Slanderers," "Sir Peter Teazle"* (Princeton, 1986), and offer a fascinating view of linguistic revisions and emendations in the drafts for *The School for Scandal*. Cecil Price has, moreover, focused particularly on antecedents for the auction scene, which did not appear in the early manuscripts. He also makes mention of auction-related entertainments that appeared in 1775, and writes "Some connection is possible" (*Dramatic Works*, vol. 1, p. 296). He identifies two other possible contemporary associations with a Jewish man, as aforesaid, and with usury in general (ibid., vol. 1, pp. 300–303). However, there is no mention made of the part actual auctioneers may have played in Sheridan's times and in the history of Drury Lane Theatre proprietorship. Price concludes his investigation, writing: "So there seems to be evidence available to suggest that the play was completed rapidly, and that Sheridan threw in some interesting topical

allusions. Of course, these were soon dated, and were omitted from later performances"
(ibid., vol. 1, p. 303).

[29] See also a young and energetic Sheridan's words about Lacy: "Leasy is utterly unequal
to any department in the theatre. He has an opinion of me, and is very willing to let the
whole burthen and responsibility be taken off his shoulders. But I certainly should not
give up my time and labor (for his superior advantage, having so much greater a share)
without some exclusive advantage" (Moore, *The Life*, vol. 1, p. 125, in letter to Thomas
Linley, 31 January 1776).

[30] Price, *Letters*, vol. 1, p. 105, n. 2; p. 166, n. 1; and p. 168, n. 2.

[31] Ibid., vol. 1, p. 169, n. 2.

[32] Moore, *Memoirs*, vol. 1, pp. 128–9.

[33] Price, *Letters*, vol. 1, pp. 104–8.

[34] Ibid., vol. 1, p. 168, n. 2.

[35] Smith, *Auctions*, p. ix.

[36] Smith: "auctions serve as rites of passage for objects shrouded in ambiguity and uncertainty"
(ibid., p. x).

[37] Ibid., p. 4.

[38] Ibid., p. 17.

[39] Cynthia Wall, "The English Auction: Narratives of Dismantlings," *Eighteenth-century
Studies,* 31/1 (1997): 1, 2, 6. Wall also emphasizes the great ambiguities of class and status
that made auctions disturbing – even traumatizing – spaces of social and cultural negotiation
and sometimes crisis ("English Auction," p. 4). Indeed, the terror of disintegration and
dissolution of individual or collective identity that lies barely concealed behind auctions
is notable ("English Auction," p. 11).

[40] For the firm of Abraham Langford, described as the foremost auctioneer of his times, see
The Concise Dictionary of National Biography (3 vols, Oxford, 1992), vol. 2, p. 11, and
The Dictionary of National Biography (22 vols, Oxford, 1921–22), vol. 11, p. 539.

[41] See for instance *A catalogue of the large and valuable collection of Greek, Roman, British,
Saxon, English and foreign medals, medallions, ... of James West, ... which ... will be sold
by auction, by Mess. Langford's, ... on Tuesday the 19th day of January 1773, ...*(London,
1773); *A catalogue of the large and capital collection of pictures, by the most admired
Italian, French, Flemish and Dutch masters; also prints and drawings, ... of James West, ...
which ... will be sold by auction, by Mess. Langford's, ... on Wednesday the 31st of this instant
March 1773, ...* (London, 1773); *A catalogue of the valuable library of James Burges, esq;
late of Old Burlington Street, deceased; consisting of a fine collection of the best editions
of the Greek and Roman classics, many on large paper, and neatly bound. Which ... will
be sold by auction, by Mr. Langford and Son, on the premises, on Thursday the 16th of this
instant May 1771, and the four following days ...* (London, Printed for Abraham Langford
and Son [1771]); *A catalogue of a collection of Italian and other pictures, belonging to
the Hon. Charles Hamilton, brought from Painshill ... which will be sold by auction by
Mess. Langford's ... on Thursday and Friday the 11th and 12th of this inst. March 1773 ...*
(London, 1773); *A catalogue of the curious collection of books, chiefly relating to medals
and antiquities; of Dr. James Davis, ... which ... will be sold by auction, by Mr. Langford
and Son, ... on Wednesday evening, the 23d of this instant January 1771 ...*(London, 1771);
*A catalogue of the genuine and curious collection of Roman and English coins and medals,
in gold, silver and brass; (many of which are very rare, and in the finest preservation;)
of a gentleman, lately gone abroad. Which will be sold by auction, by Mr. Langford and*

Son, ... on Wednesday ... the 12th ... of this instant February 1772 ... ; A catalogue of the large collection of silver and copper coins and medals, formed by Doctor Phillips, ... Which will be sold by auction, by Mr. Langford and Son, ... on Thursday the 16th of July 1772, ... (London, 1772); *A catalogue of the valuable collection of coins and medals, of Philip Carteret Webb, ... which ... will be sold by auction, by Mr. Langford and Son, ... on Saturday the 16th of this instant* February 1771, ... (London, 1771); *A catalogue of the curious collection of coins and medals, of James Michell Hannott, ... which will be sold by auction, by Mr. Langford and Son, ... on Saturday the 24th of this instant February 1770...* (London, 1770); *A catalogue of the collection of coins, medals, and antiques; of the late ingenious Mr. Thomas Snelling; which will be sold by auction, by Mess. Langfords, ... on Monday the 31st of this instant January 1774, ...* (London, 1774)**.**

42   Choudhury, "Sheridan, Garrick," p. 314.

43   Ibid., p. 318.

44   Horace Walpole, *Horace Walpole's Correspondence*, ed. W. Lewis (43 vols, New Haven, 1973), vol. 10, p. 43; emphasis mine.

45   Ibid., vol. 21, p. 173.

46   Ibid., vol. 22, p. 523.

47   Ibid., vol. 31, p. 339; original emphasis.

48   Ibid., vol. 25, pp. 604–6.

49   Hannah Cowley, *The Belle's Stratagem*, in J. Douglas Canfield and Maja-Lisa Von Sneidern (eds), *The Broadview Anthology of Restoration and Early Eighteenth-century Drama* (Peterborough, Ont., 2001), p. 1849.

50   Ibid., p. 1826.

51   Ibid., p. 1832; emphasis mine.

52   Ibid., p. 1826.

53   Ibid.

54   *The Connoisseur. A Satire on the Modern Men of Taste* (London, 1735).

55   Ibid., p. 10.

56   Cowley, *The Belle's Stratagem*, p. 1834.

57   Ibid., p. 1826.

58   Sheridan, *School for Scandal*, p. 29.

59   Ibid.

60   Again, Horace Walpole comments repeatedly on such misjudgments, usually to Horace Mann (Walpole, *Correspondence*, vol. 23, pp. 298–9 [1771]; pp. 568–70 [1774]).

61   *Connoisseur*, pp. 15–16.

62   See *A catalogue of the entire collection of scarce and curious prints, books of prints, and drawings, of James West, ... which ... will be sold by auction, by Mess. Langford's, ... on Tuesday the 19th of January 1773.*

63   *Connoisseur*, pp. 16–17.

64   Thomas Martyn, *The English Connoisseur*, Facsimile of 1st edn (2 vols, Dublin, 1767; repr. Farnborough, 1968), vol. 1, pp. 103–4.

65   The most striking perception of such privatization and transnationalization grows on the reader who studies Thomas Martyn's catalogue of the contents of Houghton – the Walpole seat – in Martyn's *English Connoisseur*. From another perspective such a collection might be considered transnational plunder (Martyn, *English Connoisseur*, vol. 1, pp. 48–70). I would also invite consideration of the striking similarity of Charles Surface's room of pictures to the description of the Supping Parlor at Houghton (ibid., vol. 1, p. 49).

66 Smith, *Auctions*, p. 33.

67 Ibid., p. 35.

68 Ibid., p. 39.

69 Ibid., p. 48.

70 Ibid., p. 49.

71 An instance in which a private collection marked a transnational moment or experience appears in Thomas Martyn's *The English Connoisseur*: "Marshall *Tallard*, who, when he had been entertained here [in Chatsworth] a few days by the Duke of *Devonshire* said, 'That when he returned to *France*, and reckoned up the Days of his Captivity in *England*, he should leave out those he spent at *Chatsworth*'" (Martyn, *English Connoisseur*, vol. 1, p. 17). The public imperial rivalries of England and France had momentarily been superseded by the establishment of camaraderie between a Frenchman and an Englishman in a private collection.

72 Martin Postle, *Sir Joshua Reynolds: the Subject Pictures* (Cambridge; New York, 1995).

73 See Pierre Bourdieu, *Distinction: A Social Critique of the Judgment of Taste*, trans. Richard Nice (Cambridge, MA, 1984).

74 Martyn, *English Connoisseur*, vol. 1, pp. i–iii; emphasis mine.

75 Ibid., vol. 1, pp. iv–v.

76 Cowley, *Belle's Stratagem*, p. 1835.

77 Ibid.

78 Ibid., p. 1838. The covetous secretiveness of the connoisseurial, but especially the collector character was frequently brought up in general discourse. See my discussion of Cobb's *The Humourist* and Inchbald's *Lovers no Conjurors* (Chapter 3).

79 Cowley, *Belle's Stratagem*, p. 1838.

80 Ibid.

81 Ibid., p. 1841. Charles Smith gestures at exactly this dilemma of valuation when he writes: "auctions … are equally capable of resolving questions of ownership, the allocation of goods, and proper classification, which may be only tangentially related to price; people may be uncertain as *to whom an object belongs or ought to belong or how an item or items are to be categorized or graded*. These uncertainties are often augmented by doubts and questions regarding *who should be allowed to participate in resolving them and the means by which this should be done*" (*Auctions*, p. 3; emphasis mine). See also Wall, "English Auction," p. 2.

82 Walpole, *Correspondence*, vol. 20, p. 268 (18 June 1751). See also ibid., p. 254.

83 Cowley, *Belle's Stratagem*, p. 1844. See Smith, *Auctions*, pp. 13, 56, 73, about the community-building work of a successful auctioneer.

84 Wall, "English Auction," p. 8.

85 See George Taylor (ed.), *Plays By Samuel Foote and Arthur Murphy* (Cambridge, 1984), p. 71.

86 Cowley, *Belle's Stratagem*, p. 1844.

87 These are painters whose works figure frequently in English interiors as described by Thomas Martyn in *The English Connoisseur*.

88 Cowley, *Belle's Stratagem*, p. 1844.

89 John Picker, "Disturbing Surfaces: Representations of the Fragment in *The School for Scandal*," *English Literary History*, 65/3 (Fall 1998): 642.

90 Picker gestures at this by suggesting that the breakdown of family "values" in the picture

auction scene is redolent of the commercialization of society as a whole.
91 Picker, "Disturbing Surfaces," p. 644. Joshua Reynolds' theory of portraiture in his *Discourses on Art* (ed. Robert R. Wark [New Haven, 1975]), a dominant contemporary aesthetic, demanded a poetic unlikeness, non-resemblance to the original.
92 Jack D. Durant, "Sheridan's Picture Auction Scene: A Study in Contexts," *Eighteenth-century Life*, 11/3 (1987), p. 34.
93 Ibid., p. 37.
94 In No. 79 of *The Idler*, 20 October 1759, found in W.J. Bate, J.M. Bullitt, and L.F. Powell (eds), *"The Idler" and "The Adventurer,"* (New Haven, 1963), p. 246.
95 Durant, "Sheridan's Picture Auction Scene," p. 37.
96 Ibid., p. 38; original emphasis.
97 Sheridan, *School for Scandal*, Act I, Scene i and Act II, Scene ii.
98 Reynolds, *Discourses on Art*, p. 171.
99 Durant, "Sheridan's Picture Auction Scene," p. 46, n. 8.
100 Mark Auburn, "Theatre in the Age of Garrick and Sheridan," in James Morwood and David Crane (eds), *Sheridan Studies* (Cambridge, 1995), p. 19; emphasis mine.
101 Ibid., p. 20.
102 Richard C. Taylor, "'Future Retrospection': Rereading Sheridan's Reviewers," in James Morwood and David Crane (eds), *Sheridan Studies*, p. 50.
103 Debbie Lee, "Yellow Fever and the Slave Trade: Coleridge's The Rime of the Ancient Mariner," *English Literary History*, 65 (1998), p. 688.
104 Lee writes: "doctors blamed commerce for destroying environmental balances that otherwise kept epidemics at bay. People who carried on the national dirty work of commerce brought [yellow] fever home" ("Yellow Fever," p. 690).
105 Sheridan, *The School for Scandal*, p. 24.
106 Ibid., p. 25.
107 See the discussion of Hume's linkage of taste, public utility, and national greatness in Chapter 2.
108 For discussions of her collecting propensities and her lineage, see Shteir, *Cultivating Women*, pp. 47–8; and Landry, *The Invention of the Countryside*, pp. 146–7. As Anne Shteir writes, colonial wives were often commissioned for botanical exotica collection (*Cultivating Women*, pp. 5, 191–3; also see pp. 49–50 on Lady Anne Monson, great granddaughter of Charles II, in India in the mid-eighteenth century).
109 Skinner, *A catalogue of the Portland Museum: lately the property of the Duchess Dowager of Portland, deceased : which will be sold by auction, by Mr. Skinner and Co. on Monday the 24th of April, 1786* (London, 1786), pp. iii–iv.
110 Wall, "English Auction," p. 10.
111 See Langford and Sons, *A Catalogue of the Entire Collection of Scarce and Curious Prints, Books of Prints, Drawings, of James West, Esq.; Deceased; Late President of the Royal Society. Which (by Order of the ADMINISTRATRIX) Will be sold by AUCTION, by Mess. Langford's, At their House in the Great Piazza, Covent Garden, On Tuesday the 19th of January 1773, and in the TWELVE following Evenings (Sundays excepted)*. I have consulted the Houghton Library copy of this catalogue.
112 Wall writes of James Christie: "Orally, Christie reimagines or reconstructs for the bidders what he intends to redistribute among them; textually, he separates what the buyer will put together" ("English Auction," p. 3). See also ibid., pp. 11, 13–14, for the incoherence of the typical auction's display.

113   Colley has discussed the strategic importance of this region for the British in the mid-century (*Captives*); original emphasis.

114   See *A CATALOGUE OF THE CAPITAL COLLECTION OF COINS AND MEDALS, in the highest Preservation, AND Beautiful Painted GLASS, OF John Ives, Esq.; F.R.S. F.S.S.A. And Suffolk Herald Extraordinary of Yarmouth, Deceased; Which (by Order of the Executrix,) Will be Sold by AUCTION, by Mess. LANGFORD, At their House in the Great Piazza, COVENT-GARDEN, ON Thursday the 13th of this Instant February 1777, and the following Day* (Houghton Library copy, B1705.464). No specific provenance is given for the single lot of non-western exotica closely associated with British experiences of captivity and torture in "barbaric" foreign parts.

115   Sheridan, *The School for Scandal*, p. 43.

116   Price, *Letters*, vol. 1, p. 50.

117   Ibid., vol. 1, pp. 49–54.

118   Ibid., vol. 1, p. 55.

119   Ibid., vol 1, pp. 61–2.

120   As in "the *hoard* and *arrear* of collected evil" (Sheridan, *Speeches*, vol. 1, p. 379 [Begum speech of 3 June 1788]).

121   Sheridan, *The School for Scandal*, p. 83.

122   Writing of the auction scene entirely in terms of pictorial and portrait theories of Taste, Durant says that Charles' "taste provides a valuable index to his character" (Durant, "Sheridan's Picture Auction Scene," pp. 42–3). Indeed, it is useful to remember that the discourse on aesthetic value in this scene strengthened the mutual regard Sheridan and Reynolds, fellow artists and connoisseurs of taste, had for each other. Sheridan highly valued Reynolds' portrayal (1775) of Elizabeth Linley Sheridan as St Cecilia, and Reynolds valued the tribute to his theory of painting in the auction scene (1777) (ibid., p. 44).

123   It is no coincidence but an exact measure of the pervasive expanse of the cultural anxieties unleashed by British commerce that literature would be replete with its condemnation. Thus, in 1777 William Roscoe would publish the anti-slavery poem *Mount Pleasant* where appeared the following description of depredations in India, a description that in a decade would mirror the content of the charges against Warren Hastings:

> Each feature reddens with a tinge of shame,
> Whilst PATNA'S plain, and BUXAR'S field I name;
> How droops BENGAL beneath Oppression's reign!
> How groans ORISSA with the weight of slain!
> To glut her [Commerce's] rage, what thousands there have bled,
> What thrones are vacant, and what princes dead! (Wood, *Poetry of Slavery*, pp. 56–7)

Again, in 1787, the same year that Sheridan gave his momentous speeches in Parliament, Roscoe published his *Wrongs of Africa*, wherein the slave trader and the eastern despot are rolled into one:

> His mad ambition, send in dread array,
> His messengers of terror …
> … He, amidst the spicy climes
> Of Asia, where prolific nature pours
> Her unappropriate, and superfluous wealth,
> Within his hoarded magazine confines

A nations' produce; and around its doors,
With lifted hands, and unaccusing voice,
Hears the meek native supplicate for food,
[a reference to the Bengal famine]
And bids him perish; and as tho' he fear'd
Some happier spot of earth should yet remain,
That bore not bleeding witness of his guilt,
He from their parent-shore, relentless tears
The sons of Afric; to the madding wave,
To strange diseases, to the piercing taunts
Of wanton insolence, and all the wrongs
That man from man can suffer, doom their days! (Wood, *Poetry of Slavery*, p. 63).

124   Sheridan, *The School for Scandal*, p. 64.

125   Ibid.

126   Ibid.

127   Jack D. Durant provides an excellent comparison of the play and the speech of 13 June, 1788 and their investments in filial piety in "Prudence, Providence, and the Direct Road of Wrong: *The School for Scandal* and Sheridan's Westminster Hall Speech," in *Studies in Burke and His Time*, 15 (1974): 241–51. See also Sheridan's *Speeches*, vol. 1, p. 417.

128   Again, an excellent source for this idea is Dalrymple, *White Mughals*.

129   Sheridan, *Speeches*, vol. 1, p. 194.

130   Ibid., vol. 1, p. 224.

131   Sheridan, *Speeches*, vol. 1, p. 229. See also Moore, *Memoirs*, vol. 2, p. 15.

132   Yet, he himself did not hesitate to use the stereotypical negative images of India when it suited him so to do; thus, in condemning Hastings' representation of British justice, he calls that representation "this base caricature, this Indian pagod" (Moore, *Memoirs*, vol. 2, p. 27).

133   Thomas Moore: "the projected impeachment was but tardy and feeble in its movements, and neither the House nor the public went cordially along with it ... The iniquities, too, of Indian rulers were of that gigantic kind, which seemed to outgrow censure, and even, in some degree, challenge admiration" (ibid., vol. 1, p. 287).

134   See for instance *The debate on the charge relating to Mr. Hastings' conduct to Cheyt Sing, at Benares, in the House of Commons, on the 13th of June, 1786* (London, 1786), pp. 11–12. In this debate, Mr Nicholls is also reported as drawing "a parallel between the European, and chiefly the British, and the Oriental constitutions; in the former, the Government was strong, and could indulge its subjects in the liberties of opposing its measures, which the latter could not with safety do" (p. 12).

135   His *Speeches* include the following report from Lord Cornwallis, the governor-general who succeeded Hastings in India: "as long as the demands of the English government upon the revenue of Oude should remain unlimited, he (the nabob [of Oudh]) could have no interest in establishing any system of economy; and whilst the English should continue to interfere in the internal government of his country, it would be vain for him to attempt any salutary reform; for his subjects knew he was only a cipher in his own dominions, and therefore laughed at and despised his authority and that of his ministers" (Sheridan, *Speeches*, vol. 1, p. 369). Srinivas Aravamudan has also read Hastings' impeachment trial as a "complicated positive levantinization" (*Tropicopolitans*, p. 225) of the Burkean Sublime: "Burke becomes one of a growing number of voices that rejects the idea that

Islamic rule in India corresponded to oriental despotism" (ibid, p. 224). Historians have of course argued for an adjusted optic on the eastern "despotism" issue; thus, Chris Bayly shows how such regimes often went through "'developmental cycles' in which periods of relative centralization were followed by decentralization, and then sometimes by attempts at recentralization" (*Birth of the Modern World*, p. 33); so did most older regimes, and in India especially religious diversity was often approached via the dictates of political expediency (ibid., pp. 31–5), resulting in tolerance of "complexity and difference" (ibid., p. 34).

136   *Debate on ... Cheyt Sing*, pp. 24–5.

137   Ibid., pp. 14–16.

138   In this regard, see an anonymous poem entitled *Cheyt Singh. A Poem. By a Young Lady of Fifteen* (Salisbury, 1790), which incarnates and materializes the east as vividly as anything in Sheridan's parliamentary speeches. The poem states:

> The imperial cap, that late his [Cheyt Singh's] forehead grac'd,
> Warm from his brow, upon the ground he plac'd;
> With suppliant form the awful silence breaks,
> And thus th'*offended* to th'*offender* speaks.
> 'What would my friend? – to him I all resign,
> My wealth, – my royalty, – my life be thine:'
> ...
> 'Be hence,' he (Hastings] cries, 'nor more my anger brave,
> Tis not for me to parley with a slave!'
>
> Now proud Oppression opens all her hoard;
> Prepares her fetters, and unsheathes her sword;
> In vain the subject to his sov'reign flies,
> His alter'd state a new distress supplies (pp. 21–7).

The copy of this poem in the Houghton Collection of Harvard Library appears among Sheridan materials and indeed the poem contains many rhetorical allusions and touches that recall Sheridan.

139   Moore, *Memoirs*, vol. 2, pp. 19–20; see also Sheridan's speech of 20 March 1796, on the west Indian Maroon rebels' right to liberty and national self-determination (Sheridan, *Speeches*, vol. 3, pp. 52–3). And Sheridan's 17 March 1807 speech on the (gradual) Abolition of West Indies Slavery bill is also notable in this regard (ibid., vol. 3, pp. 511–13).

140   The parliamentary representation of the case of the Begums of Oudh, a case which stood out as one of the most famous rhetorical moments of the Hastings Impeachment trial, has been described by many as one of the most unparalleled exertions of rhetorical prowess; see Moore, *Memoirs*, vol. 1, pp. 289–90. Indeed, in an additional twist of reportage one of the most significant issues of the trial as reported is that of the rhetorical contamination of the English parliament by what was considered to be a scandalous, inflammatory eastern influence; see ibid., vol. 2, p. 17. See also Sheridan, *Speeches*, vol. 1, pp. 88–9, on what he evinces as unfavorable colonial reception of British parliamentary assaults on British constitutional rights. Moore writes: "in Sheridan ... the vehemence is evidently more in the words than in the feeling, the tone of indignation is theatrical and assumed, and the brightness of the flash seems to be more considered than the destructiveness of the fire ..." (Moore, *Memoirs*, vol. 2, p. 25). The implication here is that Sheridan himself was under the transnational influence, and almost infected the British Parliament therewith. Be that as it may, Burke, Fox and Pitt

were memorably and vocally moved by Sheridan's flourishes (Sheridan, *Speeches*, vol. 1, p. 222). In this regard, it is amusing to read Major Scott fulminating thus: "In every public street in London you may see a print of the High Court in Westminster Hall, in which the great orator [Burke] appears, detailing those detestable stories, that I have too much respect for decency to mention; next Mr. Fox and the Managers, with grief and horror upon their countenances; a peeress fainting (which, by the way, was not the fact), and the whole Court, Commons, Spectators, and Judges, are faithfully represented, with such an expression in the appearance of each, as the relation of such horrible cruelties would naturally produce" (*A Third Letter from Major Scott to Mr. Fox, on the story of Deby Sing; two letters relative to the expences attending the trial of Warren Hastings, esquire; and a letter to Mr. Burke* [London, 1789], p. 8). Hastings' trial began on 13 February, 1788, and the second Begum speech was begun by Sheridan on 3 June, 1788 (Price, *Letters*, vol. 1, p. 181) and created the greatest public sensation (Fintan O'Toole, *A Traitor's Kiss: the Life of Richard Brinsley Sheridan, 1751–1816* [London, 1995], p. 225; Sheridan, *Speeches*, vol. 1, p. 369).

[141] Price, *Dramatic Works*, vol. 1, p. 403.

[142] Sheridan, *Speeches*, vol. 1, p. 376.

[143] Moore, *Memoirs*, vol. 2, p. 247; emphases mine.

[144] Sheridan, *Speeches*, vol. 1, pp. 228–9; emphasis mine.

[145] Moore, *Memoirs*, vol. 1, p. 292; emphasis mine.

[146] Moore's understanding of the pre-history of Sheridan's charge, echoed by Sheridan's other biographers, is given in ibid., vol. 2, pp. 8–10.

[147] Ibid., vol. 2, p. 14; see also Sheridan, *Speeches*, vol. 1, pp. 374–5.

[148] Ibid., vol. 1, p. 82.

[149] Ibid., vol 1, p. 216; on this diamond also see Dalrymple, *White Mughals*, p. 88.

[150] O'Toole, *Traitor's Kiss*, p. 51.

[151] Ibid., pp. 174–8.

[152] Ibid., p. 231.

[153] *Debate on ...Cheyt Sing*, pp. 30–31.

[154] On Britons' changing perceptions of their own imperial ventures abroad in the eighteenth century, see Linda Colley's *Captives*; she also argues that in our present day "the segregation of British domestic history from the histories of varieties of Britons overseas cannot stand" (ibid., p. 18).

[155] Sheridan's political views on liberty and the hierarchy of nations – as expressed in parliamentary speeches – are briefly summarized by Durant in "Sheridan and the Wider World," in John McVeagh (ed.), *1660–1780: All Before Them* [2 vols, London, 1990], vol. 1, p. 265).

[156] See Sheridan, *Speeches*, vol. 1, p. 230 ("plundering these aged women"); p. 231 ("sacrificing female dignity and distress to parricide and plunder"); p. 232 ("plunder the Begums of their treasure"); p. 375 ("treasures in the Zenana"); p. 376 ("Mr. Hastings ... her *plunderer*"); p. 377 ("treasure of the Begums"); p. 385 ("treasures of the Begums"), and so forth.

[157] Ibid., vol. 1, p. 397.

[158] Durant, "Sheridan's Grotesques," p. 27. He also writes in the same context: "It [the grotesque] imposes a comic perspective on the troubling aspects of experience and thus renders them less formidable to consciousness than they might otherwise be, but it never wholly neutralizes the threat they offer" (p. 27).

[159] O'Toole, *Traitor's Kiss*, p. 225; Sheridan, *Speeches*, vol. 1, p. 367.

[160] Of the intimate theatricality of English politics and the politics of English theater, few

better accounts can be found than Marc Baer's study of the 1809 Old Price riots (Baer, *Theatre and Disorder in Late Georgian England* [Oxford, 1992], esp. pp. 189–221).

[161] Wall, "English Auction," p. 2.

[162] Wall, "English Auction," pp. 2–3. Christie himself had to struggle with his humble social status and his aspirations to greatness, as Sheridan did (ibid., p. 7). Christie trained his son in classics and made him a "gentleman," just as Sheridan's family had struggled to climb the hierarchy of social rank and become "gentlemen." However, as Wall writes, it is never evident that the friendships Christie claimed with socially eminent men such as Reynolds, Gainsborough, Sheridan, Garrick, and Horace Walpole were regarded as anything other than patronage and condescension by those eminent persons themselves: "Christie himself, as his contemporaries perceived him, was an auctioneer trying to be a gentleman" (ibid.). Sheridan struggled all his life, also, to cast off the stigma of being an actor's son and a theater manager.

[163] O'Toole, *Traitor's Kiss*, pp. 85–7.

[164] Price, *Letters*, vol. 1, pp. 79–80. In 1775 Sheridan wrote again to Thomas Linley objecting to Elizabeth Linley's sister Mary's prospect of appearing on the Drury Lane stage at the invitation of no less a person than Garrick, calling the theater "the greatest Nursery of Vice and Misery on the Face of the Earth" (O'Toole, *Traitor's Kiss*, p. 87).

[165] Though more work needs to be done to explore the material history of this substitution, it is noteworthy that the site of the Royal Academy when it opened in 1769 was the "Great Auction Room" near the Haymarket that James Christie had recently vacated, moving his auction enterprise to Pall Mall (Wall, "English Auction," p. 6, n. 28.)

[166] *Letters of Sir Joshua Reynolds*, ed. F.W. Hilles (Cambridge, 1929), pp. 190–91.

[167] O'Toole, *Traitor's Kiss*, p. 459, n. 18, citing evidence from Rene Wellek and Alvaro Ribeiro (eds), *Evidence in Literary Scholarship: Essays in Memory of James Marshall Osborn* (Oxford, 1979), p. 319. See also Moore, *Memoirs*, vol. 2, pp. 303–4 on this picture and other relics of Sheridan.

[168] Wall writes: "the Auction House became the formal space that systematically manufactured the idea as well as the event of a collection open for dismemberment to the publicly highest bidder, whoever he or she happened to be" ("English Auction," p. 6). And an interesting correlation of public and private collections and access to them also obtained in the world of art, wherein it was considered to be highly condescending and magnanimous for nobility to open up their private collections to indigent artists-in-training for their practice, at least until the Royal Academy came into being.

[169] Fintan O'Toole writes confirming the interlinked dichotomy of culture and commerce that I am tracing throughout this book: "The idea of reputation was at the heart of the Enlightenment's attempts to understand what, in the late eighteenth century, it meant to be modern. In fact, it was a specifically modern concern, arising from the emergence of a phenomenon that had not been experienced before, namely urban life on a large scale" (*Traitor's Kiss*, p. 124).

[170] A good discussion of the transactions associated with this event may be found in Ian Donaldson, "New Papers of Henry Holland and R.B. Sheridan: (II) The Hyde Park Corner Operas and the Dormant Patent," *Theatre Notebook: A Journal of the History and Technique of the British Theatre*, 16 (1962), pp. 122–3.

[171] See letter "To the Proprietors of the Drury Lane and Covent Garden Theatres," 1777, in Price, *Letters*, vol. 1, pp. 116–21.

[172] Ibid., vol. 1, p. 117.

173 Ibid., vol. 1, pp. 118, 120.

174 These comments, though they appeared in an application in 1784 or 1785 by Harris to the Lord Chamberlain, are indebted, Ian Donaldson states, to Sheridan's 1783 plans as they appear in Moore, *Memoirs*, vol. 2, p. 263 (Donaldson, "New papers," pp. 118–19; Donaldson, however, uses a different edition and gives different page numbers for this text). I have already cited above the letter that demonstrates Sheridan's cogitations upon such plans in 1773.

175 Donaldson, "New papers," p. 120. Mark Auburn has written eloquently about the noise of the London theaters, in "Theatre in the Age of Garrick and Sheridan," pp. 14–15.

176 Letter to the Duke of Bedford, Price, *Letters*, vol. 1, pp. 215–19. Henry Holland was also the manager of Carleton House renovations, 1787–90; see Figure 4.4 above. These "improvement" projects were thus simultaneous and semi-public.

177 David Wilkinson, *The Duke of Portland: Politics and Party in the Age of George III* (New York, 2003), p. 61.

178 Wilkinson, *Duke of Portland*, pp. 64–7, wherein Wilkinson describes how the Duke objected to privileging the commercial potential of his possessions – especially of the park at Welbeck – over their connoisseurial and "improvement" prospects.

179 Ibid., pp. 62–3.

180 Ibid., p. 73.

181 Ibid., p. 66.

182 Ibid., p. 67.

183 Wilkinson writes that Portland was in debt to the amount of £529,900 when he died in 1809 (ibid., pp. 61–2). Charles James Fox was in debt to the tune of £140,000 when he was only 24 (James Connelly, "The Prospect Before Us," in *The School for Scandal: Thomas Rowlandson's London* [Lawrence, Kansas, 1967], p. 15).

184 O'Toole, *Traitor's Kiss*, pp. 96–8.

185 Donaldson, "New Papers," pp. 124–5.

186 O'Toole, *Traitor's Kiss*, pp. 348–9.

187 Ibid., p. 348.

188 Ibid., pp. 347–8.

189 Ibid., pp. 348–50.

Chapter 5

Transatlantic Flight: Phillis Wheatley's Copies with a Difference

Phillis Wheatley was Sheridan's short-lived slave contemporary. She was born somewhere in west Africa, around 1753, and brought to the new world in a ship that gave her her first name. Caught and framed in the nomenclature of the misery spanning the Middle Passage and the burden of slavery to John Wheatley of Boston, Phillis Wheatley quickly acquired "English and Classical Literature (especially poetry), geography and history, as well as the Bible, some Latin, and Christianity."[1] Wheatley's writing reveals – as I will argue in this chapter – a curious blend of new world intertextuality and textual flight from the world which, taken together, stands for a unique new world expression of transnational identity: simultaneously embodied, localized, migratory, and virtual. The flight I will explore here is not only the flight of audacious language-stealing – Wheatley's appropriation of the neoclassical muse – though that is also a part of my focus,[2] but her flight imagery as a broader metaphorical apparatus to inscribe slavery and the longing for freedom within the freedoms granted by poetic talent and religious fervor.

Carole Boyce Davies writes: "If following Judith Butler, the category of woman is one of performance of gender, then the category Black woman, or woman of color, exists as multiple performances of gender and race and sexuality based on the particular cultural, historical, geopolitical, class communities in which Black women exist."[3] Wheatley's writing, including her 1765 letter to Samuel Occom, the Mohegan minister, her famous inaugural elegy on the death of George Whitefield (1770), and her deft citations and transformations of English neoclassical and Latin classical traditions show a brilliant if involuntary transcultural and transnational imagination, ranging – so to speak – above the creeping lines alone permitted, according to Pope, by neoclassical poetry to its practitioners.[4] Wheatley's poetry, with its interleaved accounts of claustrophobic containment and soaring transcontinental, indeed transgalactic flight, pioneers an imaginative manifesto of neoclassicism rewritten as transnationality.[5] When Davies writes, "Black women's writing cannot be located and framed in terms of one specific place, but exists in myriad places and times, constantly eluding the terms of the discussion … not so much formulated as a 'nomadic subject,' although it shares an affinity, but as a migratory subject … as diaspora assumes expansiveness and elsewhereness, migrations of the Black female subject pursue the path of movement outside the terms of dominant discourses,"[6] she is describing Phillis Wheatley.

Aravamudan has written that "[Olaudah] Equiano initiates a practice that derives Englishness from African otherness and weds the national identity to abolitionist ideals."[7] This is not quite true if one considers that with her London publication in 1773 of *Poems Religious and Moral*, it was in fact Wheatley who initiated the wedding of (trans)national identity to otherness. As Gilroy has written: "The intellectual and cultural achievements of the black Atlantic populations exist partly inside and not always against the grand narrative of Enlightenment and its operational principles ... Though African linguistic tropes and political and philosophical themes are still visible for those who wish to see them, they have often been transformed and adapted by their New World locations to a new point where the dangerous issues of purified essences and simple origins lose all meaning."[8] If, as I have argued in my introduction to this book, the political grounds of being of transnationality is the postcolonial production of the politicized copy with a difference or repetition, then Phillis Wheatley embodies a gendered transnationality regenerating a ravished identity out of her migratory and commodified black female body, transatlantic abolitionism, as well as transatlantic identity and liberatory discourses: "fluidity, multiple identities, repetition which must be multiply articulated."[9]

In his book *The Journey Back: Issues in Black Literature Criticism* (1980), Houston Baker Jr. set out to "explain *how* black narrative texts written in English preserve and communicate culturally unique meanings."[10] Baker continues by saying that "individuals who enter a culture where the language is unfamiliar may be capable (after a relatively brief period) of identifying and defining in their own terms any single word or sentence presented, and they may rapidly become adept at constructing interesting ethnographic accounts for their 'home' cultures. But they will not comprehend the overall game of language, or the culture's composite of language games, until they have fully grasped the general rules and procedures of discourse operating within the culture."[11] He then asks what might be called an original question in paradise lost, "As slaves in perpetuity, as men and women deemed lower than animals, where could the first black Americans turn?"[12] The black American woman Wheatley turned to stylistic innovations that signal her transnational gendering. According to Robert Kendrick, Wheatley generated "a sty(lus) that would always leave at least two traces, one of the two constantly masking itself under the name of the other ... the legitimated voice of the slave who had dutifully enslaved herself to the discourse of her masters and the illegitimate one of the woman who refused the imprint of the subject position that white discourse constructed for her."[13] In the also intriguing reading of Gay Gibson Cima, Wheatley's politics of copying or repetition of Tradition, or two traditions, with a difference from each, throws a highly interesting light on the conception of her as "genius" – certainly dominant in the public discourse of the times – which would have made her talents, of course, non-duplicable, and therefore non-political in the sense construed by Walter Benjamin (see Chapter 1).

In this chapter I wish to work especially with the schema of an aesthetics of repetition as a political act, particularly as produced in colonial and postcolonial settings by subaltern voices, as outlined by Walter Benjamin and Fredric Jameson.[14] However, before I engage in a more situated reading of the Wheatley corpus for an understanding of its politics of repetition with a difference – that aesthetic of mimicry which places it in the realm of the political, according to Benjamin – I will make some comment upon the other linked "duality" of Wheatley that has roused critical firestorms. Aravamudan writes, "Postcolonial criticism ought not to reify agency from the position of other or subaltern in the manner of its precursor, decolonization discourse. Rather, in an analysis of cultural and historical texts, the postcolonial critic is inclined to find resistance through acts of trading, transculturation, and hybridity as well as from those of separation, opposition, and rejection."[15] This redrawing of the postcolonial map encompasses the two antithetical directions of Phillis Wheatley criticism: the debate rages between those who condemn Wheatley for not being sufficiently a black separatist nationalist, and those who extol her achievements in singing "double consciousness." Wheatley scholarship is suffused with the contestatory and improvisational notes of a debate over whether she was African or American, what kind of African or American she was, whether she was "African-American" in our contemporary sense of that term, and whether she resisted or accommodated any or all of the above inscriptions.[16]

Indeed, as critics have remarked, Phillis Wheatley has had to take the same exam – to prove her "originality," her "genuineness," as either a cultural genius defined by Europe or as a cultural nationalist defined by black culture – twice two centuries apart.[17] Within what I would call more nuanced opinion, the New England community that Phillis Wheatley acquired and inhabited has been delineated, by William Robinson among others, as a likely explanation for what is perceived as Wheatley's "abandonment" of her race.[18] She was a Northern slave, raised in exceptionally favorable circumstances in a North that had a history of being more permissive and liberal with slaves, the prominent Germantown Quakers having issued a condemnation of slavery as early as 1688.[19] Quite a hundred years before her time, "In Virginia as well as in New York the free people of color were growing in number and social significance up to the 1670s,"[20] though by the 1690s, such freedoms of the free colored people were coming under severe restrictions, including punishments against whites for interracial sex and reproduction, sanctioned by the Board of Trade and Plantations of which John Locke was a member.[21] As late as 1794, Timothy Dwight, president of Yale University, wrote "Greenfield Hill," where he produced a comparative slavery table that depicted "slavery in the Southern states and on the East Coast as benevolent, indeed almost utopian."[22] Of course, such a depiction of Northern slavery was largely illusory, but the American North produced the earlier American poetry on slavery, if often in its defense. Closer to Wheatley's time, again, there is evidence of a resurgence of civic and political identity, petitions and lawsuits against slavery, and self-governance and public demonstrations by Northern and New England slaves.[23]

Wheatley inherited a checkered history, therefore, of black political articulation in America, one which demonstrated alternations of "creolized" freedoms and severe and restrictive repressions.[24] Donna Landry maintains something similar when she writes that despite the contestations over Wheatley's identity and cultural output, we need not "continue to separate … [her endeavors] as antithetically 'aesthetic' and 'political.'"[25]

In other words, critics have converged upon the propriety of seeing Wheatley's corpus as a "transnation." As Robinson writes, "When one is young, gifted, and black, and determined to survive, one is sometimes called upon to wear different faces in different places for the same reasons."[26] The eighteenth-century white establishment first tested Wheatley on her ability to assume authorship when being an author was tantamount to having an "original" or genealogically originary relationship with western tradition, one that she so obviously lacked. The first publication of Wheatley's first collected volume, *Poems on Various Subjects, Religious and Moral* (1773),[27] demonstrates Wheatley's obligatory reproduction of Tradition with a difference, the poet wearing the slave's face emulating a corpus that required review and authentication by a panel of Boston worthies considered guardians of Tradition.[28]

In speaking of Wheatley's "successors" such as W.E.B. Du Bois and Richard Wright, Paul Gilroy writes: "The specificity of the modern political and cultural formation I want to call the black Atlantic can be defined, on one level, through this desire to transcend both the structures of the nation state and the constraints of ethnicity and national particularity."[29] Gilroy's critique of cultural nationalism is pertinent here, because within the "frame"-work of the published book over which the Boston worthies sat guard as the keepers of tradition, Phillis Wheatley produced a political transnation of capture, slavery, and flight, a mythopoesis of identity as a copy with a significant difference drawn from experiences that her Boston "framers" would never grasp or know,[30] even though a few years later some of them would be compelled to take flight themselves across the Atlantic. As Walt Nott writes, "The two poles of public identity represented by ... 'uncultivated Barbarian' and 'Poetical Genius' – suggest the possibilities open to Wheatley in eighteenth-century Anglo-American culture ... Wheatley's symbolic transformation in the eyes of contemporary white Anglo-American culture from 'Barbarian' to 'Genius' suggests her successful crafting of a public persona, her subsequent participation in the public discourse of her time, and, most important, her acquisition of a power such public participation entailed."[31] Nott is stating what Davies has also discussed as the significance of "positionality": "it is location which allows one to speak or not to speak ... The politics of location brings forward a whole host of identifications and associations around concepts of place, placement, displacement ... It is about positionality in society based on class, gender, sexuality, age, income. It is also about relationality and the ways in which one is able to access, mediate or reposition oneself, or pass into other spaces given certain other circumstances."[32] It is about transnation.

If in the eighteenth century the question was whether the black, Phillis Wheatley, could be called a "poet," in the twentieth century it was frequently debated whether Phillis Wheatley deserves to be called a "black" poet. The reinstatement of Wheatley in a "black" literary canon has indeed only been recent.[33] Even "sympathetic" comments hint broadly at her complicity with her captors: "In her poetry, Phillis did not concern herself with social and moral protest against the plight of the slaves; and though she has been criticized for this, one would have to admit that her lack of courage is understandable – after all, Phillis Wheatley, because of the unusually good circumstances of her life while living with the Wheatleys, and because of her training, was not likely to view her being brought to America as something to protest."[34]

All of the critical response to her "blackness" or "whiteness" of soul have been posthumous to Wheatley, and steeped in the identity politics and conflicts of *their* own day. I hope, in this chapter, to return the cultural genealogical investigations of Wheatley to the terms and perceptions of *her* own day. Only more recent commentators have taken this more nuanced, historicist view of Wheatley's life and works, but as Gates and Robinson have pointed out, such interpretations are needed. Near the conclusion of this book on the transnational urges and forces in eighteenth-century British and transatlantic literatures, it seems quite simply a necessity to "read" Wheatley as an eminent artist of "transnation," that liminal consciousness of multiple psychosocial geneses that produces the complex moral genealogies of the transnational eighteenth century and its subjectivities.

I acknowledge the widely prevalent reception of the Wheatley phenomenon as a literary curiosity, a connoisseurial undertaking (needing scrutiny and authentication by various powerful men of her times),[35] and yet aim to show how Wheatley gives voice to Yarico, shows her ability and willingness to speak her own genealogy, set her own value, and utterly transcend the status of either commodity or treasure by achieving personhood within the context of transatlantic slavery.[36] Unlike Yarico, Wheatley is able to invade the drawing room as a transatlantic luminary, a commodity or unmarked object become a fetish, a connoissuerial *objet*, a treasure, by her own efforts: "Boston and London society paraded Wheatley from one genteel drawing room to another where she entertained, simply by reading her work aloud. She performed with charm and poise, assets that contributed to her growing fame. For those assembled to watch a young black female slave read poems that she had written, Wheatley seemed to be a miracle."[37]

In her thoughtful re-reading of Wheatley's classical inflections and invocations of the muses, Flanzbaum finds that Wheatley's occasional poems usually do not contain invocations of the Muse, but that the "muse materializes only when the ensuing poem has no designated audience, market function, or carefully planned route of reception. These poems offer no ostensible service to the white community ... Wheatley exploits the typical neo-classical convention of invoking the muse to cross boundaries; in fact, with the muse's help, she charts territory that her white master cannot violate."[38] Indeed, the Muse for Wheatley may also be said to be safeguard against an entire "muse"umization of Wheatley herself; to have the Muse on her side is, for Wheatley, one way of preventing being entirely a commodity or a spectacle, but to stand outside of the picture, alongside and not at the feet of her inspiration and her support system, and gaze in upon her own creation. This Muse is thus Wheatley's political as well as literary ally – this Muse is Wheatley's copier, through whom Wheatley channels her remarkable and recognizable revisionings of the political and creative aspirations of the classical west. This Muse is Wheatley's transnational double.

In the eighteenth century it was frequently debated whether Wheatley was an original genius or a servile copyist. Thus, the advertisement for *Poems* (1773) in *The*

London Chronicle and *The Morning Post and Daily Advertiser* sounded the theme early: "The Book here proposed for publication displays perhaps one of the greatest instances of pure, unassisted genius, that the world ever produced. The Author is a native of Africa, and left not that dark part of the habitable system, till she was eight years old ... The writer while in England a few weeks since, was conversed with by many of the principal Nobility and Gentry of this Country, who have been signally distinguished for their learning and abilities, among whom was the Earl of Dartmouth, the late Lord Lyttleton, and others who unanimously expressed their amazement at the gifts with which infinite Wisdom has furnished her."[39] Yet, again and again this debate resurfaces in Wheatley criticism. John Shields writes: "Many readers of her work refuse to let go of the old double canard, first that she writes in the 'detested' mode of neoclassicism, with its heroic couplets and poetic diction, and second that she is nothing better than a derivative imitator of Alexander Pope."[40]

If my argument in this chapter can stand, however, this criticism is of course a moot point. Phillis Wheatley's poetry is not about being a poetry of originality. As a writer who comes "after" and from "elsewhere" she produces aesthetic work that is politicized because it "copies" an original to produce the irreducible unease of difference and polyphony, those "acts of trading, transculturation, and hybridity as well as ... those of separation, opposition, and rejection."[41] As Kendrick writes, "Wheatley had been influenced by other constructions of repetition and mimesis, constructions that emphasized repetition as difference ... signifying similarity may not have been her goal."[42] Neither was signifying an absolutely radical difference.

Wheatley, for instance, chose not to go to Africa as a missionary upon manumission.[43] In her letter upon the subject to John Thornton she wrote in terms problematizing reception of her poetic trope of flight as an unambiguous and equivalent expression of desire for escape to Africa: "Upon my arrival [in Africa], how like a Barbarian Should I look to the Natives; I can promise that my tongue shall be quiet for a strong reason indeed being an utter stranger to the Language of Anamaboe. Now to be Serious, This undertaking appears too hazardous, and not sufficiently Eligible, to go – and leave my British & American Friends ...."[44] After making the mordant and macabre joke about the counter-image of another stripping or tying of a tongue now forever amnesiac of Africa, Wheatley insists "seriously" on her connections, her friendships, on western soil, and foregrounds her sense of transatlantic, transnational, yet forcibly circumscribed belonging – a different kind of American, British, and African.[45]

Flight is the metonym for freedom from slavery wherein Wheatley compresses an extremely complex transnational imagination. Flight and the imagery of transcendence are the crucial transnational matrix capturing and signifying Wheatley's experiences: capture and rupture from parents; middle passage and the social death of slavery; and adoption of western soil and culture. In an essay engaged in embedding Wheatley within black culture, R. Lynn Matson, in one of the earliest fuller discussions of "flight" as a trope writes: "Another of Phillis Wheatley's great concerns was death (18 of her 46 poems are elegies) ... They certainly are sentimental ... but what is overlooked is this same theme of escape, in this case, escape (freedom) through death … One must also notice in these poems the metaphors of death as a flight or a voyage over water which later became so popular in Negro spirituals."[46] Extending Matson's astute observation, I would argue for the status of flight in her poetry as a chiasmic trope effecting a series of transversals and inversions of freedom and captivity, life and death, blackness and whiteness, and physicality and spirituality, whose end-product is a highly complex articulation of identity in social death, "a continual rewriting of the boundaries of what constitutes home."[47]

In "On Virtue," she invokes that composite deity as follows:

> Auspicious queen, thine heav'nly pinions spread,
> And lead celestial *Chastity* along;
> Lo! Now her sacred retinue descends,
> Array'd in glory from the orbs above.
> Attend me, *Virtue*! thro' my youthful years!
> O leave me not to the false joys of time!
> But guide my steps to endless life and bliss.[48]

In this poem, Virtue and Chastity are assistants to her flight from sin. They are assistants because though celestial and queenly, they clearly are commanded in the lines above to become Phillis' attendant spirits, not unlike those Belinda commands in Pope's *Rape of the Lock*. Wheatley's treatment of virtue and chastity are symptomatic of her appropriation and domination of Tradition, and of her refusal to free celestial spirits from the demands of the flesh and bone body experiencing sublunary ordeals such as slavery. Even while acknowledging her allegiance and subservience to divine figures, Wheatley refuses to allow them to soar too far without acknowledging her condition, below them, firmly planted as well as transplanted, rooted as well as uprooted.[49]

Similarly in "To the University of CAMBRIDGE, in NEW-ENGLAND," she lets the students soar for a while:

> Students, to you 'tis given to scan the heights
> Above, to traverse the ethereal space,
> And mark the systems of revolving worlds.
> Still more ye sons of science ye receive
> The blissful news by messengers from heav'n,
> How Jesus' blood for your redemption flows
> …
> And share with him in the sublimest skies,
> Life without death, and glory without end.
> …
> Suppress the deadly serpent in its egg.
> Ye blooming plants of human race divine.[50]

Then she sounds a clashing note, a challenge, literally, thrown to these highfliers, these elite mandarins of the bright new world: the warning comes from an African.[51] With

"An Ethiop tells you 'tis your greatest foe" she brings these New England youths right down to the soil they inhabit in common with her, and disallows further flights of fancy of her own or of ambition on their parts.[52] Articulating an obstacle to flight primarily in terms of her racial identity as well as difference, she transfigures flight itself from trope to tropicality, the type of death-dealing benighted heathenism that Africans were traditionally stigmatized for. Only, here it is the Ethiop who impedes the "flight" of the master race into secular and heathenish ambition. Indeed, the variant of this poem preserved at the American Antiquarian Society had figured evil as "the sable monster" rather than the deadly serpent's egg.[53] The decision to change the sable monster to the deadly serpent's egg is significant especially because the moral symbology of the Ethiop otherwise functions in the poem as a constant reminder of the dangers and pleasures of unrestrained flight, soaring, wandering, and cathects the western obsession with knowledge and power with the African's sad fantasy of flight.

Betsy Erkkila writes: "In Wheatley's writings, the memory of the African sun worship merges with the language of evangelical Christianity and the language of revolutionary freedom to produce a poetics of ascent and liberation. In this poetics the sun/son is the central figure of a constellation of images that moves from dark to light, white to black, sin to redemption, bondage to deliverance."[54] I find, however, a more complex and ambiguous movement in her flight imagery than ascent and liberation. Flight here is metonymically riveted to its opposite, slavery, as well as to its plenary topos of liberty, and neither term – liberty or slavery – is privileged or settled in the metonymic flight; instead the antipodal liberty and slavery slide and overlap over the wide expanse and ethereal scope of flight to meet each other in an affective synthesis conveying both ecstasy and terror.[55] This is the sort of chiasmus that is conveyed in the famous lines: "Remember, Christians, Negros, black as Cain,/ May be refin'd, and join th' angelic train" (in "On being brought from AFRICA to AMERICA").[56]

John C. Shields explains the flight motif in Wheatley's poem as an effect of the Sublime.[57] He is quite right, especially about the fact that the Sublime is nowhere more clearly enacted in her flight metaphor than in the incompleteness of those aspirations to what is incomparably beyond the self: "she represents the most powerful mode of ascent in the negative pleasure of sublimity. Both in Kant and in Wheatley, the inexorable attempt of the human mind to grasp totalities and the equally inexorable failure to do so incites the feeling of the sublime."[58] This incompleteness, however, that in Kantian terms might be understood as the imagination's mediation between reason and feeling – and that Shields terms "negative representation" following the impossibility of the sublime's ultimate goal of "freedom," especially in Wheatley's case[59] – in postcolonial and transnational terms might be better understood as the negotiation of the interstitiality, ambivalence, and hybridity of identification with hegemony. Kendrick has also seen the production of the sublime experience as Wheatley's reproductions of an original with a difference, in the "negating difference/ distance that lies between the knowable 'copy' and the presumed 'original,'"[60] but I would repeat that Wheatley's art of copying with difference produces as much the political and the "postcolonial" as the "Sublime." What Shields sees as a definitely poetic and pious incompleteness,[61] I would propose as a deliberate political manifesto.[62]

The only persons apparently allowed unfettered flight in her poems are generally clergymen and preachers, as in "On the Death of the Rev. Dr. Sewell. 1769,"[63] and "On the Death of the Rev. Mr. GEORGE WHITEFIELD. 1770."[64] A comparison of the two eulogies/elegies is interesting. Of the "flight" of Rev. Sewell, her own pastor, Wheatley writes thus:

> Come, let us all behold with wishful eyes
> The saint ascending to his native skies;
> From hence the prophet wing'd his rapt'rous way
> To the blest mansions in eternal day.
> Then begging for the Spirit of our God,
> And panting eager for the same abode,
> Come, let us all with the same vigour rise,
> And take a prospect of the blissful skies.[65]

Of George Whitefield, the Countess of Huntingdon's chaplain, she writes:

> Behold the prophet in his tow'ring flight!
> He leaves the earth for heav'n's unmeasur'd height,
> And worlds unknown receive him from our sight.
> There *Whitefield* wings with rapid course his way,
> And sails to Zion through vast seas of day.
> Thy pray'rs, great saint, and thine incessant cries
> Have pierc'd the bosom of thy native skies.[66]

Notable similarities between the two flight images include sanctification of Sewell and Whitefield, ascribing prophetic status to them, ascribing to them Christlike mediating roles vis-à-vis those left below, reading their flight as a rapturous religious sublime (as in "eternal day," "tow'ring flight," "umeasur'd height," "vast seas of day"), and as beings both cathected yet to their congregations in their mediating roles. Sewell models vigour sufficient to rouse the congregation to attempt the sublime if not attain it; Whitefield proves analogous to slave saints whose suffering brought them closer to heaven. Yet both perform an identity of difference and indeed alienation that captures the strategic transnationality that Wheatley produces.[67] The disappearing saint is reluctantly relinquished yet appropriated by the irreducible remainder of slavery – the slave congregation – experiencing the trans-/trance state in its most local, painfully vulnerable and embodied condition. The giddiness and semi-blindness induced by the rapid flight of departing saints into ethereal realms is never truly allowed to erase the concept of the responsibilities saints have to their flocks, as in the second half of the elegy upon Whitefield, where Whitefield is charged with conducting Americans *and* Africans to Christ. A popular and general resurrection of slaves and orphans[68] precedes Whitefield's own ultimate last day, as in the final verse Whitefield, asthmatic and hoarse, is brought back to the dust shared by these common folks, not far differently than the Cambridge students were:

> But, though arrested by the hand of death,
> Whitefield no more exerts his lab'ring breath,
> Yet let us view him in th'eternal skies,
> Let ev'ry heart to this bright vision rise;
> While the tomb safe retains its sacred trust,
> Till life divine re-animates his dust.[69]

Examining the engraving preceding Wheatley's "Elegiac Poem On the Death of that celebrated Divine, and eminent Servant of JESUS CHRIST, the late Reverend and pious George Whitefield" is also instructive in this regard. Thus in four 1770 editions of this poem, the frontispiece or title engraving depicts Whitefield laid to his rest with the coffin beside him (see Figure 5.1). This engraving is described by an advertisement in the *Massachusetts Spy* (9–11 October 1770, p. 1) as "a plate, representing the posture in which the Rev. Mr. Whitefield lay before and after his interment at Newbury-Port."[70] Of the poem Mukhtar Ali Isani has written that "by Wheatley's time, the funeral elegy, once the prerogative of the clerics, was almost entirely the work of laymen, including those with no special call to letters ... The didactic emphasis and the use of mortuary detail continued, but the latter was declining. Wheatley's use of pentameter couplets and emphatic mortuary reminders is in the tradition of the New England funerary verse."[71]

I offer an additional explanation for Wheatley's iconography and imagery in this elegy: while Whitefield's death is depicted in conventional iconography of memento mori for the viewer, when contrasted with the textual images of soaring, the engraving starkly dichotomizes Whitefield as rigorously confined both within the broad dark borders of the engraving itself, and in the posture and narrow space of a coffin. This image, awe-inspiring as memento mori within the western classical context, is also resonant with memories of slavery and the slave trade and its resulting confinements and foregrounding of the immobilized body. In its haunting if accidental evocation of the slave trade, it is interstitial. It lies between the lines that spell Whitefield's service to western Christianity, his flight to heavenly domains, and the interdicted flight of those African-Americans and Afro-Britons such as Wheatley[72] whom he had served in life. In death, then, not only is Whitefield kept confined by both the language and imagery of Wheatley's published piece, but he is further imagined in a resemblance with a difference, as a copy, of Wheatley's kind. However this image was derived, whether or not Wheatley had any say in its choice, the apparently stark contrast of the image and the poem belies a more tensely semblant paradox in both.

This refusal to loosen the link, to relinquish the bond between the heavenly and the earthly, marks Wheatley's own performative masquerade of transnational consciousness throughout her works, as when she comforts parents for the loss of their children:

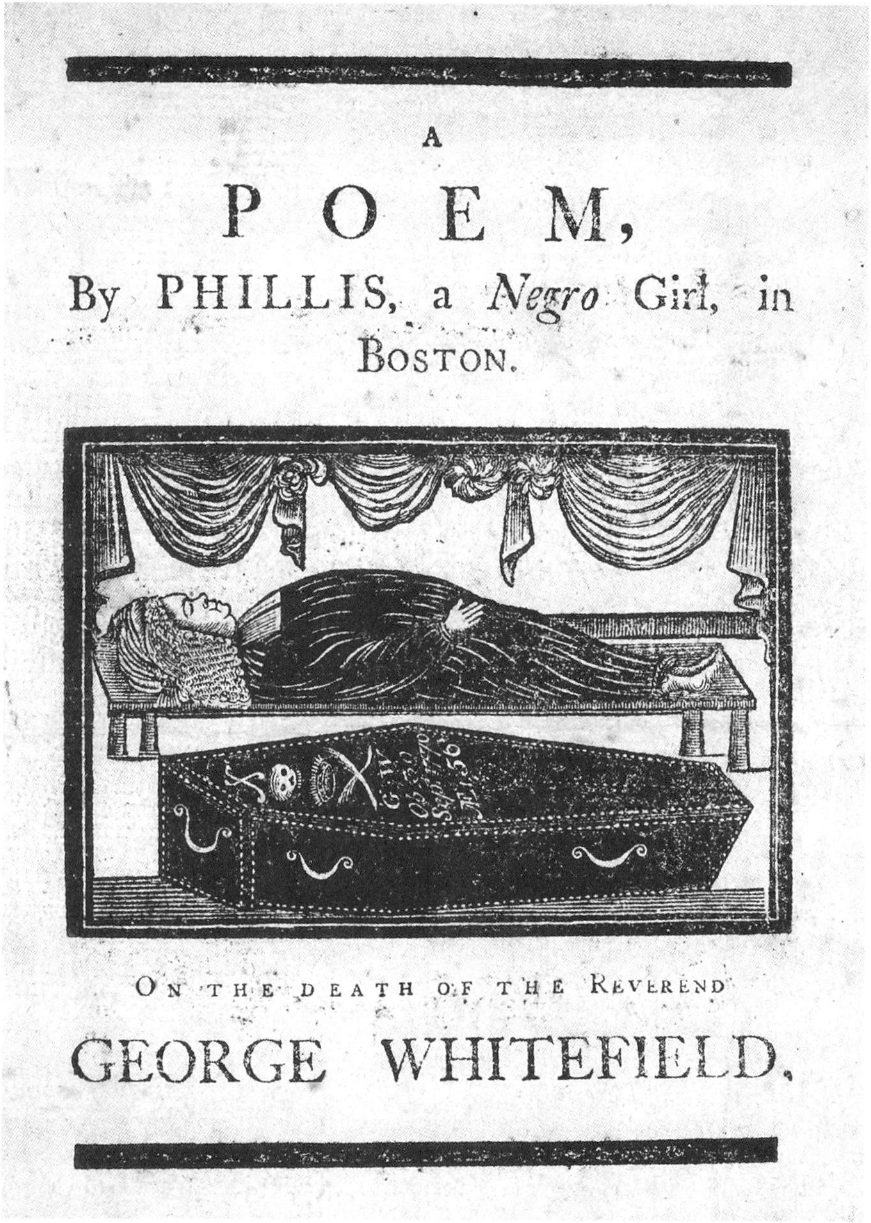

Figure 5.1   Frontispiece. In *Elegiac Poem, On the Death of ... George Whitefield*. Boston: Russell and Boyles, 1770. Yale Collection of American Literature, Beinecke Rare Book and Manuscript Library.

> Perfect in bliss she from her heav'nly home
> Looks down, and smiling beckons you to come
> ("On the Death of a young Lady of Five years of Age"[73])

And:

> Look gracious Spirit, from thine heav'nly bow'r,
> And thy full joys into their bosoms pour;
> The raging tempests of their grief control,
> And spread the dawn of glory through the soul,
> To eye the path the saint departed trod,
> And trace him to the bosom of his God
> ("On the Death of a young Gentleman"[74])

The beloved dead are never quite dead, children are never quite fully sundered from their parents. Isani writes: "The entry into the poem is swift and effective, and the apotheosis may come at the beginning rather than near the climax ... The dialogue of solace between the dead and the living is not common in the poetry of the time."[75] Instead of reading such articulations of incomplete or partial flights in Wheatley's poetry as purely conventional, it is instructive to regard them as evidence pointing to Wheatley's need to maintain the viability of distant links, sundered identifications, transcultural ruptures and transnational connections: a politics of location, not of embodiment per se. In earlier equating her articulation of the "trans-" within the condition of the "trance" in her poetry, I mean to emphasize her distinctly aesthetic project of spatially re-membering things forcibly sundered, of rewriting terror as ecstasy, flight as return, resignation as triumph, and subordination as ordination.[76]

To the parents of "J.C. an infant" she writes:

> Not as a foe, but friend converse with *Death*,
> Since to the port of happiness unknown
> He brought that treasure which you call your own.
> The gift of heav'n intrust to your hand
> Chearful resign at the divine command:
> Not at your bar must sov'reign *Wisdom* stand.[77]

The dead are also never entirely released from longing for reunion with their earthly loved ones, as in several elegies including "On the Death of General Wooster," wherein a petition for slave emancipation is also found bracketed within Wheatley's elegiac mode. Wooster, in dying, says:

> But how, presumptuous shall we hope to find
> Divine acceptance with th'Almighty mind –
> While yet (O deed unegenerous!) they disgrace
> And hold in bondage Afric's blameless race?

> Let virtue reign – And though accord our prayers
> Be victory our's, and generous freedom theirs[78]

Even while being an abolitionist mouthpiece with his last breath, Wooster is not freed from his connection to his wife, Mary Wooster, to whom Wheatley addressed the unpublished poem thus:

> A little moment steals him from thy Sight
> He waits thy coming to the realms of light
> Freed from his labours in the ethereal Skies
> Where in succession endless pleasures rise![79]

Again, in "To a Lady on the Death of Three Relations," while the Lady's brother is found to be "From bondage freed," yet "Lost in our woe for thee, blest shade, we mourn."[80] This poem exhibits a struggle between the exultation of the heaven-bound dead, and the pathos of familial loss. The religious passion of the spirit in flight from the chains of the earth is palpable enough, yet who can discount the grief of those bereaved by this "flight"? Once again, flight stands in for a problem complicating Wheatley's position vis-à-vis slavery and transnationality: it can be both a release from sublunary chains and a failed attempt to disavow those left behind.

In the secular eulogy "On IMAGINATION," the living Wheatley herself synecdochically ascends skyward in the first part of the poem:

> Now here, now there, the roving *Fancy* flies,
> Till some lov'd object strikes her wand'ring eyes,
> Whose silken fetters all the senses bind,
> And soft captivity involves the mind.[81]

Wheatley's paean approaches her funeral elegies in tempo and momentum in such lines as,

> Imagination! who can sing thy force?
> Or who describe the swiftness of thy course?
> …
> We on thy pinions can surpass the wind,
> And leave the rolling universe behind:
> From star to star the mental optics rove,
> Measure the skies, and range the realms above.
> There in one view we grasp the mighty whole,
> Or with new worlds amaze th'unbounded soul.[82]

Yet these rapturous flights on imagination's wings are brought dolorously down by the speaker's consciousness of her limitations:

> But I reluctant leave the pleasing views,
> Which *Fancy* dresses to delight the *Muse*;

> *Winter* austere forbids me to aspire,
> And northern tempests damp the rising fire;
>   They chill the tides of *Fancy's* flowing sea,
> Cease then, my song, cease the unequal lay[83]

While seeming to acknowledge the challenges of authorship for herself, Wheatley outwitted colonial patriarchy and hegemony to position herself into a situational selfhood beyond embodied commodification. Perhaps some of her strategic transnationalism was serendipitous or coincidental; indeed, though proposals for publishing her *Poems* by subscription appeared repeatedly in the *Boston Censor* with assurances that irreproachable guardians of Tradition had reviewed and authenticated not merely the work but Wheatley's authorial identity itself, her volume had no takers in America; that had to wait her transatlantic migration and her near-adoption of an Afro-British rather than Afro-American identity.[84]

In this migration, Wheatley herself came deliriously closer to achieving the conditions of "flight," that is, freedom, by exploiting the potential for liberation generated by the Somerset case (1772), but Wheatley's transnational imagination rejected this option and opted to reverse her migratory course back to American shores where, with the influence of her British connections, she achieved a freedom that was obviously a greater "moral" conquest.[85] This complex history of her manumission mirrors, in essence, her elegiac poems' retooling of "flight" as a metonym for freedom that remains also cathected to its opposite, the various constraints on "liberation" unequally experienced by her subjects and Wheatley. It would not do to ignore that Wheatley's poetry appeared just previous to the Revolution, that momentous period prior to actual Abolition when slavery became charged with highly volatile meanings of oppression by Britain, hence doubly disgraceful.[86] Of course, this cognition of Americans of their own "enslaved" condition had highly ambiguous results – not necessarily happy for African slaves – as had the same recognition by Britons in preceding centuries and up to that point (see Chapter 3). But that the slavery question – the "odious model in the relation of master to slave"[87] – had a bifurcated destiny in national identity-construction just around the time of Wheatley's eminence is without question.[88]

Seizing this moment was part of the strategic transnationalism, of the extra-ordinarily complex production of Phillis Wheatley, Poet, that demonstrates her rewriting of those devices that attempt to frame and corporealize her within her published volume. Thus it has been shown that the biographical account supposedly by John Wheatley, Phillis' master, that forms the prefatory matter of the original London edition of her *Poems*, is actually in Wheatley's handwriting.[89] Thomas Wooldridge wrote to the Earl of Dartmouth of "a very Extraordinary female Slave," that he had visited her and once again given her the obligatory test of authorial ability, and that "I send you an account signed by her master of her Importation, Education &c they are all in her own hand."[90] Thus, Wheatley was able to deploy, so to speak, transatlantic power nexuses to authorize herself, to break the chains of ownership by a particular individual, however benevolent, and to write the terms of her own representation.[91]

Once again, the politics of embodiment was replaced by that of location or even dislocation. Vincent Carretta has drawn attention to her skilful crafting in "To the Right Honourable WILLIAM, Earl of Dartmouth" (written 1772) of the interwoven petitions for American and African freedom that had an explicit English audience and an implicit American one.[92] It has not been sufficiently discussed that her addressees and patrons comprised both General Washington (the leader of the revolutionary army), as well as the Earl of Dartmouth (the organizer of the British counterinsurgency). Betsy Erkkila writes that "the signatures of the royalist Governor Thomas Hutchinson and the leader of Boston resistance John Hancock were joined for a brief moment over the body of her *Poems*,"[93] but I would argue that Wheatley maneuvered her patronage precisely so as to make her writing and body a self-theorizing, hence non-commodified one that nevertheless positioned itself in geographies of oppression and resistance.

Moreover, though compelled to leave England physically when on the very threshold of recognition as author of a remarkable and much acclaimed volume of poetry, Wheatley nevertheless maneuvered her connections there into virtual guarantees of artistic as well as personal freedom. Though as Susanna Wheatley's (pet) slave she had no choice but to return to New England from London when Susanna Wheatley fell dangerously sick in July 1773,[94] she did establish friendships in England that would at least indirectly aid her attainment of freedom.[95] Thus, she sent to Israel Mauduit in England the document of her manumission as a transatlantic trail of evidence that her mistress had indeed freed her.[96]

Contemporaries evinced consciousness of her racial and national liminality, both a choice and a necessity. In the *Massachusetts Gazette* of 1 March 1773, p. 1, "L." described Wheatley as an "*African* (so let me call her, for so in fact she is)."[97] Notably, Wheatley's ethnicity and "nationality" are foregrounded in this letter, though subsumed later on within the rubric of her identity as a slave to her "master." Again, in a funeral elegy upon Wheatley's death in 1784, the anonymous poet "Horatio" writes "colorblind" in the *Boston Magazine* (December 1784, pp. 619–20), citing her status both as an elegiac poet who thereby served her "community" and as young, gifted, and black:

> And shall the honour, which she oft apply'd,
> To other's reliques, be to hers deny'd?
> …
> What tho' her outward form did ne'er disclose
> The lily's white, or blushes of the rose;
> Shall sensibility regard the skin,
> If all be calm, serene, and pure within?
> But ah! Can beauty, or can genius save?
> Genius and beauty moulder in the grave.
> …
> Such the sad ruins of the human race,
> That reptiles riot on the fairest face![98]

Wheatley's own elegiac mode, while fairly conventional in the context of the New England elegy,[99] also gave impetus to this poet Horatio's vision of her afterlife, which duplicates what Wheatley envisioned for others:

> Tho' now the body mixes with the clay;
> The soul wings upward to immortal day;
> Free'd from a world of wo [sic], and scenes of cares,
> A lyre of gold she tunes, a crown of glory wears.

> Seated with angels in that blissful place,
> Where she now joins in her Creator's praise,
> Where harmony with louder notes is swell'd,
> Where her soft numbers only are excell'd.[100]

In instating her in the ethereal context wherein Wheatley imagined others of pure soul, "Horatio" invariably is brought to compare a dark outside with a luminous inside, and thereby perhaps unconsciously model Wheatley's own cocooning act for her many elegy subjects who could with difficulty be completely detached from their earthly moulds, their gross physical bodies. Wheatley, Horatio suggests, has had in life to confront and control the paradox that most others experience in death, the challenge of reconciling being with biology, ontology with physiology, teleology with scatology.[101] Thus, it could be said from the poem's concluding lines, particularly, that Wheatley is experiencing a revival and resurrection of herself and her style, not unlike the one which she had perpetuated and popularized, but with her own difference as a transformative internal condition of the trope.

"Horatio's" lines of course must be contrasted with the notorious Jeffersonian view of black biology versus being:

> The first difference which strikes us is that of color ... And is this difference of no importance? Is it not the foundation of a greater or less share of beauty in the two races? Are not the fine mixtures of red and white, the expressions of every passion by greater or less suffusions of color in the one, preferable to that eternal monotony, which reigns in the countenance, that immovable veil of black which covers the emotions of the other race? Add to these, flowing hair, a more elegant symmetry of form, their own judgment in favor of the whites, declared by their preference of them, as uniformly as is the preference of the Oran-ootan for the black woman over those of his own species ... Besides those of color, figure, and hair, there are other physical distinctions proving a difference of race. They have less hair on the face and body. They secrete less by the kidneys, and more by the glands of the skin, which gives them a very strong and disagreeable odor.[102]

Jefferson's racial science leads to a racial biology that is an aesthetic blackhole; he can not or will not transact the inside-outside "Horatio" revels in deconstructing. Hence, he cannot but proceed from an aesthetic inaccessibility to an intellectual disability: "in memory they are equal to the whites; in reason much inferior, as I think one could scarcely be found capable of tracing and comprehending the investigations of Euclid;

and that in imagination they are dull. Tasteless and anomalous … never yet could I find that a black had uttered a thought above the level of plain narration …."[103] Jefferson is providing the grounds for Wheatley to respond in her own voice, and she indeed dismantles the Jeffersonian racial conundrum leading to aesthetic revulsion by uncovering again and again its roots in material inequities of racialization and dominance, thus reversing foundational assumptions about personhood and cultural ability, base and superstructure. The tension that informs her dialectic of flight and entrapment or entombment and that eventually transforms that dialectic into mutually constitutive aspects of self-construction, is unavailable and unimaginable for Jefferson, who can only perceive the "immovable veil of black" as a static, near-lifeless surface.[104]

Carretta's brief discussion of Wheatley's well-known frontispiece is also significant in this regard. He writes of her frontispiece portrait that while it was probably painted by a fellow African artist, Scipio Moorhead, it performs a representational chiaroscuro highlighting now Wheatley's intellectuality, now her blackness, now her gentility, and again her intellectuality (see Figure 5.2). Yet, he writes, the whole play of her many identities is contained within the framework of her status as property of John Wheatley of Boston, as the framing words of the frontispiece declare.[105] While Carretta's conclusion is worthy of consideration – the artistic pretensions of the frontispiece are indeed modest, as was Wheatley's domestic status – this conclusion cannot be transferred to Wheatley's ability to transact a theory of virtualized transnational identity, a political manifesto of her freedom through art. Both her art and her self-representation strain against the "frame" within which she was sought to be contained.[106]

This self-representation, akin to what I have earlier called a political manifesto, anticipates in some degree future black identity discourses. Hortense Spillers has made the radical argument that to see African-American identity as essentially matrilinear, to contribute to the mythos of the matriarchal black family and the indestructible and omnipotent black mother/woman, is to refuse to see the account of black female "flesh" with its history of manglings and violations in favor of seeing the "body" of the black woman that produces and reproduces both a black labor force and a teleological narrative for white masters:

> I would make a distinction … between 'body' and 'flesh' and impose that distinction as the central one between captive and liberated subject-positions. In that sense, before the 'body' there is the 'flesh,' that zero degree of social conceptualization that does not escape concealment under the brush of discourse, or the reflexes of iconography. Even though the European hegemonies stole bodies – some of them female – out of West African communities in concert with the African 'middlemen,' we regard this human and social irreparability as high crimes against the flesh, as the person of African females and African males registered the wounding … A female body strung from a tree limb, or bleeding from the breast … This materialized scene of unprotected female flesh – of female flesh 'ungendered' – offers a praxis and a theory, a text for living and for dying.[107]

Published according to Act of Parliament, Sept.ᵣ 1, 1773 by Arch.ᵈ Bell, Bookseller N.º 8 near the Saracens Head Aldgate.

Figure 5.2   Frontispiece portrait of Phillis Wheatley. In *Poems on various subjects, religious and moral. By Phillis Wheatley, negro servant to Mr. John Wheatley, of Boston, in New England.* London, 1773. Courtesy, American Antiquarian Society.

Houston Baker calls this theoretical privileging of the flesh over the body an attempt to return to theory and bypass history: theory serves the woman herself, history serves white folks.[108] Gay Gibson Cima has argued of nineteenth-century American print culture that "While white women cultural critics have often entered political discourse and the theatrical and literary marketplace by choosing strategic anonymity and aligning themselves with what Lauren Berlant calls the 'abstract person' of the (implicitly white male) bodiless citizen, black women have traditionally not been allowed to claim that abstracted body on or for their own."[109]

Thus, when she was "framed" by powerful white male approval of her poetry, Wheatley was framed in terms of her embodied race, her "body."[110] From such scenes of critical rereading of the black woman slave's corpus as flesh and not body, theory and not history, one can argue that Wheatley herself was interested in theorizing her experience, not historicizing her body;[111] in one sense, avoidance of this "marking" of this "problematic and enforced positionality for black women critics"[112] is what her famous autobiographical reticence might amount to. In terms of Spillers' and Spivak's arguments examined here and in Chapter 1, the strategic essentiality of unmemorializd black female flesh, a repressed substance that jump-starts theory, is exemplified in Wheatley's construction of transnationalism as a strategic arena for politicizing the aesthetic. The politicization of the aesthetic and the theorizing of flesh are, in a sense, mirror activities: inverted duplicates.

She was not, for instance, interested in reproducing the slave universe or experience narrated by Robert Southey's protagonist in his poem "The Sailor Who Had Served in the Slave Trade":

> I sail'd on board a Guinea-man
> And to the slave-coast went;
> …
> But some were sulky of the slaves
> …
> One woman sulkier than the rest
> Would still refuse her food,–
> O Jesus God! I hear her cries–
> I see her in her blood!
> …
> She twisted from the blows – her blood
> Her mangled flesh I see –
> And still the Captain would not spare–
> Oh he was worse than me!
> …
> I did not close my eyes all night,
> Thinking what I had done;
> …
> They flung her overboard; – poor wretch
> She rested from her pain,–
> But when – o Christ! o blessed God!
> Shall I have rest again![113]

In this account of the war waged upon the African woman's raw flesh, she never has the chance to theorize her pain, her experience; instantly it becomes the property of the white sailor, whose history her body becomes. The slave-trading record erased the "fleshed" experiences of African women and children. The only possible expression allowed that scene of the unspeakable might have been that of embodiment, domestication, and hyper-feminization in the maternal or the maternal surrogate, as Spillers has argued.[114] Even more so, that scene of the "flesh" would be totally subsumed in an exploration of white angst. This dynamic emerges in the white sailor's traumatized imaginary, which immediately appropriates torn slave flesh in the whitewashed history of the body in pain, producing in its turn as surplus value the white art of the soul in guilt-laden and anguished freedom.[115]

Probably to avoid this fate, Wheatley pre-empts the nudging towards self-disclosure and preserves a tight-lipped silence broken only by formal manipulation which gives her the theoretical edge and does not allow control over the "body" of her experience, showing her "less interested in joining the ranks of gendered femaleness than gaining the *insurgent* ground as female social subject."[116] Helen Burke, who writes of the "literary subject, or the subject in discourse, as a fiction that makes it difficult to see the position of the historical subject ..."[117] is also describing something of Wheatley's strategic refusal of embodiment. Wheatley could not – I would insist would not – come forth as the historical black subject, and her literary liminality, her differentiated relation to whiteness, allowed her more unfettered possibilities.

As Nott has commented, "in Wheatley's portrait the inherent power of her public poetic enterprise becomes evident ... this portrait constitutes the graphic representation of Wheatley's public presence and the power it produces."[118] Operating as property and implicitly as commodity, Wheatley nevertheless found strategies in her artistic explorations and connections – what Shields calls "donning a mask"[119] – to foreground her transnationality over her enslavement.[120] Carretta alludes to the political and legal environment in England that Wheatley significantly exploited to strengthen her case for her own freedom: one such factor was the recent Somerset case decision (22 June 1772), which decreed that a slave on British soil could not legally be resold to the colonies. Though this decree did not in fact bring freedom to British slaves as much as it differentiated Britain from the colonies on the question of slave-trading versus slave-holding,[121] it operated very favorably for Wheatley.[122] Carretta asks: "how aware was Wheatley of the contested status of slavery in England ... and how willing was she to take advantage of the opportunity it offered her?" He cites the *Boston Gazette* reporting on Monday 21 September 1772 on the Mansfield decision and concludes that "Mansfield's judgment was the talk of the town and would have been known to Wheatley either in print or by word of mouth."[123] This is highly plausible, and consequently, it made Wheatley's (willing?) return to America at her mistress' request an assertion of her agency even if she could not legally claim the right to be freed and remain on English soil. Interestingly, Wheatley became a poetic celebrity at the very moment of crossing the Atlantic a third and final time: "*Poems*, the first book by an English-speaking black writer, went on sale ... while Wheatley was still at sea."[124] This historical coincidence, I hope, adds some piquancy to my argument about her strategic transnationality. It was in her transatlantic "flights" at the beck and call of others that Wheatley found herself.

Notes

1   Vincent Carretta (ed.), *Phillis Wheatley: Complete Writings* (New York, 2001), pp. xiii–xiv.
2   It is more exclusively the focus of Donna Landry in *The Muses of Resistance*: "*Les voleuses de langue*, the thieves of language, steal but also fly: Wheatley will mount and soar poetically after all, thanks to the indulgence of rich white patrons" (p. 250).
3   Davies, *Black Women*, pp. 8–9.
4   Carretta, *Phillis Wheatley*, p. xiv; .Houston Baker Jr, *The Journey Back: Issues in Black Literature and Criticism* (Chicago, 1980), pp. 12, 19–21.
5   Donna Landry has seen this politicization of the aesthetic as staging "ideological conflict within neoclassical imitation" (*Muses of Resistance*, p. 248). I am indebted to Landry for some of this chapter's ideas about Wheatley's politics of mimicry, but extend Landry's argument beyond the concept of politics as resistance to politics as strategic transnationalism.
6   Davies, *Black Women*, pp. 36–7.
7   Aravamudan, *Tropicopolitans*, p. 236.
8   Gilroy, *Black Atlantic*, p. 48.
9   Davies, *Black Women*, p. 48; see also Betsy Erkkila: "What appears to be repetition is in fact a form of *mimesis* that mimics and mocks in the act of repeating" ("Revolutionary Women," *Tulsa Studies in Women's Literature*, 6/2 [Fall 1987]: 206). Also, Donna Landry repeatedly invokes Wheatley's mimicry and hybridity (*Muses of Resistance*, pp. 243, 248).
10 Baker, *Journey Back*, p. xii.
11 Ibid., p. xiv.
12 Ibid., p. 3.
13 Robert Kendrick, "Snatching a Laurel, Wearing a Mask: Phillis Wheatley's Literary Nationalism and the Problem of Style", *Style*, 27/2 (Summer 1993): 241–2.
14 The concept of a political aesthetic of repetition is to be found in Benjamin, "The Work of Art," as discussed in the introductory chapter here, and I quote again therefrom: "reproduction emancipates the work of art from its parasitical dependence on ritual. To an ever greater degree the work of art reproduced becomes the work of art designed for reproducibility. From a photographic negative, for example, one can make any number of prints; to ask for the 'authentic' print makes no sense. But the instant the criterion of authenticity ceases to be applicable to artistic production, the total function of art is reversed. Instead of being based on ritual, it begins to be based on another practice – politics," in "The Work of Art," p. 736. Jameson's now also famous thesis is that the postcolonial realm produces an aesthetic that is characterized better as a politics ("Third World Literature").
15 Aravamudan, *Tropicopolitans*, p. 14.
16 A highly readable recent account is Henry Louis Gates Jr., *The Trials of Phillis Wheatley* (New York, 2003). William Robinson (*Critical Essays on Phillis Wheatley* [Boston, 1982])

remains the best compiler of a dazzling array of speculations about Wheatley as an original (and African nationalist) genius or a servile mimic of the west, and thus an enigma. In 1974, Angeline Jamison wrote probably one of the most vitriolic attacks on Wheatley's insufficient blackness ("Analysis of Selected Poetry of Philis Wheatley," ibid., pp. 128–35). Terence Collins, who gets some facts of her life wrong such as her non-meeting with the Countess of Huntingdon in England, sees her transnationality as the crux of her ambiguous "slave mentality" ("Phillis Wheatley: The Dark Side of the Poetry," ibid., pp. 147–58); Margaret Burroughs has documented, however, her involvement with British radicals like the Earl of Dartmouth, the Countess of Huntingdon, and of course George Whitefield, who appear to have supported and financed slave insurrections in America ("Do Birds of a Feather Flock Together?," ibid., pp. 136–45). Mukhtar Ali Isani writes: "Wheatley ... remembered the separate identity and different fortunes of her race" (ibid., p. 213). See also Mary McAleer Balkun, "Phillis Wheatley's Construction of Otherness and the Rhetoric of Performed Ideology," *African American Review*, 36/1 (Spring 2002): 123.

[17] Baker, *Journey Back*, p. 9.

[18] The "abandonment" camp has forgotten that the pen is mightier than the sword, of course; Wheatley's poetry was an inspiration to the great abolitionist Thomas Clarkson who quoted her in his 1786 *Essay on the Slavery and Commerce of the Human Species, Particularly the African* (Robinson, *Critical Essays*, pp. 6–7).

[19] Blackburn, *Making of New World Slavery*, p. 211; Paula Bennett, "Phillis Wheatley's Vocation and the Paradox of the 'Afric Muse,'" *PMLA*, 113/1 (1998): 65. However, see Charles W. Akers in Robinson, *Critical Essays*: "Boston newspapers attacking the tyranny of the British ministry also announced slave auctions and advertised for sale scores of skilled and well-behaved slaves to be uprooted and subjected once more to the inhumanity of the market for no fault but 'want of Employ'" (p. 162; see also p. 167). The war of independence naturally exacerbated the contradiction.

[20] Blackburn, *Making of New World Slavery*, p. 266.

[21] Ibid., p. 265.

[22] Wood, *Poetry of Slavery*, pp. xii–xiii.

[23] Sterling Stuckey, *Slave Culture: Nationalist Theory and the Foundations of Black America* (New York, 1987), pp. 73–79; Frank Shuffelton, "On Her Own Footing: Phillis Wheatley in Freedom," in Vincent Carretta and Philip Gould (eds), *Genius in Bondage: Literature of the Early Black Atlantic* (Lexington, 2001), pp. 178–80; Erkkila, "Revolutionary Women," pp. 204–5.

[24] Blackburn, *Making of New World Slavery*, p. 266.

[25] Landry, *The Muses of Resistance*, p. 242.

[26] Robinson, *Critical Essays*, p. 5; see also Landry, *Muses of Resistance*, pp. 243–4.

[27] Carretta, *Phillis Wheatley*, p. xvi. Archibald Bell published the volume with an attestation and legitimation by a panel of Boston's hierarchy – including the governor Thomas Hutchinson – of Wheatley's poetic abilities and her authorship. This attestation and her master's testimony of her arrival on the American and literary scenes were reproduced in the numerous subsequent transatlantic editions of this work and have drawn much critical and cultural fury and passion.

[28] Ibid., p. xvi; Helen Burke, "The Rhetoric and Politics of Marginality: The Subject of Phillis Wheatley," *Tulsa Studies in Women's Literature*, 10/1 (Spring 1991): 34. Baker sees this Boston jury as an entirely monolithic power structure: "there was, for all too long, no tangible, literate, accessible black collectivity to answer the black writer's query,

Is there anybody there? There were only whites intent on cultural hegemony. There was only what has come to be called the white literary critical establishment engaged in a discourse built on the prevailing, publicly articulated, white notions of black America. Questions of artistic form, judgment, and effect all seemed to have been answered by a white 'other' when Wheatley compiled her *Poems on Various Subjects, Religious and Moral ....*" (*Journey Back*, pp. 140–41). Of course, Wheatley was hardly the only woman rewriting Tradition at this time; as Donna Landry long ago noted, "in order to engage in public self-representation, cultural intervention, social criticism, or the 'literary,' women of the lower classes in this period had to learn to write like the privileged masters of high-literary discourse" (Landry, *Muses of Resistance*, p. 12). However, she was black and working-class, and the two together made a difference of transnational proportions.

29 Gilroy, *Black Atlantic*, p. 19.

30 On the preservation and perseverance of "African" traditions in African-American cultural expressions, see Stuckey, *Slave Culture*, and Rosemary Fithian Guruswamy, "'Thou Has the Holy Word': Jupiter Hammon's 'regards' to Phillis Wheatley," in Vincent Carretta and Philip Gould (eds), *Genius in Bondage*, pp. 190–98.

31 Walt Nott, "From 'Uncultivated Barbarian' to 'Poetical Genius': The Public Presence of Phillis Wheatley," *MELUS: The Journal of the Society for the Study of the Multi-Ethnic Literature of the United States*, 18/3 (Fall 1993): 21–2; see also Burke's discussion of Wheatley as the "connected critic" (Burke, "Rhetoric and Politics," p. 37).

32 Davies, *Black Women*, p. 153.

33 See Hilene Flanzbaum, "Unprecedented Liberties: Re-reading Phillis Wheatley," *MELUS: The Journal of the Society for the Study of the Multi-Ethnic Literature of the United States*, 18/3 (Fall 1993): 72; Robinson, *Critical Essays*, pp. 2, 8–9.

34 Anne Applegate, "Phillis Wheatley: Her Critics and Her Contribution," *Negro American Literature Forum*, 9 (1975), p. 124.

35 The *Critical Review* called her just that, a "literary phaenomenon [sic]" because "The Negros [sic] of Africa are generally treated as a dull, ignorant, and ignoble race of men, fit only to be slaves, and incapable of any considerable attainments in the liberal arts and sciences. A poet or a poetess among them, of any tolerable genius, would be a prodigy in literature" (September 1773, quoted in Isani, "The British Reception of Wheatley's Poems on Various Subjects," *Journal of Negro History*, 66/2 [Summer 1981]: 145). As Isani has also suggested, it may have been Richard Gough, the antiquary, who gave Wheatley's poetry glowing reviews in the *Scots Magazine* (September 1773) and the *Gentlemen's Magazine* (September 1773); see ibid., pp. 146, 148, and 149, n. 5. Hilene Flanzbaum writes that her book "served to signify more than itself" ("Unprecedented Liberties," p. 71). Flanzbaum's either unconscious or deliberate choice of words also points to Wheatley's doubled identity.

36 Arthur P. Davis seems to have been the first twentieth-century critic to emphasize a subjective element in Wheatley; see Davis, "The Personal Elements in the Poetry of Phillis Wheatley," *Phylon: The Atlanta University Review of Race and Culture*, 12/2 (2nd Quarter, 1953): 191–8, reprinted in Robinson, *Critical Essays*, pp. 93–101. See also R. Lynn Matson, "Phillis Wheatley – Soul Sister?" (ibid., pp. 113–22); Merle A. Richmond, "On 'The barter of her soul'," (ibid., pp. 123–7).

37 Flanzbaum, "Unprecedented Liberties," p. 71.

38 Ibid., p. 75.

39 Carretta, *Phillis Wheatley*, pp. xvii–xviii.

40   Shields, "Phillis Wheatley's Subversive Pastoral," *Eighteenth-Century Studies*, 27/4
      (Summer 1994): 632. A thorough discussion of Wheatley's neoclassical achievement is
      also to be found in Albertha Sistrunk's "The Influence of Alexander Pope on the Writing
      Style of Phillis Wheatley" (in Robinson, *Critical Essays*, pp. 175–88). However, see
      also Abraham Cowper's sentimental poem *Charity* and its conclusion that resembles
      Wheatley's lines in "On Being Brought from AFRICA to AMERICA"; Cowper
      ventriloquizes the slave:

> I was bondsman on my native plain,
> Sin forg'd and ignorance made fast the chain;
> Thy lips have shed instruction as the dew,
> Taught me what path to shun, and what pursue;
> Farewell my former joys! I sigh no more
> For Africa's once lov'd, benighted shore,
> Serving a benefactor I am free,
> At my best home if not exiled from thee (Wood, *Poetry of Slavery*, p. 86).

      After Wordsworth, Cowper was the poet most reprinted by American abolitionists (ibid.,
      p. 83).
41   Aravamudan, *Tropicopolitans*, p. 14.
42   Kendrick, "Snatching a Laurel," p. 224. Kendrick lists the following as "possible African
      aspects of her style": "the use of coincidental as opposed to subordinate rhyme, the
      appropriation of voices by the poet as modes of signification, the use of the lyric and the
      panegyric, and the positioning of the poet-signifier as mime, as manifested by the Signifying
      Monkey and by the pan-African figure of Esu-Elegbara" (ibid.).
43   Carretta, *Phillis Wheatley*, p. xxxiii.
44   Ibid., p. 159; Bennett, "Phillis Wheatley's Vocation," p. 69.
45   In his 1953 essay given especially to exploring Wheatley's subjective disclosures in
      poetry, Arthur P. Davis explains this reluctance to self-identify as "African" as due to
      Wheatley's Christian sensibility and belief (Davis, reprinted in Robinson, *Critical Essays*,
      p. 97), while also seeing her religiosity itself as a boundary and not core of her identity
      (ibid., p. 100). Sistrunk explains the same "dispassion" as the outcome of "the fact that
      depersonalization and objectivity were the overriding concerns during the eighteenth
      century" (Robinson, *Critical Essays*, p. 186). Her response to the mission scheme was
      not a necessarily common response for blacks in her time; in 1773, Massachusetts blacks
      were willing to settle on the coast of Africa because they saw nothing about to change
      in American life for them (Baker, *Journey Back*, p. 122). For theorizing of "home" for
      black diasporic women, see Davies, *Black Women*, pp. 49–51, 113. Carmen Birkle writes,
      "She was consciously African-American" ("Border Crossing and Identity Creation in
      Phillis Wheatley's Poetry," in Udo J. Hebel (ed.), *The Construction and Contestation of
      American Cultures and Identities in the Early National Period* [Heidleberg, 1999], p. 61).
      Her undecidability remains a conundrum for many critics, as perhaps she had intended?
46   Matson, in Robinson, *Critical Essays*, pp. 117–18; See also Isani, "Phillis Wheatley and
      the Elegiac Mode" (ibid., pp. 208–14). Compellingly similar are George Moses Horton's
      aspirations to "soar" as a "gifted Negro" almost one hundred years later: "Then I forbid
      that my productions should ever fall to the ground but rather soar as an eagle above the
      towering mountains and thus return as a triumphant spirit to the bosom of its God who
      gave it birth though now confined in these loathsome fetters" (John W. Blassingame [ed.],

Slave Testimony: Two Centuries of Letters, Speeches, Interviews, and Autobiographies [Baton Rouge, 1977], p. 59).

47 For a discussion of the trope of flight, return and home, see Davies, *Black Women*, p. 129, and her discussions of the works of Toni Morrison, Zora Neale Hurston, Barbara Smith, and June Jordan, pp. 148–50. See also Bennett: "Merging the material and the spiritual, she transforms death into a multivalent trope for gaining access to everything that matters in life as well as death ..." ("Phillis Wheatley's Vocation," p. 69).

48 Carretta, *Phillis Wheatley*, p. 11.

49 Kendrick argues that in the elegy on Whitefield (1770), Wheatley in fact performs also a chiasmic role-substitution with Whitefield as a saint and as a stylist ("Snatching a Laurel," p. 237).

50 Carretta, *Phillis Wheatley*, pp. 11–12.

51 See Davis, in Robinson, *Critical Essays*, pp. 94–5, for emphasis on this point.

52 See Shuffelton, "On Her Own Footing," p. 177.

53 Carretta, *Phillis Wheatley*, p. 106.

54 Erkkila, "Revolutionary Women," p. 208.

55 I do not focus especially on the quality of Wheatley's piety, though this has certainly preoccupied many other critics of her work. For an articulation of the "terror" versus "ecstasy" that I have just contrasted, thought, one might see Baker; he certainly acknowledges the power of religion in reconciling "the slave, staring into the heart of whiteness around him ...." (Baker, *Journey Back*, p. 31). It might also be noted that Blackstone's commentary on the status of slavery in England – the soil where Wheatley breathed the inspiration for freedom according to Carretta and others – retained a sense of the "Christian" slave's obligation to serve his or her master as an indentured servant would: the freedom of religious belief became a further necessary obligation of servitude according to this peculiar legal logic (Carretta, "Phillis Wheatley, the Mansfield Decision of 1772, and the Choice of Identity," in Klaus H. Schmidt and Fritz Fleischmann (eds), *Early America Re-explored: New Readings in Colonial, Early National, and Antebellum Culture* [New York, 2000], p. 204).

56 Carretta, *Phillis Wheatley*, p. 13.

57 Shields, "Phillis Wheatley and the Sublime" (in Robinson, *Critical Essays*, pp. 189–209).

58 Ibid., p. 197.

59 Ibid., p. 201.

60 Kendrick, "Snatching a Laurel," p. 243.

61 Shields, in Robinson, *Critical Essays*, pp. 201–2.

62 For this see also Vincent Carretta and Philip Gould (eds), *Genius in Bondage: Literature of the Early Black Atlantic* (Lexington, 2001), pp. 3–4. Their discussion of "creative engagement" between black and white languages in the eighteenth century particularly bears on this chapter's subject.

63 Carretta, *Phillis Wheatley*, p. 13.

64 Ibid., pp. 15–16.

65 Ibid., p. 13.

66 Ibid., p. 15.

67 Scholars have argued that such an ambiguous or loose linkage of race and slavery would have obtained in an earlier period than Wheatley's in America: "In Jefferson's day, ideas of both race and slavery were still in the process of being transformed from rather fluid and unrelated notions to their modern status as frequently conflated categories" (Alexander O.

Boulton, "The American Paradox: Jeffersonian Equality and Racial Science," *American Quarterly*, 47/3 [September 1995]: 468–9). Carretta and Gould confirm this (*Genius in Bondage*, p. 5).

68	Carretta, *Phillis Wheatley*, p. 16.

69	Ibid.

70	Robinson, *Critical Essays*, p. 18; Robinson writes, "Variously worded, this advertisement was widely reprinted in Boston, New York, and Philadelphia newspapers through October, 1770" (p. 18, n. 5).

71	Isani in Robinson, *Critical Essays*, p. 209. In the same collection (pp. 215–30), H.L. Gates Jr. writes: "Wheatley's elegies are threnodic, after the fashion of the 'Renaissance Elegy,' in that they are meant 'to praise the subject, to lament the death, and to comfort the bereaved.' Yet, they are 'Medieval' rather than 'Elizabethan' insofar as they prefer a sublime resignation to an unrestrained death-force, and seem to avoid the protest against it" ("Phillis Wheatley and the Nature of the Negro," in Robinson, p. 228).

72	Carretta explains that before the American Revolution, all African-Americans were also Afro-Britons, and many chose to preserve that identity even afterwards (Carretta, "Phillis Wheatley," p. 201). I have adopted this rationale.

73	Carretta , *Phillis Wheatley*, p. 16.

74	Ibid., p. 18.

75	In Robinson, *Critical Essays*, pp. 210–11.

76	The chiasmic figure surrounding death, flight, and rapture/rupture is so pervasive in her funeral elegies that textual quotations of such could pile up to a rather towering flight of exegesis, hence I shall only make brief reference here to the titles of other elegiac poems with the motif of flight dominating the experience of transfiguration. These are "To a Lady on the Death of her Husband" (Carretta, *Phillis Wheatley*, pp. 18–19); "Thoughts on the WORKS of PROVIDENCE" (ibid., pp. 26–9); "To a Clergyman on the Death of his Lady," (ibid., pp. 30–31); "A Funeral POEM on the Death of C.E. an Infant of Twelve Months" (ibid., pp. 37–9); "On the Death of J.C. an Infant" (pp. 49–50); "To Mr. And Mrs. –, on the Death of their Infant Son, by Phillis Wheatly [sic]" (ibid., pp. 94–6); "A Poem on the Death of Charles Eliot, Aged 12 Months," variants 1 and 2 (ibid., pp. 125–7); and "*To the Hon'ble* Thomas Hubbard, *Esq; On the Death of Mrs.* Thankfull Leonard" (ibid., pp. 131–2).

77	Carretta, *Phillis Wheatley*, p. 50.

78	Ibid., p. 93.

79	Ibid.

80	Ibid., p. 30.

81	Ibid., p. 36.

82	Ibid.

83	Ibid., p. 37.

84	The proposals for printing the poems by subscription were published in the *Boston Censor* on 29 February, 14 March and 11 April 1772 (Robinson, *Critical Essays*, p. 19). The proposal contained the following cajoling language: "The Poems having been seen and read by the best judges, who think them well worthy of the Publick View; and upon critical examination, they find that the declared author was capable of writing them" (ibid.). Also see ibid., p. 24 for the language of the 1773 "Proposals for printing *in London* by Subscription, a volume of Poems, Dedicated by permission to the Right Hon. The Countess of Huntingdon Written [sic] by Phillis, a Negro Servant to Mr. Wheatley, of Boston in

New England" which were printed in the *Boston Post Boy*, 16, 19 and 22 April 1773, and in the *Boston Weekly Newsletter*, 16 April 1773.

85   See Carretta, "Phillis Wheatley," p. 219. Indeed, a part of her decision to return to America may have included her canny recognition that the British abolition movement and the Somerset decision did not, in fact, give slaves freedom on British soil (ibid., 213). Massachusetts abolished slavery in 1783, though Wheatley probably could not have imagined, let alone anticipated, that historical moment. Scholars have noted that the British campaign was, until 1807 at least, mainly directed against the slave trade and not against circumatlantic slavery per se (see Shuffelton, "On Her Own Footing," p. 180; Wood, *Poetry of Slavery*, p. xvii; Kerr, *Reflections*, p. 13 [a pro-trade argument]). However, Wood also reminds us that it was in North America and not in Britain that anti-abolition forces were most stormy and violent (Wood, *Poetry of Slavery*, pp. xxviii–xxix).

86   Boulton, "American Paradox," p. 475. As Boulton writes: "It was out of the conflict of the American Revolution that a national language was created in which slavery and freedom were eternally at war … The more Americans relied on a philosophy of freedom as a doctrine of rights for each individual to better his or her situation, the more apt they were to use the conception of natural differences to explain the persistent causes of inequality" (ibid., p. 476). See also Erkkila, "Revolutionary Women," p. 191.

87   Boulton, "American Paradox," p. 475.

88   Shuffelton writes: "In a shifting and unstable world Wheatley positioned herself aesthetically in terms of the Atlantic civilization of the old empire, patriotically within the context of an emergent national culture, and politically in the possibility of a new community of free people of color in New England" (Shuffelton, "On Her Own Footing," pp. 176, 185–6); however, see also ibid., p. 182 for the limitations her self-positioning suffered because of the Revolution).

89   Robinson writes of this account dated Boston, New England 12 October 1772 and bearing Nathaniel Wheatley's signature that it was written in Wheatley's hand. He notes that "The sketch of 112 words was expanded into 152 words and bore the name of John Wheatley, Nathaniel's father, and the date of '*Boston, Nov. 14*, 1772,' and was part of the prefatory matter to one of the original London editions of Wheatley's *Poems*; it also prefaced several American reprintings of the *Poems*" (Robinson, *Critical Essays*, p. 21).

90   Ibid., pp. 20–21.

91   Vincent Carretta writes, "paradoxically the Atlantic slave trade, which through death and dislocation stripped many millions of people and their descendants of their natal identities as Africans, offered at least a very few of those people opportunities to choose alternative public selves other than or in addition to that of slave" (Carretta, "Phillis Wheatley," p. 201).

92   Ibid., pp. 211–12.

93   Erkkila, "Revolutionary Women," p. 202.

94   Carretta, *Phillis Wheatley*, p. xvii.

95   The *Monthly Review* stated: "The people of Boston boast themselves chiefly on their principles of liberty. One such act as the purchase of her freedom, would, in our opinion, have done them more honour than hanging a thousand trees with ribbons and emblems" (reproduced in Carretta, *Phillis Wheatley*, p. xxii; see also ibid., p. xxiii; Isani, "British Reception," p. 145).

96   See letter to David Worcester, Boston 18 October 1773, in Carretta, *Phillis Wheatley*, pp. 146–7.

97   Robinson, *Critical Essays*, p. 22.

98   Ibid., pp. 39–40.

99   See Vernon Loggins, *The Negro Author: His Development in America to 1900* (New York, 1931), pp. 22–9, reprinted in Robinson, *Critical Essays*, pp. 88, 92.

100 Ibid., p. 40.

101 Baker writes of the slave: "His [sic] being had to erupt from nothingness" (*Journey Back*, p. 31). See Shields, who emphasizes her neoclassicism and contends that she reproduces topoi of Africa in the trope of "pastoral" ("Phillis Wheatley's Subversive Pastoral," p. 644) and generally deploys classicism in the invocation of freedom (ibid., p. 645).

102 *The Writings of Thomas Jefferson*, ed. Albert E. Bergh (20 vols, Washington, DC, 1903), vol. II, pp. 192–6, reprinted in Robinson, *Critical Essays*, p. 42. See also Boulton, "American Paradox," pp. 472–5.

103 Robinson, *Critical Essays*, p. 42; however, William Snelling in the nineteenth century would not even give Wheatley credit for her memory: "It has been seen that she could remember but one solitary fact, connected with her life, previous to her seventh year. The memory of other children reaches much further back. When she composed, she could not retain her own compositions in her mind, and was obliged either to lose it or commit it instantly to paper" (Robinson, ibid., p. 64). See also "Anonymous" in *Knickerbocker or New York Monthly Magazine*, August 1834; "Anonymous" in *Memoir and Poems By Phillis Wheatley* (Boston, 1834), pp. 7–12, both in Robinson, *Critical Essays*, pp. 66, 74.

104 A variant, but I would argue only a minor variation, of Jefferson's aesthetic huff over the veil of blackness is to be found in nineteenth- and twentieth-century criticism's repeated appeals to remove that autobiographical veil so that her white interlocutors – romantic and conservative alike – might see Wheatley the slave woman better (see Robinson, *Critical Essays*, pp. 79, 80, 87, 89, 91).

105 Carretta, *Phillis Wheatley*, pp. xviii–xix. Contrast this with Shields' view that "Wheatley sits non-humbly and aggressively before a writing desk, on which one sees paper with writing on it, holding a pen and striking a contemplative pose, obviously promising still more writing to come" (Shields, "Phillis Wheatley's Subversive Pastoral," p. 634). Also see Baker, *Journey Back*, pp. 6–7; Erkkila, "Revolutionary Women," p. 202.

106 Cima has described Wheatley's performances of her poetry in white drawing rooms, and her "authentication" as poet by privileged white men as attempts at embodied framing ("Black and Unmarked: Phillis Wheatley, Mercy Otis Warren, and the Limits of Strategic Anonymity," *Theatre Journal*, 52/4 [December 2000]: 468, 475, 479.

107 Spillers, "Mama's Baby," pp. 67–8.

108 Baker, *Workings of the Spirit: The Poetics of Afro-American Women's Writing* (Chicago, 1991), pp. 13–19, 21, 37. See also Valerie Smith, "Black Feminist Theory and the Representation of the 'Other'", in Cheryl A. Wall (ed.), *Changing Our Own Words: Essays on Criticism, Theory and Writing by Black Women* (New Brunswick, 1991); and Cima, "Black and Unmarked," pp. 468, 470. See a rather vitriolic refutation of the "theorizing" claims for black writers by Baker and Spillers in Sandhu, Sukhdev and David Dabydeen (eds), *Slavery, Abolition and Emancipation* (2 vols, London, 1999), vol. 1, p. 1, which seems to imply that autobiographical blemishes make eighteenth-century black writers incapable of self-reflexivity and complex modes of resistance.

109 Cima, "Black and Unmarked," p. 467; see also Sussman, *Consuming Anxieties*, p. 141.

110 Cima, "Black and Unmarked," 467, n. 8. Cima states that "The Countess of Huntington [sic], one of her English patrons, insisted that Wheatley's likeness accompany the

publication of her work, so Wheatley's *Poems* opened with an engraving of Wheatley as well as a preface by her master and a statement of authenticity signed by prominent male Bostonians" (p. 475; see also Sandhu and Dabydeen, *Slavery, Abolition*, vol. 1, p. 57).

111   As in Houston Baker's language, "Theory's relentless tendency is to go beyond the tangible in search of *metalevels* of explanation. A concern for metalevels, rather than tangible products, is also a founding condition of Afro-American intellectual discourse. Africans uprooted from ancestral soil, stripped of material culture, and victimized by brutal contact with various European nations were compelled not only to maintain their cultural heritage at a *meta* (as opposed to a material) level but also to apprehend the operative metaphysics of various alien cultures. Primary to their survival was the work of *consciousness*, of nonmaterial counterintelligence" (*Workings*, p. 38). Baker apotheosizes Wheatley in this work as the arch black critic, using – tellingly – her frontispiece as a point of departure (pp. 39–45). See also Joan Scott's "Experience," in Sidonie Smith and Julia Watson (eds), *Women, Autobiography, Theory: A Reader* (Madison, WI, 1998), pp. 57–71, for the distinction here proposed between the embodiment and theorization of experience.

112   Cima, "Black and Unmarked," pp. 467, n. 8, 471.

113   1799, in Wood, *Poetry of Slavery*, pp. 220–21.

114   Spillers, "Mama's Baby," pp. 70–73.

115   See ibid., pp. 74–8 on the slave woman's body reproducing white surplus value in reproduction, truly a moment of production, of commodity creation. How, Spillers asks, can this reproduction be called motherhood, or the production of a family, cultural responsibilities that black women have been charged (exhortatorily) and charged (pejoratively) with? Houston Baker draws on her and incidentally pins Southey's sailor down for this production of white surplus value, or morally tasteful sentiment: "Afro-American feminist scholars (in the twentieth century) were praised and rewarded – sometimes even by their sisters in Women's Studies – for keeping the historical faith, for refusing to give way to the complexities and demands of, say, deconstruction or other theoretical modes of discourse. One might say that the historical situation of Afro-American women in Black Studies, as I have described it, can be read as a latter-day instance of the fugitive being asked to turn a scarred and essential back to a white audience as proof both of the fugitive's authenticity as fugitive … and of the white audience's moral superiority and intellectual complexity" (*Workings*, p. 17).

116   Spillers, "Mama's Baby," p. 80.

117   Burke, "The Rhetoric and Politics of Marginality," p. 33.

118   Nott, "From 'Uncultivated Barbarian,'" p. 25.

119   Shields, "Phillis Wheatley's Subversive Pastoral," p. 640.

120   See also Nott, pp. 26, 28.

121   See Folarin Shyllon's very useful and classic study of the Somerset case (Folarin Shyllon, *Black People in Britain 1555–1833* [New York, 1977]).

122   Carretta, "Phillis Wheatley," pp. 216–17.

123   Carretta, *Phillis Wheatley*, p. xxv; Carretta, "Phillis Wheatley," pp. 207–8, 210–11, 221, n. 6; he provides an excellent overview of Wheatley's "prospects" while she was in England, including her meetings with Granville Sharp, the leading anti-slavery advocate of the time, that might have encouraged her to remain in England where a slave was "free" because though owned as property she or he could not be sold as a commodity at will (*Phillis Wheatley*, pp. xxiii–xxviii, xxxii). See my discussion of this distinction between property and commodity and its application to Yarico's tragedy in Chapter 2.

Carretta ("Phillis Wheatley," pp. 203–7) refers to the loose intepretation of the Mansfield Decision by persons as eminent as Edmund Burke "as the practical implementation of the proscription of slavery under the unwritten British constitution, as described by William Blackstone" (ibid., pp. 203–4) and that "Advertisements for sales of slaves, notices of runaway slaves, and attempts to enforce colonial slave laws in Britain – all already rare in England – disappeared after the Mansfield ruling" (ibid., p. 203). See also Sandhu and Dabydeen, *Slavery, Abolition*, p. xvi.

[124] Carretta, *Phillis Wheatley*, p. xvii.

Chapter 6

Postscript

In C.A. Bayly's terms, only in the transition from "archaic" to "proto-capitalist" globalization, for instance, "the capture of slaves, once a strategy in the building of the archaic great household in Africa and the Ottoman world, became a brutal proto-capitalist industry."[1] Bayly calls this another manifestation of an "industrious revolution" that was based simultaneously on demand-side economic rationales, European social transformations including the rise of mercantilism, and on brutality and subjugation as the order of the day.[2] I began this book on the note that the woof of transnationalism stands out from the fabric of globalization – archaic or contemporary – in the production of a conscious discourse of identity. Bayly claims that European colonization and European dominance were driven as much by ideological transformations, or "new types of sociability,"[3] or "the intellectual buoyancy of the European idea of the advance of knowledge,"[4] or by "the density of civil institutions"[5] as by commercial and technological advances. This seems feasible at first glance because demand could in fact be generated anywhere once a certain economic, ideological, and social order had become worldwide and dominant, and migrations were merely routine and multivalent. However, I would like to argue that the propulsion of European colonial interests to world centrality and dominance is less well explained as the byproduct of ideological developments, than as one of the result of the history, patterns, and inequities of migrations of things and people.

It is true that the migrations back and forth that characterized the frenetic eighteenth-century world (whose globalization was distinguished from ours, some might say, only by the relatively longer time taken for non-virtual transactions) created polyphonic nationalities and racializations.[6] The routineness and the multivalence of migration can be instantiated and substantiated by data. On the one hand, Robin Blackburn has written that "England was exceptional in the mobility of its population and in their willingness to emigrate."[7] On the other hand, in his classic study, *The Atlantic Slave Trade: A Census*, Philip Curtin slices through layers of data about the number, distributions, and re-exportations and migrations of slave and free in the circumatlantic rim to write: "As a measure of human misery, 2 million slaves brought to the Americas is already such a terrifying thought that no multiplier could make it seem any worse. As a measure of the relative importance of recent inter-continental migrations, any figure in the range indicated [less than 8,000,000 or more than 10,500,000] is smaller than the nineteenth- and twentieth-century movement of Europeans overseas. And it is equally clear that more Africans than Europeans arrived in the Americas between, say, 1492 and 1770."[8] These comments encourage us to reconsider yet again demographic distributions upon the map of the early modern world; where the west and the non-west ended and began may have been a matter less of objective reckoning than of subjective flows and processes of becoming. But this polyphonic, polymorphous, and polydirectional migration was both differentiated and differential and unequal in outcomes to the migrants themselves.

Indeed, as is true today of globalization (and its discontents, to borrow Sassen's phrasing), the paradox of uneven and unequal globalization explains the mutual underpinning of free migrations of capital and unfree migration of labor. Europeans moved in ways that usually benefited them; non-Europeans often moved in ways that disadvantaged them. Today there are movements, resettlements, and concentrations of labor that represent plantation cultures. Today, capital is deterritorialized and even denationalized while unfree labor gathers – denaturalized – in the shadows of globalization's vast corporate edifices. There is thus a difference between the fates of things or services and people, between corporate capital and labor, which mirrors the eighteenth-century patterns of differential migrations and transnational identity-formations. The transnational consciousness represented in this book articulated in a variety of ways the truth of patterns of dominance and unequal fortunes in global migrations. European capital and people moved relatively voluntarily and frequently to their advantage; non-European labor and resources often moved unfreely, and to their disadvantage. When a Phillis Wheatley did crisscross the Atlantic, her cultural power was extended and transnationalized, but not unshackled. When a Sheridan did negotiate Irishness in the British parliament and on the stage, the taint of origins never left him, though he was able to rewrite a part of imperial discourse and indeed to empower a certain slave in America called Frederick Douglass a hundred or so years later. Transnational consciousness reckons with and accounts for the twinned acts of powerlessness and power, mobility and constraint, in ways that leave hegemonic globalization from above on alert.[9]

As we have seen throughout the preceding chapters, identity is a form of polymorphousness, and polymorphousness a suppressed memory of otherness allowed expression only as a traditional European plot device. This book has been concerned with unearthing the perpetual chiaroscuro of polymorphous memories of racial and colonial domination, and the transformative tricks they have played on the western cultural consciousness and moral conscience.

The polyphonic articulations of race and nationalism that sprinkle or perhaps even flood European memory are theorized, in a sense, by the literary output that I have discussed in this book. While grounding themselves in debates over personhood versus property, civilization versus race, use versus exchange value, treasure versus commodity, symbolic versus commercial capital, and social life versus social death, this literature and its author functions complicated the transnational and thereby ambivalent profile of eighteenth-century identity. Of course, the transatlantic migrations underpinned each other; because slaves could be moved and labor could be supplied, Europeans could move and settle beyond European borders. And in fact, if nations actually emerged and solidified as economic and political units in the eighteenth century, they did so because things and people moved and moved again, albeit in increasingly more regulated ways, across what would become national boundaries and borders.[10] As Bayly writes: "Europe connected, subjugated, and made tributary other peoples' industrious revolutions."[11] Which led to other revolutions that Europe and America have since been repressing but which refuse to go away despite global uniformities.[12] That Europeans repressed this memory was inevitable as well as remarkable considering the frequent and easy elisions of peripheral and metropolitan identities and interests in such phenomena as the "guinea," that venerable English coin which was issued by the Company of Royal Adventurers to Africa (granted a slave trade monopoly in 1663) as a barely suppressed memento of their activities in Western Africa.[13] I express this rather less eloquently than Etienne Balibar, who writes: "Europe is not and never has been made up of separate regions … but rather of overlapping sheets or layers … and … its specificity is this overlapping itself … it is from the whole world that the discourse, capitals, labor powers, and sometimes the weapons of Europe come back … as an aftershock."[14] On the other hand, neither is it necessary to see this repression as producing only blindness; in Spivak's insightful words, "Repression is then seen as a species of production. There is no need to valorize repression as negative and production as positive."[15] I might add that, in all the major literary works discussed in this book, the positive potential of production sets up a resonant and iterative tension with the negativity of repression.

Today's globalization is not free of human conditions similar to those of colonialism and slavery. There are still slaves, some of them children, in the world today.[16] Where are the voices that would tell the stories of such individuals and help locate them in the ongoing story of transnationality? Marcus Wood writes: "What would the Whitman who sang the 'body electric' have done with the sale of thousands of Thai children into the European and American sex industries? What would his art have done with those who auction teenaged Filipina girls off to European and American men, via the World Wide Web? If these acts of enslavement are subjects for art we do not seem to have the poets capable of dealing with them any more."[17] Perhaps more than denationalization and colonization, the narrative of economic and social displacement and disempowerment should be recognized as the key theme of eighteenth-century transnational consciousness.

Though this theme of global economic and national citizenship being at remarkable odds is now beginning to inflect theories of transnationalism, studying European eighteenth-century colonial powers and their valuation of goods and people presents an earlier clue to the irresolvable conflict then and now at the heart of transnationalism within unequal globalization: commitment to commerce, slavery, and colonialism on the one hand, and intense transnational responses to that such as abolition, postcolonial national movements, and tragically clashing civilizations or fundamentalisms.[18] In the heat of the battle – the clash – the new transnational, migrant subject has been born, however. The antislavery response to the irresistible scourge of slavery, as some imagined, was a return invasion whose catastrophic figure has also become familiar in the twenty-first century's "clash of civilizations" with no apparent mitigation of the problems of capitalist accumulation, unequal globalizations, and global neocolonialism. Thomas Day's dying Negro prophetically breathes his last with words that have certainly taken new meaning since 2001:

No more proud Commerce courts the western gales,
But marks the lurid skies, and furls her sails;
War mounts his iron car, and at his wheels
In vain soft Pity weeps, and Mercy kneels;
He breathes a savage rage thro' all the host,
And stains with kindred blood the impious coast;
Then while with horror sickening Nature groans,
And earth and heaven the monstrous race disowns,
Then the stern genius of my native land,
With delegated vengeance in his hand,
Shall raging cross the troubled seas, and pour
The plagues of Hell on yon devoted shore

...

I see their warriors gasping on the ground,–
I hear their falling cities crash around.–
In vain with trembling heart the coward turns,
In vain with generous rage the valiant burns.–
One common ruin, one promiscuous grave,
O'erwhelms the dastard, and receives the brave–
For Afric triumphs! ...[19]

In the wake of 11 September 2001, this nightmare vision has certainly spilled beyond the borders of any literary imagining of a clash of cultures. Both the glorious and the tragic impact of transnational flows are ever-present before us now through the media, literature, and scholarship. The "who-started-it" rhetoric that has become more intense since the "clash" on the twin towers cannot find resolution in either the exultation of transnational commerce or the massive subjugation of transnational migrants. It is with an investigation of transnationalisms of the past – such as I have begun in this book – that a journey away from apocalyptic reciprocal massacres must begin.

Notes

[1] Bayly, *The Birth of the Modern World*, p. 44.
[2] Ibid., pp. 55, 58–9, p. 71.
[3] Ibid., pp. 59–61, 75.
[4] Ibid., p. 80.
[5] Ibid., p. 82. Throughout his outlining of the "social" rather than "material" infrastructural causes for the dominance of the west, Bayly seems to show the hem of a "civilizational" belief peeking under the scholarly objectivity of his approach. My point here is mainly that even the conclusion that Europe's salvation was its civil society and law and order state might usefully be subjected to a critique of Eurocentric assessments. If the Arab Wahhabis or the Indian Sikhs did produce institutions that were public, egalitarian, and critical, as Bayly acknowledges, what settles the point about the superiority of similar European civic and civil structures?

6   Colley, *Captives*, pp. 16, 69; Blackburn, *Making of New World Slavery*, pp. 228–9; Lovejoy and Richardson, "Letters of the Old Calabar Slave Trade 1760–1789," in Vincent Carretta and Philip Gould (eds), *Genius in Bondage*, p. 98; Sandhu and Dabydeen, *Slavery, Abolition*, vol. 1, pp. xi–xii.

7   Blackburn, *Making of New World Slavery*, p. 228.

8   Curtin, *The Atlantic Slave Trade: A Census* (Madison, 1969), p. 87; see also Walvin, "Black and White," p. 314.

9   In this account, I am indebted to Saskia Sassen's work on globalization in more ways than I can say.

10 Bayly, *The Birth of the Modern World*, pp. 60–64.

11 Ibid., p. 64.

12 Ibid., pp. 64–6.

13 Blackburn, *Making of New World Slavery*, p. 254; Carretta, *Phillis Wheatley*, p. xliii; Sandhu and Dabydeen, *Slavery, Abolition*, vol. 1, p. xliii.

14 Etienne Balibar, "The Borders of Europe," in Robbins and Cheah (ed.), *Cosmopolitics*, p. 225. Also see Spivak, "Explanation," Landry and Maclean (ed.), *Spivak Reader*, p. 31.

15 Spivak, "More on Power/Knowledge," in Landry and Maclean (ed.), *Spivak Reader*, p. 151.

16 Blackburn, *Making of New World Slavery*, p. 593, n. 5.

17 Wood, *Poetry of Slavery*, p. xxxiv.

18 From a very long list of critical comment on this topic I find it most useful to cite Baker, *Journey Back*, p. 18. Two more recent and controversial texts that speak to the issue of east-west encounters in our times are Samuel P. Huntington's *The Clash of Civilizations and the Remaking of World Order* (New York, 1996), and Tariq Ali's *The Clash of Fundamentalisms: Crusades, Jihads and Modernity* (London; New York, 2002). Among eighteenth-century voices, see James Grainger, *The Sugar Cane* (1764) in Wood, *Poetry of Slavery*, p. 19. Detractions of the miseries inflicted by commercial greed appear in Thomas Day's "The Dying Negro" (1773), ibid., p. 40; and William Roscoe, *Mount Pleasant* (1777), ibid., pp. 54–7. On the slave trade and trader in particular see Roscoe, *Mount Pleasant* (1777), ibid., p. 59; Samuel Jackson Pratt, *Humanity; or The Rights of Nature: A Poem* (1788), ibid., pp. 134–5. Among black or slave voices, see Olaudah Equiano in *Interesting Narrative of the Life of Olaudah Equiano* (Sandhu and Dabydeen, *Slavery, Abolition*, vol. 1, pp. 276–7), and Ignatius Sancho in *Letters of the Late Ignatius Sancho* (ibid., vol. 1, pp. 103–4).

19 Wood, *Poetry of Slavery*, p. 47.

Bibliography

Addison, Joseph, *The Spectator*, ed. Donald F. Bond (5 vols, Oxford: Clarendon Press, 1965).

Ahmad, Aijaz, "In Theory: Classes, Nations, Literatures," in Bart Moore-Gilbert, Gareth Stanton and Willy Maley (eds), *Postcolonial Criticism* (London; New York: Longman, 1997), pp. 248–72.

Albanese, Denise, *New Science, New World* (Durham: Duke University Press, 1996).

Ali, Tariq, *The Clash of Fundamentalisms: Crusades, Jihads and Modernity* (London; New York: Verso, 2002).

Andrews, William, *To Tell a Free Story: The First Century of Afro-American Autobiography, 1760–1865* (Urbana; Chicago: University of Illinois Press, 1986).

Anon., "Inkle and Yarico," *New Novelist's Magazine* (London, 1787), vol. 2, pp. 116–17.

Appadurai, Arjun, *Modernity at Large: Cultural Dimensions of Globalization* (Minneapolis: University of Minnesota Press, 1996).

Applegate, Anne, "Phillis Wheatley: Her Critics and Her Contribution," *Negro American Literature Forum*, 9 (1975): 123–6.

Aravamudan, Srinivasan, *Tropicopolitans: Colonialism and Agency, 1668–1804* (Durham; London: Duke University Press, 1999).

Ashcroft, Bill, Gareth Griffiths and Helen Tiffin, *The Empire Writes Back: Theory and Practice in Postcolonial Literatures* (London; New York: Routledge, 1989).

Auburn, Mark, "Theatre in the Age of Garrick and Sheridan," in James Morwood and David Crane (eds), *Sheridan Studies* (Cambridge: Cambridge University Press, 1995), pp. 7–46.

Baer, Marc, *Theatre and Disorder in Late Georgian England* (Oxford: Clarendon, 1992).

————, "The Ruin of a Public Man: The Rise and Fall of Richard Brinsley Sheridan as Political Reformer," in James Morwood and David Crane (eds), *Sheridan Studies* (Cambridge: Cambridge University Press, 1995), pp. 151–77.

Bagster-Collins, Jeremy F., *George Colman, the Younger* (New York: King's Crown Press, 1946).

Baker, Houston A. Jr, *The Journey Back: Issues in Black Literature and Criticism* (Chicago: University of Chicago Press, 1980).

————, *Workings of the Spirit: The Poetics of Afro-American Women's Writing* (Chicago: University of Chicago Press, 1991).

Bakhtin, Mikhail, *The Dialogic Imagination: Four Essays*, ed. Michael Holquist, trans. Caryl Emerson and Michael Holquist (Austin: University of Texas Press, 1981).

Balkun, Mary McAleer, "Phillis Wheatley's Construction of Otherness and the Rhetoric of Performed Ideology," *African American Review*, 36/1 (Spring 2002): 121–35.

Barash, Carol, "The Character of Difference: The Creole Woman as Cultural Mediator in Narratives about Jamaica," *Eighteenth-century Studies*, 23/4 (1990): 407–24.

Barrett, Lindon, *Blackness and Value: Seeing Double* (Cambridge University Press, 1999).

Basker, James G. (ed.), *Amazing Grace: An Anthology of Poems About Slavery, 1660–1810* (New Haven: Yale University Press, 2002).

Bataille, Georges, *Visions of Excess: Selected Writings, 1927–1939*, ed. and trans. Allan Stoekl (vol. 14, Minneapolis: University of Minnesota Press, 1985).

Bate, W.J., J.M. Bullitt, and L.F. Powell (eds), *"The Idler" and "The Adventurer,"* (New Haven: Yale University Press, 1963).

Bayly, C.A., *The Birth of The Modern World, 1780–1914: Global Connections and Comparisons* (Malden; Oxford: Blackwell, 2004).

Beckford, William, *Vathek*, ed. Roger Lonsdale (Oxford: Oxford University Press, 1983).

Benjamin, Walter, "The Work of Art in the Age of Mechanical Reproduction," in Leo Braudy and Marshall Cohen (eds), *Film Theory and Criticism: Introductory Readings* (New York: Oxford University Press, 1999), pp. 731–51.

Bennett, Paula, "Phillis Wheatley's Vocation and the Paradox of the 'Afric Muse,'" *PMLA*, 113/1 (1998): 64–76.

Bentley, Thomas, *The Benevolent Planters* (1789).

Berg, Maxine, and Helen Clifford, "Commerce and the Commodity: Graphic Display and Selling New Consumer Goods in Eighteenth-century England," in Michael North and David Ormrod (eds), *Art Markets in Europe, 1400–1800* (Brookfield: Ashgate Publishing, 1998), pp. 187–200.

Bhabha, Homi, "Of Mimicry and Man: The Ambivalence of Colonial Discourse," in Philip Rice and Patricia Waugh (eds), *Modern Literary Theory: A Reader* (London: Arnold, 1996), pp. 360–67.

———, "The Other Question: The Stereotype and Colonial Discourse," in K.M. Newton (ed.), *Twentieth-century Literary Theory: A Reader* (New York: St. Martin's Press, 1997), pp. 293–301.

Bhattacharya, Nandini, *Reading the Splendid Body: Gender and Consumerism in Eighteenth-century British Writing on India* (Newark; London: University of Delaware Press, 1998).

Birkle, Carmen, "Border Crossing and Identity Creation in Phillis Wheatley's Poetry," in Udo J. Hebel (ed.), *The Construction and Contestation of American Cultures and Identities in the Early National Period* (Heidelberg: Universitatsverlag C. Winter, 1999), pp. 47–66.

Black, Jeremy, "Tourism and Cultural Challenge: The Changing Scene of the Eighteenth Century," in John McVeagh (ed.), *All Before Them: 1660–1780* (London; Atlantic Highlands, NJ: Ashfield Press, 1990), pp. 185–202.

————, *The British Abroad: The Grand Tour in the Eighteenth Century* (New York: St. Martin's Press, 1992).

Blackburn, Robin, *The Making of New World Slavery: From the Baroque to the Modern, 1492–1800* (London: Verso, 1997).

Blassingame, John W. (ed.), *Slave Testimony: Two Centuries of Letters, Speeches, Interviews, and Autobiographies* (Baton Rouge: Louisiana State University Press, 1977).

Boucher, Philip P., *Cannibal Encounters: Europeans and Island Caribs, 1492–1763* (Baltimore: The Johns Hopkins University Press, 1992).

Boulton, Alexander O., "The American Paradox: Jeffersonian Equality and Racial Science," *American Quarterly*, 47/3 (September 1995), pp. 467–93.

Bourdieu, Pierre, *Distinction: A Social Critique of the Judgment of Taste*, trans. Richard Nice (Cambridge, MA: Harvard University Press, 1984).

Brewer, John, *The Pleasures of the Imagination: English Culture in the Eighteenth Century* (New York: Farrar Straus Giroux, 1997).

British Library Additional Manuscripts, 25915, original receipts and letters of James Cobb 1787–1809, Britain's Literary Heritage series, English Stage after the Restoration (series), pt 1, reel 4.

Broadley, A.M., *The Century of the Colmans (George Colman, 1732–1794; George Colman, 1764–1836). Being the Memoirs of the Colman Family. By R.B. Peake. London, 1841. And the 'Rosciad' of Charles Churchill, Amplified and Illustrated by the Insertion of Many Hundreds of Portraits, Views, and Autograph Letters, Collected and Arranged by A.M. Broadley, of the Knapp, Bridport* (2 vols, London: Karlslake and Co., 1902).

Buell, Frederick, *National Culture and the New Global System* (Baltimore: The Johns Hopkins University Press, 1994).

Burke, Helen, "The Rhetoric and Politics of Marginality: The Subject of Phillis Wheately," *Tulsa Studies in Women's Literature*, 10/1 (Spring 1991): 31–45.

Burney, Frances, *Camilla, or, A Picture of Youth*, ed. Edward A. Bloom and Lillian D. Bloom (Oxford; New York: Oxford University Press, 1999).

Carretta, Vincent, "Phillis Wheatley, the Mansfield Decision of 1772, and the Choice of Identity," in Klaus H. Schmidt and Fritz Fleischmann (eds), *Early America Re-explored: New Readings in Colonial, Early National, and Antebellum Culture* (New York: P. Lang, 2000).

———— (ed.), *Phillis Wheatley: Complete Writings* (New York: Penguin Books, 2001).

———— and Philip Gould (eds), *Genius in Bondage: Literature of the Early Black Atlantic* (Lexington: University of Kentucky Press, 2001).

The Case of Many Hundreds of Poor English-captives, in Algier, Together, with Some Remedies to Prevent their Increase, Humbly Represented to Both Houses of Parliament (London, 1680).

A Catalogue of the Collection of Coins, Medals, and Antiques; of the Late Ingenious Mr. Thomas Snelling; which will be Sold by Auction, by Mess. Langfords, ... on Monday the 31st of this Instant January 1774, ... (London, 1774).

A Catalogue of a Collection of Italian and Other Pictures, Belonging to the Hon. Charles Hamilton, Brought from Painshill ... Which will be Sold by Auction by Mess. Langford's ... on Thursday and Friday the 11th and 12th of this Inst. March 1773 ... (London, 1773).

A Catalogue of the Curious Collection of Books, Chiefly Relating to Medals and Antiquities; of Dr. James Davis, ... Which ... will be Sold by Auction, by Mr. Langford and Son, ... on Wednesday Evening, the 23d of this Instant January 1771... (London, 1771).

A Catalogue of the Curious Collection of Coins and Medals, of James Michell Hannott, ... which will be Sold by Auction, by Mr. Langford and Son, ... on Saturday the 24th of this Instant February 1770 ... (London, 1770).

A Catalogue of the Entire Collection of Scarce and Curious Prints, Books of Prints, and Drawings, of James West, ... which ... will be Sold by Auction, by Mess. Langford's, ... on Tuesday the 19th of January 1773.

A Catalogue of the Genuine and Curious Collection of Roman and English Coins and Medals, in Gold, Silver and Brass; (Many of Which are Very Rare, and in the Finest Preservation;) of a Gentleman, Lately Gone Abroad. Which will be Sold by Auction, by Mr. Langford and Son, ... on Wednesday ... the 12th ... of this Instant February 1772 ....

A Catalogue of the Large and Capital Collection of Pictures, by the Most Admired Italian, French, Flemish and Dutch Masters; Also Prints and Drawings, ... of James West, ... Which ... Will be Sold by Auction, by Mess. Langford's, ... on Wednesday the 31st of this Instant March 1773, ... (London, 1773).

A Catalogue of the Large and Valuable Collection of Greek, Roman, British, Saxon, English and Foreign medals, medallions, ... of James West, ... Which ... Will be Sold by Auction, by Mess. Langford's, ... on Tuesday the 19th day of January 1773, ... (London, 1773).

A Catalogue of the Large Collection of Silver and Copper Coins and Medals, Formed by Doctor Phillips, ... Which will be Sold by Auction, by Mr. Langford and Son, ... on Thursday the 16th of July 1772, ... (London, 1772).

A Catalogue of the Valuable Collection of Coins and Medals, of Philip Carteret Webb, ... which ... will be Sold by Auction, by Mr. Langford and Son, ... on Saturday the 16th of this Instant February 1771, ... (London, 1771).

A Catalogue of the Valuable Library of James Burges, esq; late of Old Burlington Street, Deceased; Consisting of a Fine Collection of the Best Editions of the Greek and Roman Classics, many on Large Paper, and Neatly Bound. Which ... Will be Sold by Auction, by Mr. Langford and Son, on the Premises, on Thursday the 16th of this Instant May 1771, and the Four Following Days ... (London: Printed for Abraham Langford and Son, 1771).

Caulfield, James, *Portraits, Memoirs, and Characters of Remarkable Persons ...* (London, 1819).

Chambers, William, *Plans, Elevations, Sections, and Perspective Views of the Gardens and Buildings at Kew in Surry, the Seat of her Royal Highness the Princess Dowager of Wales* (London, 1763; repr. Farnborough: Gregg Press, 1966).

Chard, Chloe, "Grand and Ghostly Tours: The Topography of Memory," *Eighteenth-century Studies*, 31/1 (1997): 101–8.

————, and Helen Langdon (eds), *Transports: Travel, Pleasure and Imaginative Geography, 1600–1830* (New Haven: Paul Mellon Centre for Studies in British Art and the Yale Center for British Art, 1996).

Cheyt Sing. A poem. By a Young Lady of Fifteen. Inscribed, by Permission, to the Right Hon. Charles James Fox, ... (London: Printed for the author and sold by J. Woodhouse, no. 10, Brook-street, Grosvenor-square; Fuller, Newbury; Collins and Johnson, Salisbury, 1790).

Choudhury, Mita S., "Sheridan, Garrick, and a Colonial Gesture: *The School for Scandal* on the Calcutta Stage," *Theatre Journal*, 46 (1994): 303–21.

————, "Imperial Licenses, Borderless Topographies, and the Eighteenth-century British Theatre," in Michal Kobialka (ed.), *Of Borders and Thresholds: Theatre History, Practice, and Theory* (Minneapolis: University of Minnesota Press, 1999), pp. 70–109.

————, *Interculturalism and Resistance in the London Theatre, 1660–1800* (Lewisburg, PA: Bucknell University Press, 2000).

Cima, Gay Gibson, "Black and Unmarked: Phillis Wheatley, Mercy Otis Warren, and the Limits of Strategic Anonymity," *Theatre Journal*, 52/4 (December 2000): 465–95.

Clayton, Christopher, "The Political Career of Richard Brinsley Sheridan," in James Morwood and David Crane (eds), *Sheridan Studies* (Cambridge: Cambridge University Press, 1995), pp. 131–50.

Clifford, James, *The Predicament of Culture: Twentieth-century Ethnography, Literature and Art* (Chicago: University of Chicago Press, 1986).

Clissold, Stephen, *The Barbary Slaves* (Lanham, NJ: Rowman and Littlefield, 1977).

Cobb, James, *The Contract; or, Female Captain*, 2 act Farce (1779).

————, *The Humourist; or, Who's Who*, Farce in 2 acts (1785).

————, *The Strangers at Home (*London, 1786).

————, *The First Floor: A Farce, in Two Acts* (1787).

————, *Calcutta or Twelve Hours in India* (1788).

————, *The Doctor and the Apothecary: A Musical Entertainment in Two Acts* (London, 1788).

————, *Love in the East; or, Adventures of Twelve Hours* (London, 1788).

————, *Letter to Richard Brinsley Sheridan* (1790), BL Add. Ms. 25912, f. 3.

————, *The Age of Moliere. A comedy in twenty-two scenes* (179–?).

————, *Comedy in Five Acts, untitled*, with notes by R.B. Sheridan (? by Cobb). (17—).

————, *Lausus and Lydia: A Musial Drama in two acts* (17—).

————, *Mezentius: A Tragedy, In 5 acts (*17—), BL Add. MS. 25987.

————, *Algona: an Opera in Three Acts*, Theatre Royal Drury Lane (22 April 1802).

————, *Letter to Arthur Young* (1814), BL Add Ms. 35132, f. 132.

————, *Letter to Richard Brinsley Peake* (18—), Bodleian Ms. Montagu D.12, ff. 91–2.

————, *The Haunted Tower* (Dublin, n.d.).

————, *Letter to J.P. Kemble* (?) from East India House, n.d., mounted before p. 48 of *Farewell Dinner to J.P. Kemble Esq. on his retirement from the Stage.*

————, *The Siege of Belgrade* (London, n.d.).

Colley, Linda, *Captives: Britain, Empire and the World, 1600–1850* (London: Jonathan Cape, 2002).

Colman, George Jr., *The Mountaineers; a Play in Three Acts ... First Performed at the Theatre Royal, Haymarket, on Saturday August 3, 1793*, 2nd edn (London: Debrett, Piccadilly, 1795).

————, *Heir at Law* (Dublin, 1806).

————, *Inkle and Yarico; an Opera, in Three Acts, by G. Colman, the Younger, with Remarks by Mrs. Inchbald* (New York: D. Longworth, 1806).

————, *The Africans* (1808).

————, *Eccentricities for Edinburgh: containing poems, entitle'd, A lamentation to Scotch booksellers. Fire; or, The sun-poker. Mr. champernoune. The luminous historian; or, Learning in love. London rurality; or, Miss Bunn, and Mrs. Bunt* (repr. from Longman Hurst Rees Ormes and Brown's 1817 edn).

————, *The Dramatic Works of George Colman, the Younger with an Original Llife of the author* (Paris: Baudry, Bobee and Hingray, 1827).

————, *John Bull*, in Elizabeth Inchbald's *British Theater* (vol. 21, London, 1808).

————, *The Rodiad* (repr. Kensington: Cayme Press, 1927).

————, *Broad Grins and Eccentricities for Edinburgh* (New York: Garland Publishing, 1977).

————, *Random Records* (2 vols, ex.-ill., Huntington Library 110464).

Colman, George, the elder, *Letter to Elizabeth Inchbald* (3 March 1786, V&A F 48.G.3/12).

Colman, George Sr, *Letter to Elizabeth Inchbald* (29 November 1785, V&A F 48.G.3/11).

———— and Bonnell Thornton (eds), *The Connoisseur: by Mr. Town, Critic and Censor-General* (London, 1754–56).

The Concise Dictionary of National Biography: from Earliest Times to 1985 (3 vols, Oxford; New York: Oxford University Press, 1992).

The Connoisseur: A Satire on the Modern Men of Taste (London, 1735).

Cooper, Anthony Ashley, Third Earl of Shaftesbury, *Characteristicks of Men, Manners and Opinions* (3 vols, London, 1711).

Cowley, Hannah, *The Belle's Stratagem*, in J. Douglas Canfield and Maja-Lisa Von Sneidern (eds), *The Broadview Anthology of Restoration and Early Eighteenth-century Drama* (Peterborough, Ont.: Broadview Press, 2001), pp. 1826–73.

Craton, Michael, *Sinews of Empire: A Short History of British Slavery* (New York: Anchor Doubleday, 1974).

Curran, Stuart, "Romantic Poetry: The I Altered," in Anne K. Mellor (ed.), *Romanticism and Feminism* (Bloomington: Indiana University Press, 1988), pp. 185–207.

Curtin, Philip, *The Atlantic Slave Trade: A Census* (Madison: University of Wisconsin Press, 1969).

————, *Africa Remembered: Narratives by West Africans from the Era of the Slave Trade* (Madison: University of Wisconsin Press, 1967).

Dabydeen, David, and Sukhdev Sandhu (eds), *Black Writers*, vol. 1 of *Slavery, Abolition and Emancipation: Writings in the British Romantic Period* (London: Pickering and Chatto, 1999).

Dalrymple, William, *White Mughals: Love and Betrayal in Eighteenth-century India* (New York: Viking, 2003).

Davies, Carole Boyce, *Black Women, Writing and Identity: Migrations of the Subject* (London: Routledge, 1994).

Davis, David Brion, *Problem of Slavery in Western Culture* (Ithaca: Cornell University Press, 1966).

de Certeau, Michel, "Ethno-Graphy: Speech, or the Space of the Other: Jean de Lery," in Tom Conley (trans.), *The Writing of History* (New York: Columbia University Press, 1988), pp. 209–43.

The debate on the charge relating to Mr. Hastings's conduct to Cheyt Sing, at Benares, in the House of Commons, on the 13th of June, 1786 (London: Printed for John Stockdale, 1786).

Dictionary of National Biography (22 vols, London: Oxford University Press, H. Milford, 1921–22).

Donaldson, Ian, "New Papers of Henry Holland and R.B. Sheridan: (II) The Hyde Park Corner Operas and the Dormant Patent," *Theatre Notebook: A Journal of the History and Technique of the British Theatre*, 16 (1962), pp. 117–25.

Durant, Jack D., "Prudence, Providence, and the Direct Road of Wrong: *The School for Scandal* and Sheridan's Westminster Hall Speech," *Studies in Burke and His Time: A Journal Devoted to British, American, and Continental Culture, 1750–1800*, 15 (1974): 241–51.

————, "Sheridan, Burke, and Revolution," *Eighteenth-century Life*, 6/2–3 (1981 January–May): 103–13.

————, "Sheridan's Grotesques," *Theatre Annual: A Journal of Performance Studies*, 38 (1983): 13–30.

————, "Sheridan's Picture Auction Scene: A Study in Contexts," *Eighteenth-century Life*, 11 (1987): 35–47.

————, "Sheridan and the Wider World," in John McVeagh (ed.), *All Before Them: 1660–1780*, vol. 1 (2 vols, London: Ashfield Press, 1990), pp. 263–75.

Ehrenreich, Barbara, and Arlie Russell Hochschild (eds), *Global Women: Nannies, Maids, and Sex Workers in the New Economy* (New York: Metropolitan Books, 2003).

Equiano, Olaudah, *Interesting Narrative and Other Writings*, ed. Vincent Carretta (New York: Penguin Books, 1995).

Erkkila, Betsy, "Revolutionary Women," *Tulsa Studies in Women's Literature*, 6:2 (Fall 1987): 189–223.

Essay on the African Slave Trade (1790).

Felsenstein, Frank (ed.), *English Trader, Indian Maid* (Baltimore: The Johns Hopkins University Press, 1999).

Ferguson, Moira, *Subject to Others: British Women Writers and Colonial Slavery, 1670–1834* (New York: Routledge, 1992).

Ferris, Ina, "Narrating Cultural Encounter: Lady Morgan and the Irish National Tale," *Nineteenth-century Literature* (1996), pp. 287–303.

Flanzbaum, Hilene, "Unprecedented Liberties: Re-Reading Phillis Wheatley," *MELUS: The Journal of the Society for the Study of the Multi-Ethnic Literature of the United States*, 18/3 (Fall 1993): 71–81.

Fried, Michael, *Absorption and Theatricality: Painting and Beholder in the Age of Diderot* (Berkeley: University of California Press, 1980).

Gates, Henry Louis Gates Jr., *The Trials of Phillis Wheatley* (New York: Basic, Civitas Books, 2003).

Gilroy, Paul, *The Black Atlantic: Modernity and Double Consciousness* (Cambridge, MA: Harvard University Press, 1993).

Guha, Ranajit, *A Rule of Property for Bengal: An Essay on the Idea of Permanent Settlement* (Durham; London: Duke University Press, 1996).

Guruswamy, Rosemary Fithian, "'Thou Has the Holy Word': Jupiter Hammon's 'Regards' to Phillis Wheatley," in Vincent Carretta and Philip Gould (eds), *Genius in Bondage: Literature of the Early Black Atlantic* (Lexington: University Press of Kentucky, 2001), pp. 190–98.

Habermas, Jürgen, *The Structural Transformation of the Public Sphere: An Inquiry into a Category of Bourgeois Society*, trans. Thomas Burger and Frederick Lawrence (Cambridge, MA: MIT Press, 1989).

Hall, Gwendolyn Midlo, *Africans in Colonial Louisiana: The Development of Afro-Creole Culture in the Eighteenth Century* (Baton Rouge: Louisiana State University Press, 1992).

Hall, Stuart, "Cultural Identity and Diaspora," in Patrick Williams and Laura Chrisman (eds), *Colonial Discourse and Postcolonial Theory: A Reader* (New York: Columbia University Press, 1994), pp. 392–403.

Hamblyn, Richard, "Private Cabinets and Popular Geography: British Audiences for Volcanoes in the Eighteenth Century," in Chloe Chard and Helen Langdon (eds), *Transports: Travel, Pleasure, and Imaginative Geography, 1660–1830* (New Haven: Paul Mellon Centre for Studies in British Art and the Yale Center for British Art, 1996), pp. 179–205.

Hogan, Charles Beecher (ed.), *The London Stage, 1660–1800*, Pt 5 (1776–1800) (Carbondale: Southern Illinois University Press, 1968).

Hulliung, Mark, *The Autocritique of Enlightenment: Rousseau and the Philosophes* (Cambridge, MA: Harvard University Press, 1994).

Hulme, Peter, *Colonial Encounters: Europe and the Native Caribbean, 1492–1797* (London: Methuen, 1986).

————, and Ludmilla Jordanova (eds), *The Enlightenment and Its Shadows* (New York, London: Routledge, 1990).

Hume, David, *Of the Standard of Taste and Other Essays*, ed. John W. Lenz (Indianapolis: Bobbs Merrill, 1965).

Hume, Robert D., "Goldsmith and Sheridan and the Supposed Revolution of 'Laughing' against 'Sentimental' Comedy," in Paul J. Korshin (ed.), *Studies in Change and Revolution: Aspects of English Intellectual History, 1640–1800* (Menston, Yorks.: Scolar Press, 1972).

Huntington, Samuel P., *The Clash of Civilizations and the Remaking of World Order* (New York: Simon & Schuster, 1996).

Inchbald, Elizabeth, *Lovers no Conjurors*, a farce in two acts (1792), manuscript at Huntington Library, LA 952.

————, *The British Theatre* (London, 1808).

Indenture between Willoughby Lacy and Richard Niner (29 August 1780), Harvard Houghton Library Theatre Collection.

Irigaray, Luce, "Women on the Market," in *This Sex Which is Not One*, trans. Catherine Porter (Ithaca: Cornell University Press, 1986).

Isani, Mukhtar Ali, "The British Reception of Wheatley's Poems on Various Subjects," *Journal of Negro History*, 66/2 (Summer 1981), pp. 144–9.

Jacobus, Mary, "Geometric Science and Romantic History: or Wordsworth, Newton and the Slave-trade," in her *Romanticism, Writing, and Sexual Difference* (Oxford: Clarendon Press, 1989), pp. 69–93.

Jameson, Fredric, and Masao Miyoshi (ed.), *The Cultures of Globalization* (Durham: Duke University Press, 1998).

Janowitz, Anne, *England's Ruins: Poetic Purpose and National Landscape* (Cambridge: Basil Blackwell, 1990).

Johnson, Claudia, *Equivocal Beings: Politics, Gender and Sentimentality in the 1790s: Wollstonecraft, Radcliffe, Burney and Austen* (Chicago: University of Chicago Press, 1995).

Jones, Robert W., "Sheridan and the Theatre of Patriotism: Staging Dissent during the War for America," *Eighteenth-century Life*, 26/1 (Winter 2002): 24–45.

Karamcheti, Indira, "Minor Pleasures," in Gita Rajan and Radhika Mohanram (eds), *Postcolonial Discourse and Changing Cultural Contexts: Theory and Criticism* (Westport, CT; London: Greenwood Press, 1995), pp. 59–68.

Kelly, Gary, *Women, Writing and Revolution, 1790–1827* (Oxford: Clarendon Press; New York: Oxford University Press, 1993).

Kendrick, Robert L., "Snatching a Laurel, Wearing a Mask: Phillis Wheatley's Literary Nationalism and the Problem of Style," *Style*, 27/2 (Summer 1993): 222–51.

Kerr, M., *Reflections on the Present State of the Slaves in the British Plantations, and the Slave Trade from Africa* (York: J. Todd, 1789).

Kowaleski-Wallace, Beth, *Consuming Subjects: Women, Shopping, and Business in the Eighteenth Century* (New York: Columbia University Press, 1997).

Krise, Thomas (ed.), *Caribbeana* (Chicago: University of Chicago Press, 1999).

Kriz, Kay Dian, "Dido Versus the Pirates: Turner's Carthaginian Paintings and the Sublimation of Colonial Desire," *Oxford Art Journal*, 18/1 (1995): 116–32.

————, "Introduction: The Grand Tour," *Eighteenth-century Studies*, 31/1 (1997): 7–9.

Lambert, Susan, *The Image Multiplied: Five Centuries of Printed Reproductions of Paintings and Drawings* (New York: Abaris Books, 1987).

Landry, Donna, *The Invention of the Countryside: Hunting, Walking and Ecology in English Literature, 1671–1831* (New York: Palgrave, 2001).

————, *The Muses of Resistance: Laboring-class Women's Poetry in Britain, 1739–1796* (Cambridge: University Press, 1990).

————, and Gerald Maclean (eds), *The Spivak Reader: Selected Works of Gayatri Chakravorty Spivak* (New York; London: Routledge, 1996).

Langford, Abraham, *A catalogue of the valuable library of Mr. Josiah Colebrook, deceased; F.R.S. And late treasurer of the Antiquarian Society. Which (by order of the executor,) will be sold by auction, by Mess. Langford, ... On Tuesday the 20th of this instant February 1776, ... Catalogues of which may be had gratis on the days of viewing, at Mess. Langford aforesaid* (London, 1776).

Langford and Son, *A catalogue of the entire collection of scarce and curious prints, books of prints, and drawings, of James West, ... which ... will be sold by auction, by Mess. Langford's, ... on Tuesday the 19th of January 1773, ...* (London, 1773).

————, *Particulars of the valuable freehold estate of Binfield, in the county of Berks; one of the seats of William Pitt, ... Which will be sold by auction, by Mess. Langford, ... on Tuesday the 2d day of July 1776, ...* (London, 1776).

————, *A catalogue of the capital collection of coins and medals, in the highest preservation, and beautiful painted glass, of John Ives, ... which ... will be sold by auction, by Mess. Langford, ... on Thursday the 13th of this instant February 1777, ...* (London, 1777).

Lee, Debbie, "Yellow Fever and the Slave Trade: Coleridge's *The Rime of the Ancient Mariner*," *English Literary History*, 65/3 (1998): 675–700.

"Letter from Mr. Travers to James Cobb," India Office Records, *Biographical Series 1702–1948*, O/6/8, pp. 234–5.

Linebaugh, Peter, and Marcus Rediker, *The Many-headed Hydra: Sailors, Slaves, Commoners, and the Hidden History of the Revolutionary Atlantic* (Boston: Beacon Press, 2004).

Loftis, John, *Sheridan and the Drama of Georgian England* (Cambridge, MA: Harvard University Press, 1977).

Lovejoy, Paul, and David Richardson, "Letters of the Old Calabar Slave Trade 1760–1789," in Vincent Carretta and Philip Gould (eds), *Genius in Bondage:*

Literature of the Early Black Atlantic (Lexington: University Press of Kentucky, 2001), pp. 89–115.

Lowe, Lisa, *Immigrant Acts* (Durham: Duke University Press, 1996).

Lynch, Deidre, *The Economy of Character: Novels, Market Culture, and the Business of Inner Meaning* (Chicago: University of Chicago Press, 1998).

Macht, Carol, *Classical Wedgwood Designs* (New York: Gramercy, 1957).

Martyn, Thomas, *The English Connoisseur*, Facsimile of 1st edn (Dublin: T. and J. Whitehouse, 1767; Farmborough: Gregg, 1968).

Mason, Julian D. Jr (ed.), *The Poems of Phillis Wheatley: Revised and Enlarged Edition* (Chapel Hill: University of North Carolina Press, 1989).

McKeon, Michael, *The Origins of the English Novel, 1600–1740* (Baltimore: The Johns Hopkins University Press, 1987).

"Memorandum of Correspondence relative to a Pearl deposited by Mesrs. Van Groll and DeVrys as security for 2000 pounds advanced to them by the East India Company," India Office Records, *Biographical Series 1702–1948*, O/6/10, pp. 317–20.

Merchant, Peter, "Robert Paltock and the Refashioning of 'Inkle and Yarico,'" *Eighteenth-century Ficion*, 9/1 (1996): 37–50.

Michals, Teresa, "'That Sole and Despotic Dominion': Slaves, Wives, and Game in Blackstone's *Commentaries*," *Eighteenth-century Studies*, 27 (1994), pp. 195–216.

Mitter, Partha, *Much Maligned Monsters: A History of European Reactions to Indian Art* (Chicago: University of Chicago Press, 1992).

Moore, Catherine E., "Robinson and Xury and Inkle and Yarico," *English Language Notes*, 19/1 (1981), pp. 24–9.

Moore, Thomas, *Memoirs of the Life of the Rt. Hon. Richard Brinsley Sheridan* (2 vols, New York, Greenwood Press, 1858, repr. 1968).

Morton, Timothy, "Blood Sugar," in Peter J. Kitson and Tim Fulford (eds), *Romanticism and Colonialism* (Cambridge: Cambridge University Press, 1998), pp. 87–106.

Most, Andrea, "'We Know We Belong to the Land': The Theatricality of Assimilation in Rodgers and Hammerstein's *Oklahoma!*," *PMLA*, 113/1 (1998): 77–89.

Mukherjee, Sushil Kumar, *The Story of the Calcutta Theatres 1753–1980* (Calcutta: K.P. Bagchi, 1980).

Munns, Jessica, and Gita Rajan (eds), *A Cultural Studies Reader: History, Theory, Practice* (London; New York: Longman, 1995).

Nolta, David D., "The Body of the Collector and the Collected Body in William Hamilton's Naples," *Eighteenth-century Studies*, 31/1 (1997): 108–14.

North, Michael, and David Ormrod (eds), *Art Markets in Europe, 1400–1800* (Brookfield: Ashgate Publishing, 1998).

Nott, Walt, "From 'Uncultivated Barbarian' to 'Poetical Genius': The Public Presence of Phillis Wheatley," *MELUS: The Journal of the Society for the Study of the Multi-Ethnic Literature of the United States*, 18/3 (Fall 1993): 21–32.

Nussbaum, Felicity, *Torrid Zones: Maternity, Sexuality and Empire in Eighteenth-century English Narratives* (Baltimore: The Johns Hopkins University Press, 1995).

———— (ed.), *The Global Eighteenth Century* (Baltimore, London: The Johns Hopkins University Press, 2003).

Omai (London: T. Cadell, 1785).

Original Assignments of Manuscripts between Authors and Publishers, principally for Dramatic Works, from the year 1703 to 1810, collected by William Upcott of the London Institution (1825), with an engraved portrait of James Cobb, BL Add. Ms. 38728. and Add. Ms. 38730 (old f. 60).

O'Toole, Fintan, *A Traitor's Kiss: the Life of Richard Brinsley Sheridan, 1751–1816* (London: Granta, 1995).

Pascoe, Judith, "The Spectacular Flaneuse: Mary Robinson and the City of London," *The Wordsworth Circle*, 23/3 (Summer 1992): 165–71.

Paulson, Ronald, *The Beautiful, the Novel and the Strange: Aesthetics and Heterodoxy* (Baltimore: The Johns Hopkins University Press, 1996).

Peake, Richard Brinsley, *Memoirs of the Colman Family, Including their Correspondence with the Most Distinguished Personages of their Time,* originally published in 1841 (2 vols, New York: B. Blom, 1972).

Pensions to Hastings, Wellesley and Sir John Kennaway. India Office Records, *Biographical Series 1702–1948*, O/6/8, pp. 85–6.

Picker, John M., "Disturbing Surfaces: Representations of the Fragment in *The School for Scandal*," *English Literary History*, 65/3 (Fall 1998): 637–52.

Postle, Martin, *Sir Joshua Reynolds: the Subject Pictures* (Cambridge; New York: Cambridge University Press, 1995).

Pratt, Mary Louise, *Imperial Eyes: Travel Writing and Transculturation* (London; New York: Routledge, 1992).

Price, Cecil (ed.), *Letters of Richard Brinsley Sheridan* (3 vols, Oxford: Clarendon, 1966).

———— (ed.), *The Dramatic Works of Richard Brinsley Sheridan* (2 vols, Oxford: Clarendon, 1973).

————, "Pursuing Sheridan," in Rene Wellek and Alvaro Ribeiro (eds), *Evidence in Literary Scholarship: Essays in Memory of James Marshall Osborn* (Oxford: Clarendon, 1979), pp. 309–20.

Price, Lawrence, *Yarico and Inkle Album* (Berkeley: University of California Press, 1937).

Prown, Jules David, "A Course of Antiquities at Rome, 1764," *Eighteenth-century Studies*, 31/1 (1997): 90–100.

Receipts and Other Papers. Of and concerning James Cobb, 1787–1809 and undated, BL Add. Ms. 25915.

Redford, Bruce (ed.), *The Origins of* The School for Scandal: *"The Slanderers," "Sir Peter Teazle"* (Princeton: University Library, 1986).

Rifkin, Jeremy, "The Biotech Century: Human Life as Intellectual Property," *The Nation* (13 April 1998), pp. 11–19.

Roach, Joseph, *Cities of the Dead: Circum-Atlantic Performance* (New York: Columbia University Press, 1996).

Robbins, Bruce, and Pheng Cheah (eds), *Cosmopolitics: Thinking and Feeling Beyond the Nation* (Minneapolis: University of Minnesota Press, 1998).

Robinson, William H., *Critical Essays on Phillis Wheatley* (Boston: G.K. Hall, 1982).

Rousseau, George, and Roy Porter (ed.), *Exoticism in the Enlightenment* (Manchester: University Press, 1990).

Rubin, Gayle, "The Traffic in Women: Notes on the 'Political Economy' of Sex," in Julie Rivkin and Michael Ryan (eds), *Literary Theory: An Anthology* (Malden, MS: Blackwell, 1998), pp. 533–60.

Sandhu, Sukhdev, and David Dabydeen (eds), *Slavery, Abolition and Emancipation*, vol. 1: *Black Writers* (2 vols, London: Pickering and Chatto, 1999).

Sassen, Saskia, *Globalization and Its Discontents* (New York: New Press, 1998).

————, *Guests and Aliens* (New York: New Press, 1999).

Schmidt, James (ed.), *What is Enlightenment?: Eighteenth-century Answers and Twentieth-century Questions* (Berkeley: University of California Press, 1996).

The School for Scandal: Thomas Rowlandson's London; an account of his life & times & especially his depictions of the theatre, together with some discussion of the life & works of Richard Brinsley Sheridan & of his play The school for scandal as performed at the University Theatre (Lawrence: University of Kansas, Museum of Art Publication, 1967).

Scott, Joan W., "Experience," in Sidonie Smith and Julia Watson (eds), *Women, Autobiography, Theory: A Reader* (Madison: University of Wisconsin Press, 1998), pp. 57–71.

Scott, Major (John), 1747–1819, *A third letter from Major Scott to Mr. Fox, on the story of Deby Sing; two letters relative to the expences attending the trial of Warren Hastings, esquire; and a letter to Mr. Burke* (London, Printed for John Stockdale, 1789).

Searing, James, *West African Slavery and Atlantic Commerce: The Senegal River Valley, 1700–1860*, African Studies Series 77 (Cambridge: Cambridge University Press, 1993).

Shepherd, Verene (ed.), *Working Slavery; Pricing Freedom* (New York: Palgrave, 2002).

Sheridan, Richard, "Resistance and Rebellion of African Captives in the Transatlantic Slave Trade before becoming Seasoned Labourers in the British Caribbean, 1690–1807," in Verene Shepherd (ed.), *Working Slavery; Pricing Freedom* (New York: Palgrave, 2002), pp. 181–205.

Sheridan, Richard B., *The Speeches of the Right Honourable Richard Brinsley Sheridan, Edited by a Constitutional Friend* (3 vols, London: 1842, repr. New York: 1969).

————, *The School for Scandal*, in *The Dramatic Works of Richard Brinsley Sheridan*, ed. Cecil Price (2 vols, Oxford: Clarendon Press, 1973).

————, *School for Scandal*, ed. F.W. Bateson (London: A. and C. Black; New York: Norton, 1989).

Shields, John C., "Phillis Wheatley's Subversive Pastoral," *Eighteenth-century Studies*, 27/4 (Summer 1994): 631–47.

Shipton, Clifford K., and James E. Mooney, *National Index of American Imprints Through 1800: The Short-Title Evans*, vol. 2: N–Z (American Antiquarian Society and Barre Publishers, 1969).

Shteir, Ann B., *Cultivating Women: Cultivating Science: Flora's Daughters and Botany in England 1760–1860* (Baltimore; London: The Johns Hopkins University Press, 1996).

Shuffelton, Frank, "On Her Own Footing: Phillis Wheatley in Freedom," in Vincent Carretta and Philip Gould (eds), *Genius in Bondage: Literature of the Early Black Atlantic* (Lexington: University of Kentucky Press, 2001), pp. 175–89.

Shyllon, Folarin, *Black People in Britain 1555–1833* (New York: Oxford University Press, 1977).

Sichel, Walter, *Sheridan* (Boston: 1909).

Simms, Norman, "A Silent Love Affair: Frances Seymour's 'Inkle and Yarico' (1726)," *AUMLA*, 85 (May 1996): 93–101.

Skinner and Co., *A catalogue of the Portland Museum: lately the property of the Duchess Dowager of Portland, deceased: which will be sold by auction, by Mr. Skinner and Co. on Monday the 24th of April, 1786 ...* Catalogues may now be had on the premises, and of Mr. Skinner and Co ... (London: 1786).

Smith, Charles, *Auctions: the Social Construction of Value* (Berkeley: University of California Press, 1989).

Smith, Valerie, "Black Feminist Theory and the Representation of the 'Other,'" in Cheryl A. Wall (ed.), *Changing Our Own Words: Essays on Criticism, Theory and Writing by Black Women* (New Brunswick: Rutgers University Press, 1991).

Soane, Sir John, *Plans, Elevations, and Sections of Buildings Erected in the Counties of Norfolk, Suffolk ...* (1788).

Spillers, Hortense, "Mama's Baby, Papa's Maybe: An American Grammar Book," *Diacritics*, 17/2 (Summer 1987): 65–81.

Spivak, Gayatri C., *In Other Worlds* (London; New York: Methuen, 1987).

————, "Can the Subaltern Speak?," in Bill Ashcroft, Gareth Griffiths and Helen Tiffin (eds), *The Post-colonial Studies Reader* (London; New York: Routledge, 1995), pp. 24–8.

Stuckey, Sterling, *Slave Culture: Nationalist Theory and the Foundations of Black America* (New York: Oxford University Press, 1987).

Sussman, Charlotte, *Consuming Anxieties: Consumer Protest, Gender, and British Slavery, 1713–1833* (Stanford: Stanford University Press, 2000).

Sutcliffe, Barry (ed.), *Plays by George Colman the Younger and Thomas Morton* (Cambridge; New York: Cambridge University Press, 1983).

Tasch, Peter A. (ed.), *The Plays of George Colman the Younger* (2 vols, New York: Garland, 1981).

Taylor, George (ed.), *Plays By Samuel Foote and Arthur Murphy* (Cambridge: Cambridge University Press, 1984).

Thomas, Nicholas, *Entangled Objects: Exchange, Material Culture, and Colonialism in the Pacific* (Cambridge, MA: Harvard University Press, 1991).

Thompson, James, *Models of Value: Eighteenth-century Political Economy and the Novel* (Durham: Duke University Press, 1996).

————, "'Sure I have seen that face before': Representation and Value in Eighteenth-century Drama," in J. Douglas Canfield and Deborah Payne (eds), *Cultural Readings of Restoration and Eighteenth-century Theater* (Athens: University of Georgia Press, 1996), pp. 281–308.

Tobin, Beth Fowkes, *Picturing Imperial Power: Colonial Subjects in Eighteenth-century British Painting* (Durham, NC: Duke University Press, 1999).

Trumpener, Katie, *Bardic Nationalism: The Romantic Novel and the British Empire* (Princeton: Princeton University Press, 1997).

Wainwright, Clive, *The Romantic Interior: The British Collector at Home 1750–1850* (New Haven and London: Yale University Press for Paul Mellon Center for Studies in British Art, 1989).

Wall, Cynthia, "The English Auction: Narratives of Dismantlings," *Eighteenth-century Studies*, 31/1 (1997): 1–25.

Walpole, Horace, *Horace Walpole's Correspondence*, ed. W. Lewis (43 vols, New Haven: Yale University Press, 1973).

Walvin, James, "Black and White: Slaves, Slavery and British Society, 1600–1807," in Verene Shepherd (ed.), *Working Slavery, Pricing Freedom: Perspectives from the Caribbean, Africa and the African Diaspora* (London: St. Martin's Press, 2002), pp. 303–19.

Wechselblatt, Martin, "Gender and Race in Yarico's Epistle to Inkle: Voicing the Feminine/Slave," *Studies in Eighteenth-century Culture*, 19 (1989), pp. 197–223.

Welsh, Alexander, *Strong Representations: Narrative and Circumstantial Evidence in England* (Baltimore: The Johns Hopkins University Press, 1992).

Wertheimer, Eric, *Imagined Empires: Incas, Aztecs, and the New World of American Literature, 1771–1876* (Cambridge; New York: Cambridge University Press, 1999).

Wheatley, Phillis, *Phillis's poem on the death of Mr. Whitefield* (Boston: Printed by Isaiah Thomas, 1770).

————, *To Mrs. Leonard, on the death of her husband* (Boston: s.n., 1771).

————, *Poems on various subjects, religious and moral. By Phillis Wheatley, negro servant to Mr. John Wheatley, of Boston, in New England* (London: Printed for A. Bell; and sold by Messrs. Cox and Berry, Boston, 1773).

————, *An elegiac poem, on the death of that celebrated divine, and eminent servant of Jesus Christ, the Reverend and learned George Whitefield ... Who made his exit from this transitory state, to dwell in the celestial realms of bliss, on Lord's-Day,*

30th of September, 1770 ... at Newbury-Port, near Boston, New-England. ... by Phillis, a servant girl, of 17 years of age, belonging to Mr. J. Wheatley, of Boston: – she has been but 9 years in this country from Africa. (Boston: Printed and sold by Ezekiel Russell, in Queen-Street, and John Boyles, in Marlboro'-Street, 1770).

Wheatley, Phillis, An elegy, sacred to the memory of the great divine, the Reverend and learned Dr. Samuel Cooper, who departed this life December 29, 1783, aetatis 59. by Phillis Peters (Boston: Printed and sold by E. Russell, in Essex-Street, near Liberty-Pole, 1784).

———, *Liberty and peace, a poem. by Phillis Peters* (Boston: Printed by Warden and Russell, at their office in Marlborough-Street, 1784).

———, *Poems on Various Subjects* (Philadelphia: Cruikshank, 1786).

———, *Poems on Various Subjects* (Philadelphia: James, 1787).

———, *Poems on various subjects, religious and moral. By Phillis Wheatley, negro servant to Mr. John Wheatley, of Boston, in New-England* (London; Philadelphia: repr. and sold by Joseph Cruikshank, in Market-Street, between Second and Third-Streets, 1789).

Wheeler, Roxann, "'My Savage,' 'My Man': Racial Multiplicity in *Robinson Crusoe*," *English Literary History*, 62/4 (1995): 821–61.

———, "The Complexion of Desire: Racial Ideology and Mid-eighteenth-century British Novels," *Eighteenth-century Studies*, 32/3 (1999): 309–32.

Whitefield, George, *A True Copy of the Last Will and testament of ...* (n.p., 1770).

———, *Two Funeral Hymns, Composed by... George Whitefield...who Departed... the Thirtieth of September, 1770* (Boston: Russell and Boyles, 1770).

Wiesenthal, Christine S., "Representation and Experimentation in the Major Comedies of Richard Brinsley Sheridan," *Eighteenth-century Studies*, 25/3 (Spring 1992), pp. 309–30.

Wilkinson, David, *The Duke of Portland: Politics and Party in the Age of George III* (New York: Palgrave, 2003).

Wind, Edgar, *Hume and the Heroic Portrait: Studies in Eighteenth Century Imagery*, ed. Jaynie Anderson (Oxford: Oxford University Press, 1986).

Wolf, John, *The Barbary Coast: Algiers Under the Turks, 1500–1800* (New York: Norton, 1979).

Wollstonecraft, Mary, *A Vindication of the Rights of Woman*, ed. Mary Warnock (London: Penguin Classics, 1992).

Wood, Marcus, *Blind Memory: Visual Representations of Slavery in England and America 1780–1865* (New York: Routledge, 2000).

———, *The Poetry of Slavery: An Anglo-American Anthology 1764–1865* (Oxford: Oxford University Press, 2003).

Wrigley, Richard, "Crossing Boundaries and Exceeding Limits: Destabilization, Tourism, and the Sublime," in Chloe Chard and Helen Langdon (eds), *Transports: Travel, Pleasure, and Imaginative Geography, 1660–1830* (New Haven: Paul Mellon Centre for Studies in British Art and the Yale Center for British Art, 1996), pp. 75–116.

Young, Hilary (ed.), *The Genius of Wedgwood* (London: V&A Museum, 1995).
Young, Robert J.C., *Colonial Desire: Hybridity in Theory, Culture, and Race* (New York: Routledge, 1995).

Index